Markus Frischhut

The Ethical Spirit of EU Law

Markus Frischhut
Management Center Innsbruck
Jean Monnet Chair "European
Integration & Ethics"
Innsbruck, Austria

This book has been kindly financed by the European Commission under Erasmus+ (Jean Monnet Chair 'European Integration & Ethics'), as well as by Management Center Innsbruck.

Website: https://jeanmonnet.mci.edu/

https://doi.org/10.1007/978-3-030-10582-2

The book is dedicated to all those who supported and inspired me during the drafting process.

Preface

The law of the European Union (EU) affects more and more areas of national law, including also some sensitive fields, for instance patentability of human life. At the same time, we can observe a tendency towards increasing references to the terms 'ethics' and 'morality' in EU law. Especially if unethical behaviour leads to legal consequences, the often missing determination of these concepts remains a challenge.

The starting point of this journey was the EU directive on patients' rights in cross-border health care, which states several rights of patients while at the same time stressing a very important limitation: unethical treatment cannot be sought abroad. Based on a comprehensive research on EU primary and especially secondary law, I managed to identify those EU legal documents that refer to the terms of ethics and morality. At the end of this paper entitled 'EU: Short for "Ethical" Union? The Role of Ethics in European Union Law' and published in 2015, I addressed those parts of EU law that were still missing. Luckily, I had some very talented and motivated students, who supported me in conducting this research, based on the identified fields and research designs.

In September 2016, the Jean Monnet Chair on 'European integration & ethics', kindly supported by the European Commission under Erasmus+, was launched, comprising teaching, research and related activities in this field (all information available under https://jeanmonnet.mci.edu). The research necessary for this book has been conducted within the comprehensive activities of this Chair, with several students and research interns having contributed to this project. The different persons having contributed to the different parts are explicitly named in the respective chapters.

This book will now put all these different pieces together and further develop them, finally resulting in 28 theses on the 'ethical spirit' of EU law. As a well-known funding requirement, this book is published open access. Even if this requirement would not exist, it makes a lot of sense for the content presented here, as I will argue that public debate on this 'ethical spirit' is of utmost importance and must be based on active citizen participation.

This book was mainly written during the summer of 2018, where the author would like to thank his home institution (MCI Management Center Innsbruck), the department to which he is affiliated (Management & Law), and especially its head Ralf Geymayer and department colleagues, for making this possible.

The author would like to thank the following colleagues (in alphabetical order) for valuable feedback and discussions during the drafting process of this book: Johan Brännmark (Lund University | VBE research group on 'science and proven experience'); Daniel Degischer (MCI | Management & Law); Marie-Luisa Frick (University of Innsbruck | Department of Philosophy); Göran Hermerén (Lund University | 2002–2011 president/chairperson of the 'European Group on Ethics in Science and New Technologies' [EGE]); Eva Lichtenberger (former Member of the European Parliament); Winfried Löffler (University of Innsbruck | Department of Christian Philosophy); Andreas Th. Müller (University of Innsbruck | Department of European Law and Public International Law); Bruno Niederbacher (University of Innsbruck | Department of Christian Philosophy); Claudia Paganini (University of Innsbruck | Department for Christian Philosophy); Barbara Prainsack (University of Vienna | Department of Political Science | EGE member | Member of the Austrian Bioethics Commission); Nils-Eric Sahlin (Lund University | VBE research group | EGE member); Karl Harald Søvig (University of Bergen | Faculty of Law); Lena Wahlberg (Lund University | VBE research group). The usual disclaimer applies.

Andreas Müller already provided very valuable feedback and exchange of ideas for the 2015 paper, and throughout the process finally leading to this book. His interdisciplinary expertise in law and philosophy was very valuable for the realization of this book.

Forming the Advisory Board of this Jean Monnet Chair on teaching and research in this field, the author would like to thank the members for valuable support, exchange of thoughts, guest-lectures at MCI, as well as mentoring (in alphabetical order): Doris Dialer (European Parliament); André den Exter (Erasmus University Rotterdam | Jean Monnet Chair EU Global Health Law); Brad Glosserman (Pacific Forum Center for Strategic & International Studies & Tama University); Dean M. Harris (The University of North Carolina at Chapel Hill | Gillings School of Global Public Health); Tamara K. Hervey (The University of Sheffield | Jean Monnet Professor of European Union Law); Othmar Karas (Member of the European Parliament); Gabriele Werner-Felmayer (Medical University of Innsbruck | Member of the Austrian Bioethics Commission).

This chair closely cooperates with 'ethucation' (https://www.i-med.ac.at/ethucation/index.html.en), an independent 'Network for Bioethics in Education and Advanced Training', chaired by Gabriele Werner-Felmayer, which provides a platform for valuable work in the field of ethics and bioethics, hence also valuable input for this book.

The author would also like to thank Lorenzo Pasculli (formerly: Kingston University, now: Coventry University), Director of the Global Integrity Research Network (GIRN), formerly: Integrity Research Group (IRG), where the author is an external member, for the pleasant and professional supervision of Matthias Pirs' Master's thesis.

The author also thanks the participants of the following events (in reverse chronological order) for valuable discussions and suggestions: 17 and 18 October 2018: meeting of the National Ethics Councils (NEC) Forum and the European Group on Ethics in Science and New Technologies (EGE), Vienna, Austria; 28 May 2018: VBE workshop 'Science and Proven Experience in the Legal Regulation of Risk', Lund University, Sweden; 3 May 2018: seminar 'Research Group Law, Democracy and Welfare', University of Bergen, Norway; 23 January 2018: seminar "Integrity Research Group (IRG)", Kingston University, London; 23 March 2017: UNESCO Chair in Bioethics 12th World Conference Bioethics, Medical Ethics & Health Law, Limassol, Cyprus; 6 January 2015: UNESCO Chair in Bioethics 10th World Conference Bioethics, Medical Ethics & Health Law, Jerusalem, Israel.

The author is also thankful for 'www.DeepL.com/Translator', which was a very useful support in translating certain terms and (parts of) sentences.

Philipp Weinkogl (MCI | Management & Law) and Margit Frischhut did a great job in proofreading the manuscript.

The author would also like to thank Anja Trautmann, Manuela Schwietzer and Raghavy Krishnan at Springer for the professional and pleasant cooperation.

Last, but not least the author would like to thank his wife Daniela and her nice location HerzensOase, where the 28 theses have been drafted, as well as daughters Lena and Lara, for their love and support throughout the drafting process. The time we enjoyed together gave me additional energy for the realization of this book.

Waidring, Innsbruck, Austria
November 2018

Markus Frischhut

Contents

Abbreviations

ACP	African, Caribbean and Pacific Group of States
Art	Article(s)
B.C.	Before Christ
BVerfG	Bundesverfassungsgericht (= German Constitutional Court)
CCNE	Comité Consultatif National d'Ethique (= French National Consultative Ethics Committee)
CETA	Comprehensive Economic and Trade Agreement (EU Canada)
CFR	Charter of Fundamental Rights of the EU
CJ	Court of Justice
CJEU	Court of Justice of the EU
CoC	Code of Conduct
CONV	European Convention document
CSR	Corporate social responsibility
DE	German language
DNA	Deoxyribonucleic acid
e.g.	exempli gratia (= for example)
EAEC	European Atomic Energy Community
EC	European Commission, European Community
ECB	European Central Bank
ECHR	European Convention for the Protection of Human Rights and Fundamental Freedoms
ECtHR	European Court of Human Rights
ed.	editor, edition
eds.	editors
EEA	European Economic Area
EEC	European Economic Community
EFTA	European Free Trade Area
EGE	European Group on Ethics in Science and New Technologies
EIB	European Investment Bank
EN	English language

EP	European Parliament
ES	Spanish language
ESA	EFTA Surveillance Authority
et al.	et alii (= and others)
etc.	et cetera (= and so forth)
ETS	European Treaty Series
EU	European Union
FR	French language
GAEIB	Group of Advisers to the EC on the Ethical Implications of Biotechnology
GC	General Court
GDPR	General Data Protection Regulation
GIRN	Global Integrity Research Network
GM	Genetically modified
GMOs	Genetically modified organisms
i.e.	id est (= that is)
ibid.	ibidem (= in the same place)
ICESC	International Covenant on Economic Social and Cultural Rights
ICT	Information and communication technologies
IEC	Independent Ethical Committee
IFAC	International Federation of Accountants
IRG	Integrity Research Group (at Kingston University, UK)
ISC	International Stem Cell
IT	Italian language
IVF	in vitro fertilization
MCI	Management Center Innsbruck
MEP	Member of the European Parliament
MS	Member State(s)
N.B.	Nota bene (= note well)
NIM	National implementation measures
No.	Number
OJ	Official Journal (of the EU)
OLAF	Office Européen de Lutte Anti-Fraude (= European Anti-Fraud Office)
p.	Page
para	Paragraph
paras	Paragraphs
pers.	Persons
pp.	Pages
pt.	Point
QCA	Qualitative content analysis
SPUC	Society for the Protection of Unborn Children
TEU	Treaty on European Union

TFEU	Treaty on the Functioning of the European Union
UK	United Kingdom
UNESCO	United Nations Educational, Scientific and Cultural Organisation
VBE	'Vetenskap och beprövad erfarenhet' (= science and proven experience; research group at Lund University, Sweden)
vs.	Versus (against)
WHO	World Health Organization

List of Figures

List of Tables

Chapter 1
Setting the Agenda

A return to principles and values, inspired by Europe's cultural, religious and humanist heritage, [...] would imbue the integration project with meaning beyond the technocratic and the market, and might enhance the connection between the rule setters and the rule takers, i.e. the companies and citizens of Europe.

René Smits, The Invisible Core of Values in the European Integration Project (Smits 2018, 221).

1.1 Point of Departure

In European Union (EU) law, we can find more and more references in different legal documents to non-legal concepts such as ethics and morality.[1] This phenomenon, observed at both the national[2] as well as the EU level,[3] has been described as an "ethicalization" of law.[4] The term of ethicalization can refer to opening clauses (references to non-legal concepts), ethics codices, as well as ethics committees,[5] thus including standards, procedures and institutions in law, which themselves are not part of the legal system.[6]

So far, at EU level, literature on EU law and ethics has covered selected sectoral topics such as research and patenting of human embryonic stem cells,[7] biotechnol-

---

[1]A first step in this regard has been high lightened by Frischhut (2015).

[2]For an ethicalization of national private law and public international law, see Paulus and Schneider (2013).

[3]Fowkes and Hailbronner (2013, p. 395) even refer to a "global trend".

[4]Vöneky et al. (2013, VI).

[5]For an intriguing overview of ethics committees, see Hermerén (2009).

[6]Gruschke (2013, p. 41).

[7]Herrmann and Rowlandson (2008); stressing different approaches in different Member States in this regard (p. 251).

M. Frischhut, *The Ethical Spirit of EU Law*,
https://doi.org/10.1007/978-3-030-10582-2_1

ogy,[8] science at large,[9] or world politics.[10] Some authors have focussed on the role of the European Commission (EC)'s key[11] ethics advisory board, the European Group on Ethics in Science and New Technologies (EGE),[12] while others have also concentrated on the references of the Charter of Fundamental Rights of the EU (CFR[13]) to moral norms.[14] However, we can still observe a gap, as we lack a comprehensive analysis of which approach EU law[15] in general takes with regard to ethics and morality.[16]

In enacting legal provision, the EU is bound to the 'rule of law' (Art 2 TEU[17]). According to the EC's recent Communication,[18] one (formal[19]) element of the rule of law is legal certainty,[20] which, according to the Court of Justice of the EU (CJEU[21]), requires amongst other things that "legislation must be clear and predictable for those who are subject to it".[22]

This applies to both, whether law refers to legal concepts, or to non-legal concepts. References from one discipline (law) to another (see Fig. 1.1) can create certain chal-

---

[8]Tallacchini (2015).

[9]Wilms (2013).

[10]Manners (2008).

[11]For another ethics advisory body, which recently issued an opinion on ethics and digitalization, see Ethics Advisory Group (2018).

[12]Busby et al. (2008), Mohr et al. (2012), Plomer (2008), Tallacchini (2015).

[13]Consolidated version: OJ 2016 C 202/389.

[14]Waluchow (2012, p. 193); "it can nonetheless be true that the EU and its Member States share a set of common *values* [...] *to which* the EU *Charter makes reference* and which its authors intended to place front and centre in the minds of those required to exercise public power *in accordance with its moral demands*" (p. 194; emphases added).

[15]For simplicity's sake, in the following, reference will always be made to today's terminology; e.g. European Union instead of European (Economic) Community. In case fundamental rights have previously been decided as 'general principles of law', reference will also be made to the relevant provision of the CFR. On the EU courts, see *infra* note 21.

[16]In the explanatory notes to what is now Art 2 TEU, the 'praesidium' of the European Convention has also taken a broader approach (i.e. surpassing Art 2 TEU and also taking into account the objectives of Art 3 TEU, the CFR, etc.) when referring to "the Union's 'ethic'"; CONV 528/03 of 6 February 2003, p. 11.

[17]Consolidated version: OJ 2016 C 202/13.

[18]EC 'A New EU Framework to Strengthen the Rule of Law', COM (2014) 158 final 11.3.2014, p. 4 and Annex 1.

[19]Craig (1997, p. 467); "the clarity of the ensuing norm (was it sufficiently clear to guide an individual's conduct so as to enable a person to plan his or her life, etc.)".

[20]Addressing challenges of opening clauses against the background of legal certainty: Gruschke (2013, p. 42).

[21]This abbreviation refers to the Court of Justice of the EU in the sense of Art 19(1) TEU, which comprises not only the Court of Justice (CJ; this also includes the abbreviation ECJ), but also the General Court (GC). When in the following reference is made to the GC, this should be understood as also comprising the formerly Court of First Instance.

[22]CJEU judgment of 12 November 1981, *Meridionale Industria Salumi*, 212 to 217/80, EU:C:1981:270, para 10. See also Venice Commission, Report on the Rule of Law,

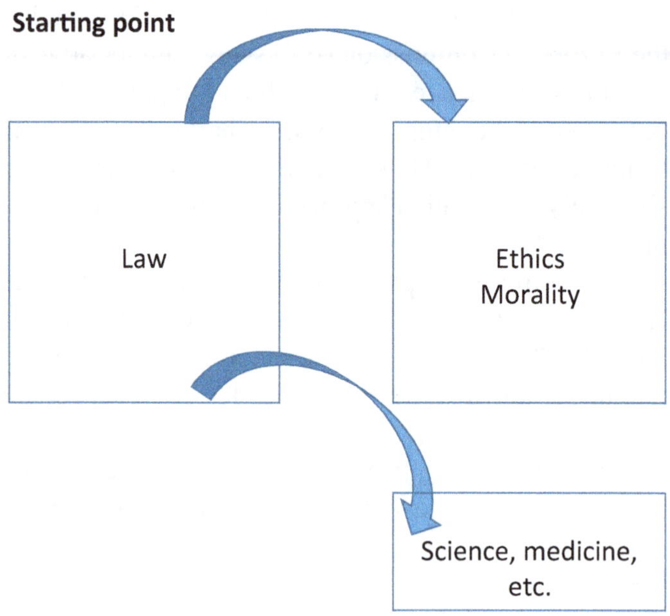

Fig. 1.1 References of law to non-legal concepts

lenges, which we already know from the interface of law and science in general,[23] as well as from EU law using concepts, which require the import of medical knowledge into the legal sphere.[24] Finally, this is also true if EU law refers to ethics, thus importing concepts of practical philosophy (i.e. normative ethical theories)[25] into law, a phenomenon, which we can increasingly observe since the 1990s.[26]

In 2009, Williams has identified a "lack of ideal constitution for the EU", as "values have not been taken seriously"[27]; hence, he addressed the question "whether

CDLAD(2011)003rev, 10 et seq.; and European Court of Human Rights (ECtHR) judgment of 29 April 2014, *L.H. versus Latvia*, 52019/07, para 47 ("the rule of law, which [...] means that the domestic law must be formulated with sufficient precision and must afford adequate legal protection against arbitrariness").

[23]This issue of responsibility and ethics in the life sciences is described by Jasanoff (2007, pp. 26–27) as follows: "A major function of policymaking for the life sciences is to create and maintain *boundaries* that correspond to people's *preexisting* ethical and social sensibilities concerning the products of biotechnology [...] politically significant boundary work also takes place in a multitude of more *specialized forums* that are less transparently in the business of boundary maintenance than *legislatures or courts*, such as *expert advisory committees*, parliamentary commissions, ethics review boards, and nongovernmental organizations"; emphases added.

[24]CJEU judgment of 12 July 2001, *Smits and Peerbooms*, C-157/99, EU:C:2001:404, para 92 ("what is considered normal according to the state of international medical science and medical standards generally accepted at international level"); see also paras 94 and 98. On an intriguing project of importing non-legal (medical) concepts in the legal sphere (VBE research group on 'science and proven experience', https://www.vbe.lu.se/) see Wahlberg and Persson (2017).

[25]As von Savigny (1951, p. 48) has emphasized in his book on legal methodology, every systematic approach leads to philosophy ("*Alles System führt auf Philosophie hin.*").

[26]See *infra* Sect. 4.2.1; Busby et al. (2008, pp. 806–808), Frischhut (2015, p. 550).

[27]Williams (2009, p. 552) also states that "existing philosophy of EU law rests upon a *theory of interpretation* at the expense of a *theory of justice*" (no emphases added). "Perhaps the most impor-

an alternative philosophy, as a first step towards constructing a more just institution, can be achieved in the context of the EU and its current law".[28] He has also argued that although it might not be satisfactory, however, "some form of philosophy *does* exist".[29] Such a 'philosophy of EU law' can either be identified from within,[30] or at the interface of law and philosophy, that is to say where EU law refers to non-legal concepts of ethics and morality (i.e. partly from the outside).[31] Thus, the focus of this book is on the 'import' of non-legal concepts of 'ethics' and 'morality'[32] into EU law.

In the following, this term of EU law comprises different 'layers' (in the sense of the hierarchy of EU law), which comprises EU primary law, EU secondary law, EU tertiary law, as well as, in between primary and secondary law, international agreements concluded by the EU[33] (i.e. a vertical perspective[34]).

From a horizontal perspective,[35] in terms of different 'areas' of EU law, this book will mainly take into account the legislative output of the EU institutions (i.e. EU secondary and tertiary law). Due to the importance of the EU's legal system, this book will also include the CJEU's approach when dealing with ethics and morality. Beyond the legislative output, this book will also cover the question of ethics in law making concerning the sensitive issue of lobbying, as well as the ethical approach of the EGE in its opinions.

As EU secondary law also comprises EU directives (referring to ethics and morality), which require implementation into national law, also the different approaches of selected MS in implementing these EU directives into national law will be covered.[36]

These different (vertical) layers and (horizontal) areas of EU law covered in this book are displayed below in Fig. 1.2.

---

tant consequence of such a diagnosis is the evaluation that whatever else the ECJ may have done, particularly through its development of general principles, it has singularly failed to countenance 'justice' as a clear ethical commitment in its own right." (p. 572).

[28]Williams (2009, p. 576).

[29]Williams (2009, p. 551); no emphasis added.

[30]For a philosophy of EU law based on EU integration itself, see Walker (2015), Williams (2009).

[31]On this ethicalization from outside versus an ethicalization form inside, see Gruschke (2013).

[32]This also comprises related terms, such as "ethical", "moral", etc. and, in the following, includes references to ethics and/or morality.

[33]In case of so-called 'mixed agreements', also by the MS.

[34]This vertical perspective concerns the hierarchy of EU law as such, but not the relationship of EU law in relation to the Member States; the latter issue will be covered in Sects. 3.1, 3.3.4 and 5.1 (see *infra*) of this book.

[35]For the application of the 'separation of powers' to the EU, see *infra* notes 48 and 49.

[36]See *infra*, Sect. 3.3.4.

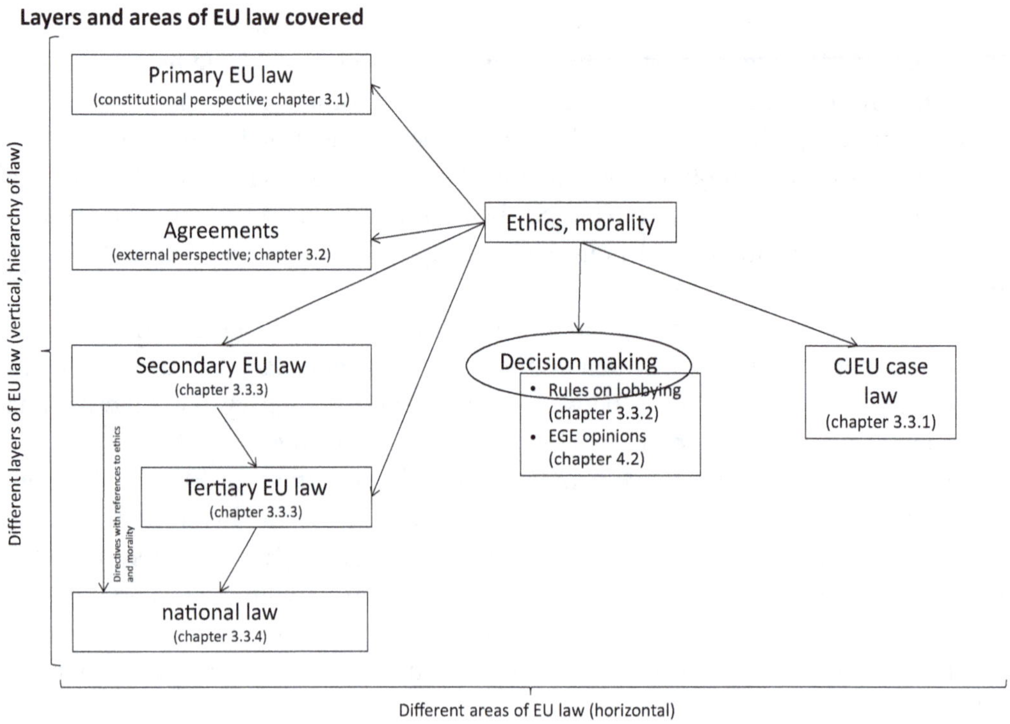

Fig. 1.2 Layers and areas of EU law covered (The vertical axis refers to the hierarchy of law, the horizontal axis to the separation of powers. The orientation of these arrows refers to the import of these non-legal concepts of ethics and morality into EU law; however, in the sense of references of EU law to them, the arrows could also be depicted in the opposite direction)

1.2 Objective and Limitations

Hence, this book is based on comprehensive research, identifying those references of EU law to the non-legal concepts of ethics and morality. While the legal order of EU law can be seen as autonomous,[37] it shall nevertheless respect principles of justice[38] (i.e. 'relative autonomy').[39]

As this book will also look at this interface of law and philosophy from a legal lens,[40] one important issue is the question, whether the references of legal texts to non-legal concepts are sufficiently determined regarding their content, so that the subject of law has enough information about the legal situation. In addition, looking

---

[37] CJEU judgment of 6 March 2018, *Achmea*, C-284/16, EU:C:2018:158, para 33 (autonomy with regard to both the MS and international law).

[38] CJEU judgment of 27 February 2018, *Associação Sindical dos Juízes Portugueses*, C-64/16, EU:C:2018:117, para 30.

[39] In this context, the CJEU also emphasizes the role of national courts: CJEU judgment of 25 July 2018, *LM*, C-216/18 PPU, EU:C:2018:586, para 50.

[40] This book will use the notion of 'lens' and not the one of 'frame' [also described as perspectives; Matthes (2014, p. 9)], as it often also has a negative connotation in the sense of being very selective and not putting an emphasis on facts; Wehling (2016, 43, 45).

at the different layers or areas of EU law, it will also be important to answer the question, of whether there is a common underlying pattern, i.e. if the references to ethics can be attributed to one (or more) particular normative theory(ies).

Based on where (in which particular sectoral fields, e.g. health, technology, finance) and to which extent we can find references to ethics and morality in EU legal documents, this book will strive to answer the following questions:

- First, are those references to ethics and morality determined in their content, or are they used without providing sufficient clarification (i.e. objective 1)?
- Second, when it comes to the implementation of relevant EU directives in national law, how have selected MS dealt with ethics and morality in the way they implemented these directives (i.e. objective 2)?
- Third, which role does the CJEU play in shaping the notion of ethics and morality in its case-law? Can we observe a phenomenon, which has been called a '*gouvernement des juges*',[41] or does the CJEU rather take a more reluctant approach, a so-called 'judicial self-restraint'[42] (i.e. objective 3)?[43]
- Finally, can we identify a certain common horizontal (or rather a specific[44]) pattern in referring to these terms of ethics and morality, and can we thus identify an ethical spirit[45] based on an analysis of these legal texts, or do we have to ascertain a gap, which has to be filled by other means (i.e. objective 4)?
- Questions to be answered are the following:
  - In EU law's references to ethics, can we identify any philosophical theory at all (question No 1)?
  - If yes, does this comprise one or more philosophical theories (question No 2)?
  - If yes, should this be understood as an unconditional reference to one or more philosophical theories, or only as pointing towards a certain idea (question No 3)?[46]

[41]Lambert (1921, p. 8), with further reference to a US study from 1911. According to Montesquieu, Charles de Secondat, Baron de (1927, p. 159), "*les juges de la nation ne sont, comme nous avons dit, que la bouche qui prononce les paroles de la loi*".

[42]Frischhut (2003, pp. 339–340), Rensmann (2005, 64–65).

[43]Theoretically, also objective 1 could refer to the CJEU; however, as we will see, in this case it is an integral part of objective 3.

[44]This question can be answered both with regard to different layers and areas of law (does the EU follow a different approach in EU secondary law, than for instance the CJEU in its case-law), or different sectoral policies (e.g. a different approach in the field of health, compared to the financial or technology sector).

[45]In CJEU judgment of 5 February 1963, *Van Gend en Loos*, 26/62, EU:C:1963:1, p. 12, the Court has referred to the "spirit" of EU law (the EEC Treaty at the time, more precisely), "the general scheme and the wording of the Treaty", when identifying the principles of primacy and direct effect. However, Williams (2009, p. 561) emphasizes that this reference to the spirit was limited by also addressing the legal objective of the Treaty.

[46]This question (concerning the philosophical lens) is separate from the other question (concerning the legal lens) of whether these notions shall be imported in an unaltered way (i.e. absolute approach), or whether they shall be imported by placing them in the legal context (i.e. relative approach).

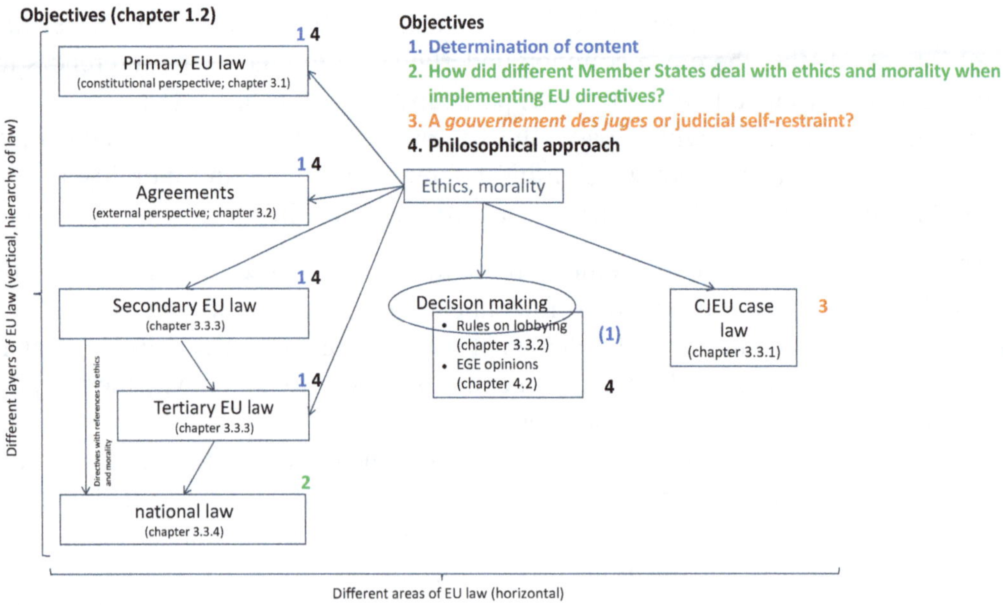

Fig. 1.3 Objectives

The relationship of these objectives to the different layers and areas of EU law covered in this book (see above Fig. 1.2) is visualized above in Fig. 1.3.

It is clearly no objective of this book to create an inventory of all the examples of EU law, which reference ethics and/or morality. Based on a comprehensive empirical research (database research in EUR-Lex and other databases), the objective of this book is rather to answer the above-mentioned questions, especially if there is a coherent ethical spirit which, thus, can be identified in EU law.

In order to guarantee a manageable scope and length of this book, certain limitations have to be emphasized.

- While the book will take a look at the law enacted by the EU[47] institutions in the sense of EU secondary law (by the European Parliament [EP] as well as the Council of Ministers) and EU tertiary law (by the EC), it will remain in this legislative field from the perspective of Montesquieu's[48] 'separation of powers'.[49] While the judiciary (i.e. the CJEU) will briefly be covered in terms of relevant case-law, the administrative branch in the sense of all the policy decisions of the EU institutions (mainly the EC) will be clearly excluded from this book, as the amount of decisions and documents to be analysed would require one or several distinct book(s).

[47] While it is clearly beyond the scope of this book, it would be equally interesting to do the same research for the Council of Europe.

[48] Montesquieu, Charles de Secondat, Baron de (1927, pp. 152–162).

[49] While the EU is clearly not a nation state and accepting that there are certain differences when applying this state related concept, we can still use it to differentiate the legislative from the administrative and the judiciary branch.

  - Hence, the objective of this book is clearly not to cover any situation where EU law and/or policy have an ethical dimension or ethical implications, irrespective of whether there is a relevant EU document for this particular situation.
  - The way in which these documents are applied by the competent authorities (at EU or at national level) is also beyond the scope of this book.

- This book will not analyse a possible clash of ethics and law, which could lead to a discussion, as it took place between law and justice. According to the Radbruch formula, for the sake of legal certainty, in principle "positive law, secured by legislation and power, takes precedence even when its content is unjust and fails to benefit the people, unless the conflict between statute and justice reaches such an intolerable degree that the statute, as 'flawed law', must yield to justice".[50] Radbruch's formula was an attempt to challenge intolerable unjust law (for example, of the Nazi regime) by the principle of justice. Radbruch's approach has to be seen against the background of legal positivism, whereby law and morality have been strictly separated.[51] However, as the objective of this paper is to depict and analyse the status quo of ethics and morality in EU law, this challenging task can be left aside.
- In the legislative field, the book will focus on the documents that explicitly refer to ethics and morality, implicit references in other legal documents cannot be taken into account.[52]
- One could also assess the ethical quality of any provision of EU law, even if it does not entail a direct (or even indirect) reference to ethics and morality. Such an analysis is also clearly beyond the scope of this book.
- When analysing EU legal documents referring to ethics and morality, this book will focus on these legal documents, which are still in force.
- While it could be interesting to address the question at which stage (right from the beginning in the Commission's proposal or later on by Parliament or Council) of the law-making process references to ethics and morality have been inserted, it is beyond the scope of this book to address this question. Hence, only the finally adopted legal document will be taken into account.[53]
- This book will also not examine how values come to matter in the EU institutions, as, for instance, it was analysed with regard to the EC.[54]

---

[50]Radbruch (2006, p. 7).

[51]Hart (1994, p. 268) put it this way "I argue in this book that though there are many different contingent connections between law and morality there are no necessary conceptual connections between the content of law and morality: and hence morally iniquitous provisions may be valid as legal rules or principles. One aspect of this separation of law from morality is that there can be legal rights and duties which have no moral justification of force whatever".

[52]Concerning rules on lobbying (*infra*, Sect. 3.3.2), also implicit references will be taken into account. Such an implicit approach has also been observed by Tallacchini (2015, p. 166) with regard to nanotechnology.

[53]Concerning the CJEU (e.g. references to ethics addressed by referring national courts in preliminary ruling procedures, respectively the EC in infringement procedures, Advocates General, or the CJEU itself), see at the beginning of Sect. 3.3.1.1.

[54]Dratwa (2014).

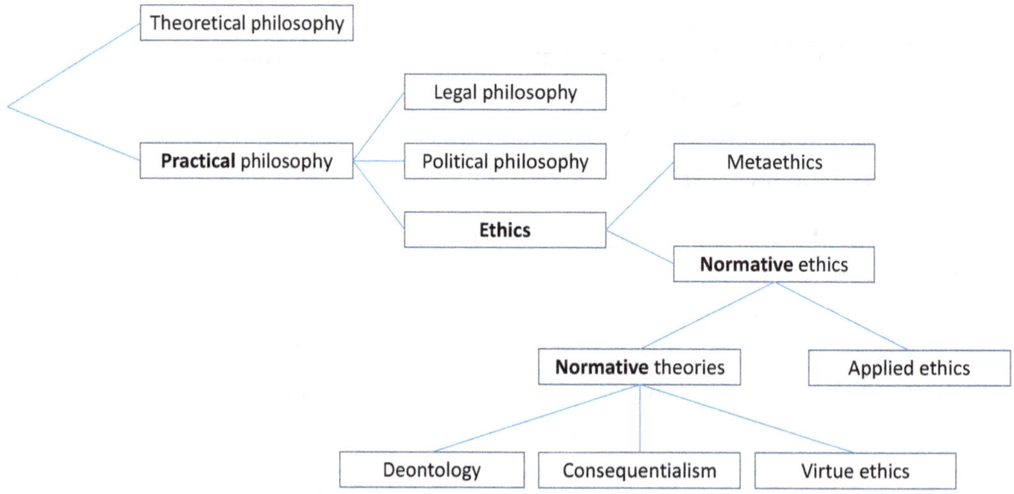

Fig. 1.4 Overview philosophy [The author would like to thank Bruno Niederbacher (University of Innsbruck | Department of Christian Philosophy) for this (non-exhaustive) overview]

- Sometimes, EU law (e.g. Directive 2001/20/EC,[55] now Regulation 536/2014[56] on clinical trials) foresees the establishment of ethics committees in the various MS. The work of these committees might have been initiated due to EU law, but is clearly beyond the objective of this book.
- While this book will cover international agreements concluded by the EU, it will not cover international law as such.[57]
- When this book also takes a philosophical lens, this only covers ethics as one part of practical philosophy, while theoretical philosophy is not covered. Within ethics, this book focuses on normative theories, thus not on meta-ethics and applied ethics (see Fig. 1.4).

1.3 Methodology

Ethics and morality[58] have not explicitly accompanied the EU integration process right from the beginning.[59] Instead, we can rather identify a process of increasing

[55]Directive 2001/20/EC of 4 April 2001 on the approximation of the laws, regulations and administrative provisions of the MS relating to the implementation of good clinical practice in the conduct of clinical trials on medicinal products for human use, OJ 2001 L 121/34, as repealed by 'Regulation clinical trials' (=note 56) [Directive clinical trials].

[56]Regulation (EU) No 536/2014 of 16 April 2014 on clinical trials on medicinal products for human use […], OJ 2014 L 158/1, as complemented by OJ 2017 L 238/12 [Regulation clinical trials].

[57]On the ethicalization of public international law see Vöneky (2013).

[58]On the terminology, see *infra* Sect. 1.5.

[59]For instance, there are no explicit references in the European Coal and Steel Community Treaty. However, the issue of values and fundamental rights has already been addressed even before the formal integration into the EU treaties; e.g. Hallstein (1979, 66–71 and 71–72). According to

references of EU law to ethics and morality since the 1990s.[60] Hence, there is no pre-determined and explicitly stated philosophical theory of ethics in the EU, which could be applied to specific topics in a deductive way. Thus, in terms of methodological approach, the above-mentioned research question (especially determination of content and possible identification of an ethical spirit of EU law) requires an indicative approach, evaluating the current situation of EU law in relation to ethics and morality, as it stands today.

Therefore, a comprehensive inductive database research, using primarily the open access EUR-Lex database, as well as Curia for the CJEU's case-law, was conducted. The language for this search was mainly English (as the most important factual working language of the EU institutions). However, also the German and French language versions were taken into account.[61]

- The first question, the determination of content (objective 1) of EU law (primary, secondary, tertiary and agreements), will be analysed by using the following inductively developed categories:

  1. References only as an argument against interference from the EU
  2. References only as a supportive argument for a certain legal solution
  3. References in order to create a parallel ethical assessment (besides the legal one)
  4. Determination via ethics committees, at EU or at national level
  5. Determination via codes of conduct, at EU or at national level
  6. Determination via references to other (international) documents
  7. Determination in document itself (some hints with regard to the content or understanding of ethics)
  8. No determination at all.

- As lobbying (i.e. influencing decision-making processes) is a topic, which is often perceived by many citizens in a very critical way, the book will analyse, if there are both explicit, as well as implicit references to ethical or moral behaviour concerning both actors and targets of lobbying.
- In terms of implementation of EU directives (objective 2), the book will analyse, how those EU directives referring to ethics and morality have been dealt with by selected MS. Have those countries been more or less ambitious, and can we observe a similar approach in these countries?
- Concerning the case-law of the CJEU (objective 3), the book will address the question, if we can observe a '*gouvernement des juges*', or rather a judicial self-restraint when dealing with ethics and morality in some sensitive fields (e.g. patentability of human life).

Calliess (2004, p. 1034), values—as part of the "magic triangle of values" (i.e. peace, economy and integration; own translation)—have been part of the integration process from the outset.

[60] See *supra* at note 26.

[61] Partially also Spanish and Italian.

- Finally, for the possible identification of a common pattern (objective 4), the book will put together the different findings of the above-mentioned layers and areas. In addition, it will analyse the opinions of the EGE, which has played an "influential role"[62] in EU law making in some sensitive fields, and whose role[63] and appointment of members[64] has been criticized in the past. Therefore, it will be essential to see if the group substantiates its ethical reasoning on certain normative ethical theories.[65]

By putting all these findings together, this inductive research will try to identify a general proposition, which can be derived from these specific examples. These findings will be analysed through two different lenses. First, these findings will allow to answer the question, if there is an underlying common normative ethical approach, and, if yes, if this can be referred to one (single or at least predominant) ethical normative theory (i.e. the philosophical lens). Second, these findings will also be placed in the legal context of the EU's common values, human rights (CFR), human dignity, and the relationship of EU law and religion (i.e. the legal lens).

1.4 Structure

After a definition of some key terms (Sect. 1.5), the book will start with a brief introduction of the three main theories of normative ethics, i.e. deontology, consequentialism, and virtue ethics (Chap. 2). The first theory rather focuses on an act, the second on its consequences, and the last one putting an emphasis on the agent itself.[66] This will provide the necessary foundations for later (Chap. 4) putting the research findings into a philosophical (i.e. ethical) context.

Taking a closer look at the different layers of EU law, this book will first focus on EU primary law (i.e. the constitutional perspective, Sect. 3.1), international agreements (i.e. the external perspective, Sect. 3.2), and EU secondary law (i.e. the internal law perspective, Sect. 3.3). The latter part will start with the question, whether in regard to the legislative and the judiciary branch of power (CJEU case-law) we can observe a '*gouvernement des juges*', or rather a judicial self-restraint (Sect. 3.3.1). This internal law perspective will then cover the law-making process in the sense of ethics in lobbying (Sect. 3.3.2), before finally turning to EU secondary (and tertiary) law (Sect. 3.3.3). As EU secondary law also comprises EU directives (referring to

---

[62]Busby et al. (2008, p. 834).

[63]This role was criticized as "ambiguous"; Busby et al. (2008, p. 842).

[64]Plomer (2008, p. 858).

[65]The opinions of the EGE were coded with the aim to derive 'rules for prediction' in an explorative way, using a latent analysis, in order to focus on the structural meaning of these opinions. The software MAQDA has been used by the research team in order to thoroughly analyse the EGE's opinions; see *infra* Sect. 4.2.2.

[66]Cf. Louden (2012, p. 504).

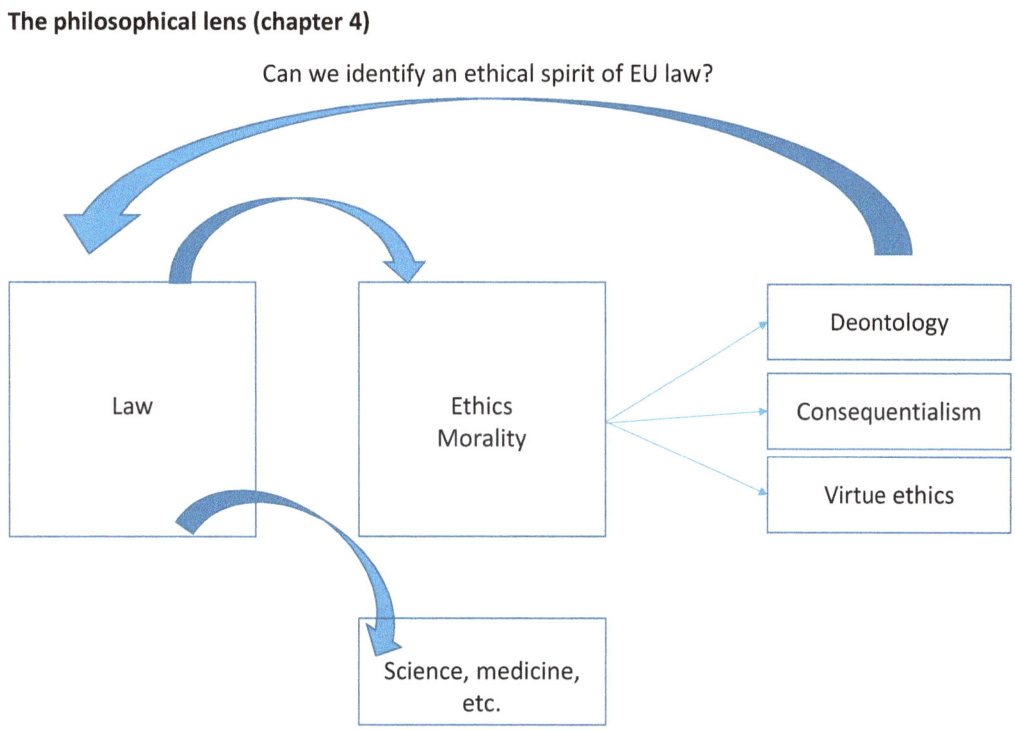

Fig. 1.5 Philosophical lens

ethics and morality) which have to be implemented into national law, also the different implementation approaches of selected MS will be covered (Sect. 3.3.4).

Both the questions regarding the determination of content of EU law referring to ethics and morality (objective 1), as well as the related question as to how selected MS have implemented the relevant directives into national law (objective 2) will mainly be answered in Chap. 3. The same is true for the CJEU's approach in this field (objective 3; Sect. 3.3.1).

Based on these findings, the question concerning the ethical spirit of EU law (objective 4) will be addressed in Chap. 4 as follows.

Section 4.1 will put all the findings (of Chap. 3) together and will relate them to the three main philosophical theories covered in Chap. 2 (i.e. deontology, consequentialism, and virtue ethics). As mentioned above, this includes the question of whether we can identify any normative ethical theory at all, and, if yes, if we can identify one or more theories (i.e. the philosophical lens). In the latter situation, the question will be if one of them is the predominant one.

As displayed above in Fig. 1.5, Sects. 4.1 and 4.2 will answer the question if at all, and to which extent we can identify an ethical spirit of EU law from the lens of practical philosophy.[67]

[67]N.B. The two arrows pointing to the right refer to references of law to non-legal domains, whereas the arrow on top addresses a different question.

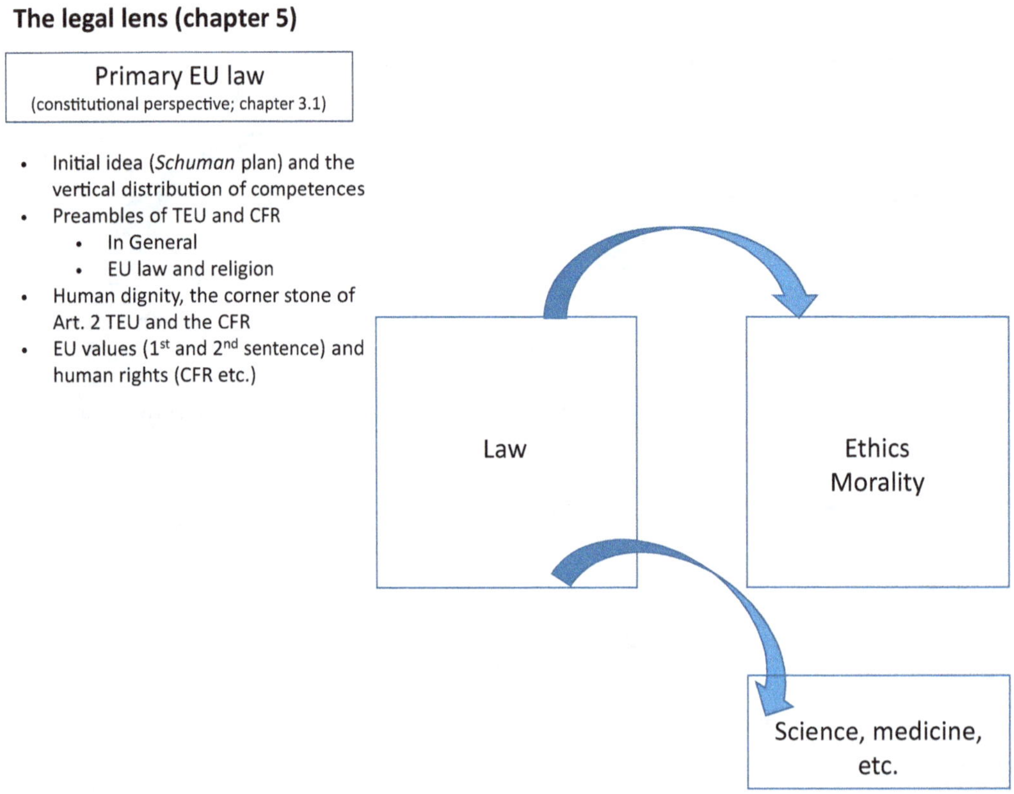

Fig. 1.6 Legal lens

As can also be seen from Fig. 1.5, references of EU law to ethics and morality address the same question as in case of references to science and medicine. That is to say, the question whether these notions shall be imported in an unaltered way (i.e. absolute approach), or whether they shall be imported by placing them in the legal context (i.e. relative approach).[68] This already takes us to the next chapter, the legal lens (see Fig. 1.6).

Finally, these findings will also be analysed from a legal lens. Chapter 5 will include the EU's values enshrined in Art 2 TEU, which have a high normative orientation function.[69] As emphasized by *Potacs*, these values have to be taken into account in the interpretation of EU law.[70] This part on the EU's values[71] will also include literature on the notion of the EU as a 'community of values' (*Wertegemeinschaft*).[72] Furthermore, this chapter will cover human rights, with a special emphasis

[68]For law and science, a relative approach has been preferred; Frischhut (2017, pp. 71–72), Wahlberg (2010, 208, 213; 2017, p. 63), Wahlberg and Persson (2017).

[69]Di Fabio (2004, p. 3).

[70]Potacs (2016).

[71]We have to accept that values do not only have a legal meaning, but also a philosophical one; cf. e.g. Scheler (1916).

[72]E.g. Mandry (2009), Reimer (2003), Rensmann (2005), Schmitz (2005, 80–85), Sedmak (2010, pp. 9–19).

on the CFR. Within the different values mentioned in Art 2 TEU,[73] a special emphasis will be put on human dignity,[74] the corner stone[75] of both the CFR and the values.

In search for the ethical spirit of EU law, also the preambles[76] of both the CFR as well as of the TEU will be taken into account,[77] as they include valuable contributions to the topic at hand.[78] This will also lead us to the heated debates in the European Convention about an *invocatio dei*, respectively a reference to (one or more) religion(s) in the process of drafting the CFR,[79] as well as the influence of religion on the notion of human dignity.[80]

Given the fact that so far, the European integration process is new and unique, one question will be whether the ethical spirit of the EU can be identified as an accomplished status quo, or whether it is a nascent one. Thus, a short look should also be taken at the *Schuman* declaration, which initiated this integration process, as well as at today's vertical separation of powers, as enshrined in articles 2–6 TFEU.[81]

All of this together will help us to answer the question about the ethical spirit of EU law. In other words, as it was described elsewhere,[82] the discovery of a common approach which can serve as a basis of understanding to the underlying philosophy of EU law. This shall help contribute to a better understanding not only of those legal documents referring to ethics and morality, but also for the rest of them.

1.5 Terminology

The word 'ethics' is partly used in the sense of 'justified morality' (the philosophers' view), partly in the sense of 'common morality' or 'social morality' (in a sociological sense). However, we should not only focus on individual moral beliefs and at the same time disregard norms embodied in institutions, in our case the EU.[83]

---

73 Another question to be answered is the different meaning of the first in relation to the second sentence of Art 2 TEU.

74 In literature, human dignity has been described as a deontological concept; Düwell (2017, p. 182).

75 Frischhut (2015, p. 532).

76 According to Art 31(2) Vienna Convention on the Law of Treaties (United Nations, Treaty Series, vol. 1155, p. 331) the context for the purpose of the interpretation of a treaty also comprises, amongst others, its preamble.

77 I.e. especially recital 2 of the CFR preamble ("spiritual and moral heritage", "indivisible, universal values of human dignity"), as well as recital 2 of the TEU preamble ("cultural, religious and humanist inheritance of Europe", "universal values of the inviolable and inalienable rights of the human person").

78 See especially Meyer (2014).

79 Cf. Meyer (2014, pp. 70–73).

80 Moyn (2014).

81 Consolidated version: OJ 2016 C 202/47.

82 Waluchow (2012, p. 199).

83 The author would like to thank Johan Brännmark (Lund University | VBE research group; see note 24) for sharing these thoughts.

In EU law, the terms of 'ethics' and 'morality' are often used in a way that leaves it open whether they are to be understood as synonymous. As we have seen above in Fig. 1.4, 'ethics' is a branch of practical philosophy which deals with what is morally right or wrong, whereas 'morality', on the other hand, is described by Beauchamp and Childress in the following way[84]:

> In its most familiar sense, the word *morality* [...] refers to norms about right and wrong human conduct that are so widely shared that they form a stable social compact. As a social institution, morality encompasses many standards of conduct, including moral principles, rules, ideals, rights, and virtues. We learn about morality as we grow up, and we learn to distinguish the part of morality that holds for everyone from moral norms that bind only members of specific communities or special groups [...].

Hence, in a very simplified way, one can say that ethics is the theoretical/philosophical approach to morality, where the latter refers to certain rules ("*mores*") and formal[85] codes of conduct in a specific (cultural, territorial and temporal) social system.[86] At least, this is the standard terminology in philosophy.

This is also true for the notion of 'public morality'[87] in EU law; while morality changes over the years (evolutionary character), it is different from country to country ("in its territory") and is based on certain values ("in accordance with its own scale of values").[88]

This collective notion of 'public morality' can be opposed to the notion of 'ethos', which has more of an individual connotation. The latter describes the special nature and attitude of a person, his convictions, customs and behaviours, which are rooted in an innate natural disposition (including the natural disposition to reason), but which can also be developed and fortified by habit, practice and adaptation according to origin.[89] Nowadays, the term of ethos is often used to refer to a certain professional group.[90] However, the notion of 'ethos' refers not only to humans, but is also used in the context of organisations.[91]

Besides 'ethics', 'morality' and 'ethos', we also need to shed some light on the notions of 'principles', 'values' and 'virtues'. This book is based on a legal, not on a

---

[84]Beauchamp and Childress (2013, pp. 2–3); no emphasis added.

[85]The author would like to thank Lena Wahlberg (Lund University | VBE research group; see note 24) for valuable feedback in this regard.

[86]Frischhut (2015, p. 536).

[87]See also *infra* Sect. 3.1.1.

[88]CJEU judgment of 11 March 1986, *Conegate*, 121/85, EU:C:1986:114, para 14.

[89]Funke (1971–2007, p. 812).

[90]See Footnote 89.

[91]CJEU judgment of 17 April 2018, *Egenberger*, C-414/16, EU:C:2018:257 (ethos of church as employer and recruitment); CJEU judgment of 11 September 2018, *IR*, C-68/17, EU:C:2018:696 (similar case, but on dismissal).

philosophical[92] understanding of the notion of 'principles',[93] whereas "principles are legal norms laying down essential elements of a legal order".[94] Principles "refer to general propositions from which rules might derive [and] relate to certain standards that might be based in law or practice, which contribute to forming a framework for decision-making and action".[95]

'Values',[96] according to one view,[97] can be explained as follows, by distinguishing them from principles[98]:

> principles possess a deontological character 'whereas values are teleological'. [...] A sense of obligation attaches to principles whereas a sense of purpose is emitted by values, which 'are to be understood as intersubjectively shared preferences.' [...] Values are therefore those ends deemed worth pursuing. Politically, they describe those qualities and states of condition that are considered desirable as shaping action or political programmes.

It is important to emphasise that values are more abstract than principles, as the former lack specific limitations, in particular with regard to specific legal consequences and addressees.[99]

Besides 'principles' and 'values', 'virtues'[100] have been described as "[t]raits of character that are judged to be morally admirable or valuable".[101] In the words of MacIntyre, virtue is understood "as a disposition or sentiment which will produce in us obedience to certain rules".[102] Virtues are usually only spoken of when they are actually lived and not just wanted, a combination of competence and performance, so to speak.[103] "Good character is not an accident. It requires discipline, reflection and responsibility."[104]

The basic virtues necessary for a virtuous life are called the 'cardinal virtues', which are temperance (*temperantia*), courage (*fortitudo*), practical wisdom (*pruden-*

---

[92]The author would like to thank Nils-Eric Sahlin (Lund University I VBE research group; see note 24; member of the EGE) for valuable discussions concerning the legal versus the philosophical understanding of this notion of 'principle' (in the context of the precautionary principle/approach) during a workshop on 3 May 2018 in Lund.

[93]On principlism, see *infra* Sect. 2.4.

[94]Bogdandy (2003, p. 10).

[95]Williams (2009, p. 559).

[96]For a detailed analysis of this term, see Hermerén (2015).

[97]The author would like to thank Lena Wahlberg for addressing the issue that sometimes also values need to be balanced against each other; hence, what we ought to do can depend on the balancing, the situation, the decision rule, etc.

[98]Williams (2009, p. 559); see also Williams (2010, pp. 256–257).

[99]Reimer (2003, p. 209). See, for a similar analysis with regard to human dignity, Advocate General (AG) Stix-Hackl opinion of 18 March 2004, *Omega*, C-36/02, EU:C:2004:162, paras 84–85.

[100]On virtue ethics, see *infra* Sect. 2.3.

[101]Louden (2012, p. 503).

[102]MacIntyre (1981, p. 227). Also adopting this definition: Williams (2010, p. 257), who furthermore points out that these three notions of values, principles and virtues "can and do overlap".

[103]Birnbacher (2013, p. 297).

[104]Kollar (2002, p. 915).

tia) and justice (*iustitia*).[105] As for all theories of ethics it has to be emphasized that those cardinal virtues can be understood in a secular (Platon), or in a religious way (Ambrose).[106] Although virtues can be relative to culture, as Kollar pointed out: "Some virtues are part of any listing of virtues: justice, prudence, generosity, courage, temperance, magnanimity, gentleness, magnificence, wisdom. Yet there is no agreed-upon list of virtues."[107]

The last term to be defined is 'humanism', which can be described as "any philosophical perspective that assigns preeminent value to human beings, their experiences, their interests, and their rights".[108] Humanism is a central notion for the EU, although a reference to humanism in an earlier version,[109] in the end, has not made it into the preamble of the CFR.

Having shed some light on these terms, let us now turn to the three main theories of normative ethics.

References

Beauchamp, T. L., & Childress, J. F. (2013). *Principles of biomedical ethics* (7th ed.). New York: Oxford University Press.

Birnbacher, D. (2013). *Analytische Einführung in die Ethik*. Berlin: De Gruyter.

Bogdandy, A. V. (2003). Doctrine of Principles: Jean Monnet Working Paper Series No. 9/03.

Busby, H., Hervey, T. K., & Mohr, A. (2008). Ethical EU law? The influence of the European Group on ethics in science and new technologies. *European Law Review (E.L.Rev.), 33,* 803–842.

Calliess, C. (2004). Europa als Wertegemeinschaft: Integration und Identität durch europäisches Verfassungsrecht? *Juristenzeitung (JZ), 59,* 1033–1084.

Craig, P. (1997). Formal and substantive conceptions of the rule of law: An analytical framework. *Public Law*, 467–487.

Di Fabio, U. (2004). Grundrechte als Werteordnung. *Juristenzeitung (JZ), 59,* 1–8.

Dratwa, J. (2014). How values come to matter at the European Commission: Ethical experimentations of Europe. *Politique Européenne*, 86–121.

Düwell, M. (2017). Human dignity and the ethics and regulation of technology. In R. Brownsword, E. Scotford, & K. Yeung (Eds.), *The Oxford handbook of law, regulation and technology* (pp. 177–196). New York: Oxford University Press.

Ethics Advisory Group. (2018). Towards a digital ethics: Report by the Ethics Advisory Group established by the European Data Protection Supervisor, the EU's independent data protection authority. Retrieved from https://edps.europa.eu/sites/edp/files/publication/18-01-25_eag_report_en.pdf.

Fowkes, J., & Hailbronner, M. (2013). Courts as the Nation's conscience: Empirically testing the intuitions behind ethicalization. In S. Vöneky, B. Beylage-Haarmann, A. Höfelmeier, & A.-K. Hübler (Eds.), *Ethik und Recht—Ethics and Law: Die Ethisierung des Rechts—The Ethicalization of Law* (pp. 395–419). Heidelberg: Springer.

---

[105] Klein (1971–2007, p. 695).

[106] See Footnote 105.

[107] See Footnote 104.

[108] Steelwater (2012, p. 674).

[109] CONV 722/03 of 28 May 2003, p. 2.

Frischhut, M. (2003). *Die Rolle der Judikative in der Ausformung der Verbandsgewalt supranationaler Organisationen: EuGH, Andengerichtshof, Supreme Court und Conseil Constitutionnel im Vergleich*. Frankfurt am Main: Peter Lang.

Frischhut, M. (2015). "EU": Short for "Ethical" Union?: The role of ethics in European Union law. *Heidelberg Journal of International Law (HJIL), 75,* 531–577.

Frischhut, M. (2017). Standards on quality and safety in cross-border healthcare. In A. D. Exter (Ed.), *Cross-border health care and European Union law* (pp. 59–86). Rotterdam: Erasmus University Press.

Funke, G. (1971–2007). Ethos. In J. Ritter, K. Gründer, & G. Gabriel (Eds.), *Historisches Wörterbuch der Philosophie* (pp. 812–815). Basel: Schwabe.

Gruschke, D. (2013). Externe und interne Ethisierung des Rechts. In S. Vöneky, B. Beylage-Haarmann, A. Höfelmeier, & A.-K. Hübler (Eds.), *Ethik und Recht—Ethics and Law: Die Ethisierung des Rechts—The Ethicalization of Law* (pp. 41–66). Heidelberg: Springer.

Hallstein, W. (1979). *Die Europäische Gemeinschaft* (5. Auflage). Düsseldorf, Wien: Econ.

Hart, H. L. A. (1994). *The concept of law* (2nd ed.). Oxford: Clarendon Press.

Hermerén, G. (2009). Accountability, democracy, and ethics committees. *Law, Innovation and Technology, 1,* 153–170.

Hermerén, G. (2015). Werte. In D. Sturma & B. Heinrichs (Eds.), *Handbuch Bioethik* (pp. 165–173). Stuttgart: J.B. Metzler'sche Verlagsbuchhandlung und Carl Ernst Poeschel Verlag GmbH.

Herrmann, J. R., & Rowlandson, M. (2008). The role of ethics and morality in EU law. *Journal of International Biotechnology Law, 5,* 241–251. https://doi.org/10.1515/JIBL.2008.39.

Jasanoff, S. (2007). *Designs on nature: Science and democracy in Europe and the United States*. Princeton, NJ: Princeton University Press.

Klein, U. (1971–2007). Kardinaltugenden. In J. Ritter, K. Gründer, & G. Gabriel (Eds.), *Historisches Wörterbuch der Philosophie* (pp. 695–696). Basel: Schwabe.

Kollar, N. R. (2002). Virtue ethics. In J. K. Roth (Ed.), *International encyclopedia of ethics* (pp. 915–916). London, Chicago, Illinois: Fitzroy Dearborn.

Lambert, É. (1921). *Le gouvernement des juges et la lutte contre la législation sociale aux États-Unis: l'expérience américaine du contrôle judiciaire de la constitutionnalité des lois*. Paris: Marcel Giard & Cie.

Louden, R. B. (2012). Virtue Ethics. In R. F. Chadwick (Ed.), *Encyclopedia of applied ethics* (2nd ed., pp. 503–510). London: Academic Press.

MacIntyre, A. (1981). *After Virtue: A study in moral theory*. Notre Dame, IN: University of Notre Dame Press.

Mandry, C. (2009). *Europa als Wertegemeinschaft: Eine theologisch-ethische Studie zum politischen Selbstverständnis der Europäischen Union. Denkart Europa: Vol. 9*. Baden-Baden: Nomos.

Manners, I. (2008). The normative ethics of the European Union. *International Affairs, 84,* 45–60. https://doi.org/10.1111/j.1468-2346.2008.00688.x.

Matthes, J. (2014). *Framing* (1. Aufl.). *Konzepte: Bd. 10*. Baden-Baden: Nomos.

Meyer, J. (2014). Präambel. In J. Meyer (Ed.), *Charta der Grundrechte der Europäischen Union* (4th ed., pp. 43–93). Baden-Baden: Nomos.

Mohr, A., Busby, H., Hervey, T. K., & Dingwall, R. (2012). Mapping the role of official bioethics advice in the governance of biotechnologies in the EU: The European Group on Ethics' Opinion on commercial cord blood banking. *Science and Public Policy, 39,* 105–117. https://doi.org/10.1093/scipol/scs003.

Montesquieu, Charles de Secondat, Baron de. (1927). *De L'esprit des Loix: Avec des notes de Voltaire, de Crevier, de Mably, de la Harpe, etc.* Nouvelle édition entièrement refondue. Tome premier. Paris: Librairie Garnier Frères.

Moyn, S. (2014). The secret history of constitutional dignity. In C. McCrudden (Ed.), *Understanding human dignity* (pp. 95–111). Oxford: Oxford University Press.

Paulus, C. G., & Schneider, F. B. (2013). Über die Ethisierung des Rechts. *Juristische Ausbildung, 12,* 1197–1205.

Plomer, A. (2008). The European group on ethics: Law, politics and the limits of moral integration in Europe. *European Law Journal, 14,* 839–859. https://doi.org/10.1111/j.1468-0386.2008.00447.x.

Potacs, M. (2016). Wertkonforme Auslegung des Unionsrechts? *Europarecht (EuR),* 164–176.

Radbruch, G. (2006). Statutory Lawlessness and Supra-Statutory Law (1946): Translated by Bonnie Litschewski Paulson and Stanley L. Paulson. *Oxford Journal of Legal Studies, 26,* 1–11. https://doi.org/10.1093/ojls/gqi041.

Reimer, F. (2003). Wertegemeinschaft durch Wertenormierung?: Die Grundwerteklausel im europäischen Verfassungsvertrag. *Zeitschrift Für Gesetzgebung,* 208–217.

Rensmann, T. (2005). Grundwerte im Prozeß der europäischen Konstitutionalisierung: Anmerkung zur Europäischen Union als Wertegemeinschaft aus juristischer Perspektive. In D. Blumenwitz, G.-H. Gornig, & D. Murswiek (Eds.), *Die Europäische Union als Wertegemeinschaft* (pp. 49–72). Berlin: Duncker & Humblot.

Scheler, M. (1916). *Der Formalismus in der Ethik und die materiale Wertethik: Neuer Versuch der Grundlegung eines ethischen Personalismus.* Sonderdruck aus: "Jahrbuch für Philosophie und phänomenologische Forschung", Bd. I und II, herausgegeben von EDMUND HUSSERL, Freiburg i. Br. Halle a. d. Saale: Verlag von Max Niemeyer.

Schmitz, T. (2005). Die Charta der Grundrechte der Europäischen Union als Konkretisierung der gemeinsamen europäischen Werte. In D. Blumenwitz, G.-H. Gornig, & D. Murswiek (Eds.), *Die Europäische Union als Wertegemeinschaft* (pp. 73–97). Berlin: Duncker & Humblot.

Sedmak, C. (2010). Europäische Grundwerte, Werte in Europa: Einleitung zum Gesamtprojekt. In C. Sedmak (Ed.), *Grundwerte Europas: Band 1. Solidarität: Vom Wert der Gemeinschaft* (pp. 9–42). Darmstadt: WBG Wissen verbindet.

Smits, R. (2018). The invisible core of values in the European integration project. *Legal Issues of Economic Integration, 45,* 221–227.

Steelwater, E. (2012). Humanism. In R. F. Chadwick (Ed.), *Encyclopedia of applied ethics* (2nd ed., pp. 674–682). London: Academic Press.

Tallacchini, M. (2015). To bind or not bind?: European ethics as soft law. In S. Hilgartner, C. A. Miller, & R. Hagendijk (Eds.), *Genetics and society. Science and Democracy: Making knowledge and making power in the biosciences and beyond* (pp. 156–175). New York: Routledge, Taylor & Francis Group.

von Savigny, K. F. (1951). *Juristische Methodenlehre: Nach der Ausarbeitung des Jakob Grimm. Herausgegeben von Gerhard Wesenberg.* Stuttgart: K.F. Koehler Verlag.

Vöneky, S. (2013). Grundlagen und Grenzen der Ethisierung des Völkerrechts. In S. Vöneky, B. Beylage-Haarmann, A. Höfelmeier, & A.-K. Hübler (Eds.), *Ethik und Recht—Ethics and Law: Die Ethisierung des Rechts—The Ethicalization of Law* (pp. 129–148). Heidelberg: Springer.

Vöneky, S., Beylage-Haarmann, B., Höfelmeier, A., & Hübler, A.-K. (2013). Vorwort. In S. Vöneky, B. Beylage-Haarmann, A. Höfelmeier, & A.-K. Hübler (Eds.), *Ethik und Recht—Ethics and Law: Die Ethisierung des Rechts—The Ethicalization of Law* (pp. V–IX). Heidelberg: Springer.

Wahlberg, L. (2010). *Legal questions and scientific answers: Ontological differences and epistemic gaps in the assessment of causal relations.* Lund: Media-Tryck.

Wahlberg, L. (2017). Legal ontology, scientific expertise and the factual world. *Journal of Social Ontology, 3,* 49–65. https://doi.org/10.1515/jso-2015-0022.

Wahlberg, L., & Persson, J. (2017). Importing notions in health law: Science and proven experience. *European Journal of Health Law, 24,* 565–590. https://doi.org/10.1163/15718093-12453308.

Walker, N. (2015). The philosophy of European Union law. In A. Arnull & D. Chalmers (Eds.), *Oxford Handbooks in Law. The Oxford handbook of European Union law* (pp. 3–27). Oxford University Press.

Waluchow, W. (2012). Constitutionalism in the European Union: Pipedream or possibility? In J. Dickson & P. Eleftheriadis (Eds.), *Philosophical foundations of law. Philosophical foundations of EU law* (pp. 189–215). Oxford: Oxford University Press.

Wehling, E. (2016). *Politisches Framing: Wie eine Nation sich ihr Denken einredet—und daraus Politik macht. Edition medienpraxis: Vol. 14.* Köln: Halem Verlag.

Williams, A. T. (2009). Taking values seriously: Towards a philosophy of EU law. *Oxford Journal of Legal Studies, 29,* 549–577. https://doi.org/10.1093/ojls/gqp017.

Williams, A. T. (2010). *The ethos of Europe: Values, law and justice in the EU*. *Cambridge studies in European law and policy*. Cambridge: Cambridge University Press.

Wilms, H. C. (2013). Ethisierung des Europarechts—Grundrechtliche Grenzen und politische Praktiken. In S. Vöneky, B. Beylage-Haarmann, A. Höfelmeier, & A.-K. Hübler (Eds.), *Ethik und Recht—Ethics and Law: Die Ethisierung des Rechts—The Ethicalization of Law* (pp. 285–298). Heidelberg: Springer.

Chapter 2
Normative Theories of Practical Philosophy

While the outcome sometimes might be the same, it is the way of reasoning which distinguishes these three theories.[1] In the following, these theories will be addressed by displaying some key characteristics, without going into all possible details, as it is beyond the scope of this book.[2]

2.1 Deontology

The word 'deontological' is derived from the Greek word '*deon*', which means 'the (moral) necessity'[3] and relates to an obligation or duty.[4] Hence, 'deontology' is sometimes referred to as the 'science of duty'.[5] Deontology refers to the form of normative ethics according to which the commitment and quality of moral actions and judgments derive from the obligation to certain behaviours or maxims of action.[6]

According to different deontological approaches, a moral obligation may result from rules defined by a religious community (church), or from personal or collective values, or be found in some objective order of duties. Thus, it can be understood in a secular, or in a religious way.

Well-known representatives of deontology are the German philosopher Immanuel Kant and William David Ross.

[1]Parfit (2011) addresses the interesting question, whether different theories (Kantianism, contractualism, consequentialism) in the end 'climb the same mountain' and whether they can be combined.

[2]The author would like to thank Bruno Niederbacher for valuable feedback on this chapter. The usual disclaimer applies.

[3]Literally, 'the necessary', and in a practical context, the 'moral necessity'.

[4]Spinello (2002, p. 219).

[5]Hallgarth (2012, p. 602).

[6]Fahrenbach (1972, p. 114).

M. Frischhut, *The Ethical Spirit of EU Law*,
https://doi.org/10.1007/978-3-030-10582-2_2

Deontology can be seen as being opposed to any form of teleological or consequentialist ethics,[7] or in other words, according to deontology, "[a]ctions are *intrinsically* right or wrong, regardless of the consequences they produce".[8] An example, which clearly follows a deontological (torture is intrinsically wrong) and not a consequentialist (even if torture would result in saving the kidnapped child's life) approach, is the famous Gäfgen[9] case of the European Court of Human Rights (ECtHR).[10] From a legal perspective, this concerns the discussions in the context of human rights on absolute versus relative rights, where the first are rights, which are not subject to exceptions (e.g. there is no possibility to torture a kidnapper in order to get the information necessary to safe the kidnapped child).[11] Otherwise, we refer to relative rights. It is worth clarifying that although often associated with deontology, deontological ethical theories can recognize absolute rights, but does not necessarily do so.[12]

In addition to types of action that are morally good or bad in themselves, one also has to address the question of good will. This good will "must be autonomous and thus rationally generated, because it is reason alone that enables the human person to overcome myriad variations of inclination and desire".[13]

We can distinguish between a hypothetical (e.g. if you want to be fit, do some sports) and a categorical imperative, where the first does not imply an absolute moral duty, whereas a categorical imperative is without option.[14] In order to determine whether, besides the good will, an action corresponds to a duty (i.e. whether it is intrinsically right) it has to follow a 'maxim'. According to Kant, reason communicates to the mind things it should do according to certain rules, which he refers to as 'maxims'.[15] "A *maxim* is the subjective principle for acting, and must be distinguished from the *objective principle*, namely the practical law."[16] The way in which a person can then test whether a maxim is of supreme moral worth is the 'categorical imperative'. As Kant is a representative of deontology, his way for determining whether a maxim for action is a genuine universal moral principle, "must be grounded in a priori principles", i.e. principles which can be justified before we can evaluate their consequences.[17]

Kant describes the categorical imperative as follows:

---

[7] See Footnote 6.

[8] Spinello (2002, p. 219); no emphasis added.

[9] ECtHR judgment of 1 June 2010, *Gäfgen vs. Germany*, 22978/05.

[10] For a case that raises similar questions (small vs. big number of victims), see Bundesverfassungsgericht (BVerfG) judgment from 15 February 2006, *Shooting down terror plane*, 1 BvR 357/05.

[11] ECtHR *Gäfgen vs. Germany*, 22978/05, para 87.

[12] Birnbacher (2013, p. 133).

[13] Hallgarth (2012, p. 608).

[14] Hallgarth (2012, p. 609).

[15] See Footnote 13.

[16] Kant (2014, p. 69 (IV 420)); no emphasis added.

[17] See Footnote 14.

- "*act only according to that maxim through which you can at the same time will that it become a universal law*"[18] (basic formula);
- "*so act as if the maxim of your action were to become by your will a* UNIVERSAL LAW OF NATURE"[19] (formula of the universal law of nature);
- "*So act that you use humanity, in your own person as well as in the person of any other, always at the same time as an end, never merely as a means*"[20] (formula of humanity);
- "to do no action on a maxim other than in such a way, that it would be consistent with it that it be a universal law, and thus only in such a way *that the will could through its maxim consider itself as at the same time universally legislating*"[21] (formula of autonomy);
- "every rational being must so act as if through its maxims it were at all times a legislating member of the universal kingdom of ends"[22] (kingdom of ends).

As we can already imagine at this stage, Kant's view is one, which can be seen to respect contemporary notions of human rights.[23] Likewise, the understanding of the concept of human dignity is very much attributable to Kant.[24] As he pointed out, "what constitutes the condition under which alone something can be an end in itself does not merely have a relative worth, i.e. a price, but an inner worth, i.e. dignity".[25] Hence, humans should be treated as subjects, not as objects.

2.2 Consequentialism

Consequentialism is described as "[a]ny ethical theory that argues fundamentally that right action is an action that produces good results or avoids bad results".[26] Consequentialist theories assume that the judgement about the moral correctness and wrongness of actions depends exclusively on the quality of the consequences of action.[27] One example in this regard are impact assessments. However, they are not required in any case, but are limited to decisions with far-reaching consequences, as in the case of national or supranational legislators.[28] Also risk assessment deals with consequences, either from a legal or from an ethical perspective.

---

[18]Kant (2014, p. 71); no emphasis added.

[19]See Footnote 18.

[20]Kant (2014, p. 87); no emphasis added.

[21]Kant (2014, p. 97); no emphasis added.

[22]Kant (2014, p. 105).

[23]Hallgarth (2014, p. 611).

[24]On Kant and human dignity, see Knoepffler (2017).

[25]Kant (2014, p. 99); no emphasis added.

[26]Hallgarth (2012, p. 602).

[27]Birnbacher (2013, p. 173).

[28]Birnbacher (2013, pp. 194–195).

To a greater extent than deontological ethics, consequentialist theories allow adjustments of moral judgement to social and scientific-technical change.[29] The effects of current action on future generations are often considered to have the same weight as the effects on the current living.[30]

The most famous form of consequentialist is 'utilitarianism'. As for every normative ethical theory, there are different variations, which due to limited space cannot be covered in the following. The axiology of utilitarianism has only one non-moral value, called 'utility', where utility is the extent of well-being brought about by an action.[31] Hence, utilitarianism is a decision procedure that is intended to promote the general welfare,[32] "according to which the rightness and wrongness of acts depends entirely on facts about the maximization of overall well-being".[33]

Well-known representatives of utilitarianism are Jeremy Bentham and John Stuart Mill. The distinction between primary and secondary principles is based on Mill, where primary principles are located at the level of ethical theory, secondary principles at the level of moral practice; the relationship between the two is the following: the primary ethical principles determine which secondary principles should apply at the level of social morality.[34] Secondary principles must then be formulated in such a way that they avoid any shortcomings of primary principles.[35]

Secondary principles must not cognitively overload the average actor and that is why he cannot be required to include future world conditions in his reasons for action; however, a responsibility for precaution is nevertheless demanded in the case of new land and risk technologies.[36] One factor to be considered when choosing secondary principles is the extent to which the obligated actor himself causally contributed to the evil (polluter pays principle).[37]

Utilitarianism is egalitarian as the well-being of each person is of equal value, and even the feelings of animals can be taken into account.[38] Characteristic of utilitarianism is a pronounced future orientation and thinking in long-term development tendencies; thus, in addition to sustainability, utilitarianism can call for present precautions for future generations.[39]

---

[29]Birnbacher (2013, p. 174).

[30]Birnbacher (2013, p. 195).

[31]Birnbacher (2013, p. 218).

[32]Habibi (2002, p. 894).

[33]Eggleston (2012, p. 452).

[34]Birnbacher (2013, p. 194).

[35]Birnbacher (2013, p. 197).

[36]Birnbacher (2013, p. 200).

[37]Birnbacher (2013, p. 203).

[38]Habibi (2002, p. 895).

[39]Birnbacher (2013, pp. 220–221).

Utilitarianism is an ethical theory, which stands for a secular, rational and scientific moral system,[40] which can almost be calculated in a mathematical way (the slogan 'the greatest good for the greatest number'). Bentham's desire was "to devise a system that would be objective and scientific".[41] The simplicity of utilitarian ethics, however, applies only in theory and not in concrete application.[42]

2.3 Virtue Ethics

Virtue ethics is described as "[a]n approach to both understanding and living the good life that is based on virtue",[43] where virtue[44] is referred to as "moral excellence of behaviour and [!] character".[45] Proponents of virtue ethics try to construct the morality demanded by normative standards from the concepts of virtue that are valid in morality; thus, values or norms are not the starting point of the analysis or construction, but virtue concepts and virtue catalogues.[46] The key question of virtue ethics obviously is what kind of traits should we develop, and, in which way does this help us in assessing the moral correctness of actions?

The notion of honesty, for instance, does not only designate the motive of wanting to be honest, but it also includes certain judgments of correctness such as the judgement that it is morally correct not to lie, etc.[47] Hence, instead of considering the requirements of morality in detail, it is often enough to describe the examples of perfect virtue.[48]

As a prominent example, we have already seen the 'cardinal virtues' of temperance (*temperantia*), courage (*fortitudo*), practical wisdom (*prudentia*), and justice (*iustitia*).[49] Together with the theological virtues of faith (*fides*), hope (*spes*) and love (*caritas*), they form the so-called seven virtues.[50] As mentioned above, virtues (character traits) can be understood in a secular, or in a religious way.[51] Hence, different cultures and religions have different catalogues of virtues,[52] which sometimes overlap (e.g. justice), while others might be more specific; for instance, love might

[40]See Footnote 32.

[41]See Footnote 38.

[42]Birnbacher (2013, p. 219).

[43]Kollar (2002, p. 915).

[44]On the notion of virtue, see also *supra* Sect. 1.5.

[45]Chara (2002, p. 912).

[46]Birnbacher (2013, p. 302).

[47]Birnbacher (2013, p. 302).

[48]See Footnote 47.

[49]Klein (1971–2007, p. 695).

[50]Chara (2002, pp. 912–914).

[51]Chara (2002).

[52]See Footnote 50.

rather occur in a religious context.[53] In terms of applied virtue ethics, virtues can also be tailored to specific needs, for instance in the fields of medical ethics,[54] business ethics, professional ethics, etc.[55] It remains to be seen, which approach EU law takes in this regard.[56]

However, sometimes even virtue ethics cannot avoid establishing principles. In this context, Birnbacher provides the following example: the virtue of justice may require principles of justice, whereas this might not be the case for virtues such as solidarity, helpfulness, or generosity.[57] Given the most controversial debate on solidarity in the context of the current migration and refugee debate, according to the author also solidarity might require a reference to principles, which provide further clarification with regard to the substance.[58]

Without going into further details, in literature virtue ethics is sometimes seen rather as a supplement, than as a basis of normative ethics.[59] In the words of Louden, "[v]irtue ethics is not competing for quite the same turf as modern consequentialist and deontological theories but is rather an attempt to return moral theory to more realistic possibilities".[60]

2.4 Excursus

As mentioned in Fig. 1.4, deontology, consequentialism and virtue ethics are the three normative theories concerning ethics. Besides these just covered theories, there are three other approaches, which deserve attention.

Although different in details, both the 'minimal ethics' approach and 'principlism' of Beauchamp and Childress do not cover the whole of morality, but only its baselines. Instead of tracing the controversial ramifications of moral views in detail, both conceptions are limited to the rough outlines of morality and reconstruct only that core set of principles which is so uncontroversial that it can be recognized by all.[61]

---

53 On the proliferation of virtues, see Halbig (2013, pp. 142–146).

54 Beauchamp and Childress (2013, pp. 37–44) address "five focal virtues" for health professionals: compassion, discernment, trustworthiness, integrity, and conscientiousness.

55 Louden (2012, p. 507).

56 See *infra* Chap. 4.

57 Birnbacher (2013, p. 304).

58 See *infra* Chap. 6.

59 Birnbacher (2013, p. 305).

60 Louden (2012, p. 509).

61 Birnbacher (2013, p. 77).

2.4.1 Minimal Ethics

Minimal ethics claims moral realism and the possibility of moral knowledge only for a core set of moral norms, while it renounces a claim to truth and knowledge for all norms that are not part of the core set. Minimal ethics combines the programme of descriptive inventory with the ambitious programme of an unassailable justification of intersubjectively valid standards. In doing so, it asserts a par excellence objective validity for the minimum set of moral norms that it has highlighted.[62] Well-known representatives are Thomas Hobbes and Bernard Gert.[63] Gert has defined ten moral rules, all of which are formulated negatively, which remind us of the 'Ten Commandments', and can be subject to exceptions.[64]

Such ethical theories, which focus on the description of the functional principles of current morality, can be assigned to the model of 'reconstructive' ethics, while an 'establishing' ethics not only describes moral principles, but also attempts to justify them.[65]

2.4.2 Principlism

Besides ethical minimalism, there is another well-known contemporary reconstructive ethical approach. Determining what is 'the right thing to do' can also be done in a substantive way, as elaborated by Beauchamp and Childress[66] in the field of medical ethics. Their 'principlism' is a system of ethics, which is based on four moral principles: autonomy (free will), nonmaleficence (do no harm), beneficence (do good), and justice (social distribution of benefits and burdens). According to Brännmark, "bioethicists like Beauchamp and Childress do not think that they have to make a choice between Kantianism and utilitarianism, because irrespective of which fundamental normative approach one adopts, one can still understand their four-principle framework as a reasonable framework in bioethics".[67] Such an approach might have the advantage of being more 'user-friendly', but a possible disadvantage can be seen in the sectoral approach, in the case of this prominent example, medical ethics 'only'.[68] As principlism is a rather new approach, to some extent on a timeline it

---

[62]Birnbacher (2013, pp. 398–399).

[63]Birnbacher (2013, p. 399).

[64]Birnbacher (2013, 82–83, 399–401).

[65]Birnbacher (2013, p. 64).

[66]Beauchamp and Childress (2013).

[67]Brännmark (2017, p. 174).

[68]On 'disunitarianism', see *infra* Chap. 6.

cannot have had a causal influence on the 'ethical spirit' of EU law. Nevertheless, it might proof useful for this book.

2.4.3 Communitarianism

Besides universalist ethical theories, which claim to be universally valid, there are also particularistic approaches. According to a particularistic moral understanding, the claim of morality can also be limited to the members of certain cultures, members of certain religious communities and ethnic groups, in extreme even to a single individual.[69]

One example is 'communitarianism',[70] which has recently emerged in political philosophy since the 1980's, and which emphasizes the rootedness of morality in the specific history and culture of a community or nation and rejects the sharp separation of moral and other cultural norms that characterizes the universalist understanding of morality.[71] Well-known representatives are Alasdair MacIntyre and Michael Sandel. MacIntyre's book 'After Virtue' was at the beginning of this "new ethic that repudiated both modern individualist liberalism and the rejuvenated conservatism of the Reagan era".[72] As described elsewhere, in this book, "MacIntyre analyzes theories of morality with regard to culture and states that virtue is found within the community, in its *ethos*, or character, and not in the individual alone".[73]

Communitarianism, a theory mainly associated with American philosophers, has been developed against the background of multiple crises, where society is "in a state of emergency", where morality has become "a virtual impossibility", and where communities, institutions and social relationships, which should make morality possible, "are quickly succumbing to a pervasive individualism".[74] One major point of criticism is that society is nothing more than a collection of individuals "with nothing in common but self-interest and the fear of death".[75] That is why communitarianism can also be opposed to liberalism, according to which "each person is to determine the good individually".[76]

Communitarianism rejects "Western culture's one-sided emphasis on individual rights and seeks to balance rights with responsibilities".[77] Thus, the community-based ethics stresses the 'common good', shared common values and emphasises

---

[69]Birnbacher (2013, p. 27).

[70]Not to be confused with 'communism'.

[71]Birnbacher (2013, p. 28).

[72]Paul (2002, p. 172).

[73]N.N. (2002, p. 519); no emphasis added.

[74]See Footnote 72.

[75]Paul (2002, p. 172).

[76]Etzioni (2012, p. 516).

[77]See Footnote 75.

individual's obligations towards society. As Etzioni has pointed out: "This is in contrast to focusing on maximizing the utility of each person, the autonomy of the self and individual rights".[78]

Communitarianism also suggests that the good should be defined by society. In the words of one well-known representative, Michael Sandel, "[a] just society can't be achieved simply by maximizing utility or be securing freedom of choice. To achieve a just society we have to reason together about the meaning of the good life, and to create a public culture hospitable to the disagreements that will inevitably arise."[79] He also points out that "[a] more robust public engagement with our moral disagreements could provide a stronger, not a weaker, basis for mutual respect",[80] which is of utmost importance for democracy.[81] To sum it up, according to Paul, "communitarianism remains one of the most promising contemporary moral philosophies".[82]

References

Beauchamp, T. L., & Childress, J. F. (2013). *Principles of biomedical ethics* (7th ed.). New York: Oxford University Press.

Birnbacher, D. (2013). *Analytische Einführung in die Ethik*. Berlin: De Gruyter.

Brännmark, J. (2017). Respect for persons in bioethics: Towards a human rights-based account. *Human Rights Review, 18,* 171–187. https://doi.org/10.1007/s12142-017-0450-x.

Chara, P. J. (2002). Virtue. In J. K. Roth (Ed.), *International encyclopedia of ethics* (pp. 912–915). London, Chicago, IL: Fitzroy Dearborn.

Eggleston, B. (2012). Utilitarianism. In R. F. Chadwick (Ed.), *Encyclopedia of applied ethics* (2nd ed., pp. 452–458). London: Academic Press.

Etzioni, A. (2012). Communitarianism. In R. F. Chadwick (Ed.), *Encyclopedia of applied ethics* (2nd ed., pp. 516–521). London: Academic Press.

Fahrenbach, H. (1972). Deontologie. In J. Ritter (Ed.), *Historisches Wörterbuch der Philosophie: Band 2: D-F* (p. 114). Basel, Stuttgart: Schwabe & Co.

Frick, M.-L. (2017). *Zivilisiert streiten: Zur Ethik der politischen Gegnerschaft. Was bedeutet das alles?: Nr. 19454*. Ditzingen: Reclam.

Habibi, D. A. (2002). Utilitarianism. In J. K. Roth (Ed.), *International encyclopedia of ethics* (pp. 894–895). London, Chicago, IL: Fitzroy Dearborn.

Halbig, C. (2013). *Der Begriff der Tugend und die Grenzen der Tugendethik*. Berlin: Suhrkamp.

Hallgarth, M. W. (2012). Consequentialism and Deontology. In R. F. Chadwick (Ed.), *Encyclopedia of applied ethics* (2nd ed., pp. 602–613). London: Academic Press.

Kant, I. (2014). *Groundwork of the metaphysics of morals* (M. Gregor & J. Timmermann, Ed. and Trans.). Cambridge: Cambridge University Press.

Klein, U. (1971–2007). Kardinaltugenden. In J. Ritter, K. Gründer, & G. Gabriel (Eds.), *Historisches Wörterbuch der Philosophie* (pp. 695–696). Basel: Schwabe.

Knoepffler, N. (2017). Menschenwürde bei Kant. In C. Sedmak (Ed.), *Grundwerte Europas: Band 7. Menschenwürde: Vom Selbstwert des Menschen* (pp. 63–80). Darmstadt: WBG Wissen verbindet.

[78] See Footnote 76.

[79] Sandel (2010, p. 261).

[80] Sandel (2010, p. 268).

[81] See Frick (2017).

[82] Paul (2002, p. 173).

Kollar, N. R. (2002). Virtue ethics. In J. K. Roth (Ed.), *International encyclopedia of ethics* (pp. 915–916). London, Chicago, IL: Fitzroy Dearborn.
Louden, R. B. (2012). Virtue Ethics. In R. F. Chadwick (Ed.), *Encyclopedia of applied ethics* (2nd ed., pp. 503–510). London: Academic Press.
N.N. (2002). MacIntyre, Alasdair. In J. K. Roth (Ed.), *International encyclopedia of ethics* (pp. 519–520). London, Chicago, IL: Fitzroy Dearborn.
Parfit, D. (2011). *On what matters. The Berkeley Tanner lectures*. Oxford: Oxford University Press.
Paul, G. E. (2002). Communitarianism. In J. K. Roth (Ed.), *International encyclopedia of ethics* (pp. 172–173). London, Chicago, IL: Fitzroy Dearborn.
Sandel, M. J. (2010). *Justice: What's the right thing to do?* New York: Farrar, Straus and Giroux.
Spinello, R. A. (2002). Deontological ethics. In J. K. Roth (Ed.), *International encyclopedia of ethics* (pp. 219–220). London, Chicago, IL: Fitzroy Dearborn.

Chapter 3
Status Quo of Ethics and Morality in EU Law

After this introduction into the relevant basics of normative ethics, let us turn to the status quo of EU law referring to ethics and morality. Following the hierarchy of EU law, let us first have a look at primary EU law.[1]

3.1 Constitutional Perspective: The Status Quo of Morality in Primary EU Law

3.1.1 'United in Diversity'

The EU's approach to ethics can best be described by its motto 'united in diversity'. On the one hand ('EU united'), the Treaty on European Union draws inspiration "from the cultural, religious and humanist inheritance of Europe"[2] and the EU Charter of Fundamental Rights which refers to the Union's "common values"[3] and "spiritual and moral heritage".[4] On the other hand the CFR requires the EU to respect "the diversity of the cultures and traditions of the peoples of Europe as well as the national identities of the Member States"[5] ('EU in diversity').

Initially, EU integration was an economic vehicle, which developed from coal and steel to an internal market, and finally to a political Union (also safeguarding fundamental rights). The internal market is still a key objective of the EU. Nonetheless, on an exceptional basis, MS are allowed to restrict the free movement of goods based on grounds of "public morality, public policy [and so forth]" (Art 36 TFEU).

[1]The following chapter is strongly based on the starting point of this research project, i.e. Frischhut (2015).

[2]Recital 2 TEU.

[3]Recital 1 CFR.

[4]Recital 2 CFR.

[5]Recital 3 CFR. See also recital 6 CFR, Art 3(3)(4) and Art 4(2) TEU.

M. Frischhut, *The Ethical Spirit of EU Law*,
https://doi.org/10.1007/978-3-030-10582-2_3

The term of 'public morality' itself is not defined in the Treaties. As a notion of EU law, it is interpreted by the CJEU. The Court leaves it to the MS to apply their understanding of public morality, as long as they do not follow a principle of public double morality.[6]

3.1.2 National Umbrella Philosophy

With the expanding case-law of the CJEU interpreting the fundamental freedoms of the internal market, some MS sought to protect their nationally determined understanding of morality. A look at the timeline exhibits the contemporaneity of a famous Irish abortion case[7] (4.10.1991) and the Maastricht Treaty[8] (signed on 7.2.1992), where one of the protocols to this Treaty provides an umbrella, protecting "Article 40.3.3 [right to life of the unborn] of the Constitution of Ireland".[9]

When Malta acceded to the EU in 2004, a similar protocol was annexed to the Accession Treaty, stating that "[n]othing [...] shall affect the application in the territory of Malta of national legislation relating to abortion".[10] Although those two instances operated without explicit reference to public morality, the intention was the same, as in the following examples.

In the very same round of accessions, Poland opted for a similar, yet different approach. This can be qualified as "less" in terms of legal significance, as Poland's concerns were only taken into account in terms of a Declaration of that acceding state. However, at the same time, it can be seen as 'broader', in the sense that the wording states as follows: "nothing [...] prevents the Polish State in regulating *questions of moral significance*, as well as those related to the protection of human life".[11]

With the entering into force of the Lisbon Treaty[12] (1.12.2009), the previously only solemnly proclaimed[13] CFR became legally binding.[14] In this context, Poland seemed to fear that the CFR[15] "might be used to challenge its freedom to regulate the availability of abortions, euthanasia and same-sex marriage".[16] Therefore, the final

---

[6] CJEU *Conegate,* 121/85, para 20.

[7] CJEU judgment of 4 October 1991, *Society for the Protection of Unborn Children [SPUC]*, C-159/90, EU:C:1991:378.

[8] OJ 1992 C 191/1.

[9] OJ 1992 C 191/94.

[10] OJ 2003 L 236/1 (947).

[11] OJ 2003 L 236/1 (983); emphasis added; see also 978.

[12] OJ 2007 C 306/1.

[13] OJ 2000 C 364/1 (Nice, 7.12.2000) and OJ 2007 C 303/1 (Strasbourg, 12.12.2007).

[14] Art 6(1) TEU.

[15] For the application of the CFR on Poland and the United Kingdom see Protocol 30, OJ 2007 C306/156; see also CJEU judgment of 21 December 2011, *N. S.*, C-411/10 and C-493/10, EU:C:2011:865, paras 116–117; Arnull (2014, pp. 1595–1596).

[16] Arnull (2014, p. 1601). Nowadays, on same sex-marriage and EU citizenship, see CJEU judgment of 5 June 2018, *Coman*, C-673/16, EU:C:2018:385.

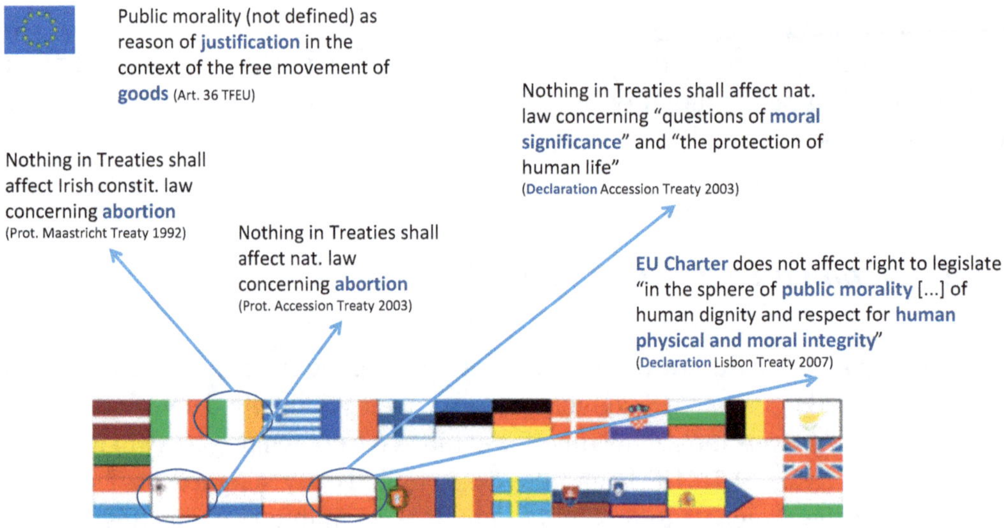

Fig. 3.1 National umbrella philosophy

act of the 13.12.2007 signed Lisbon Treaty contained a declaration by Poland on the CFR, whereby "[t]he Charter does not affect in any way the right of Member States to legislate in the sphere of *public morality*, family law, as well as the protection of human dignity and respect for human physical and moral integrity".[17] Some MS, those present at the time of accession, were united in a position diverse to the Polish one, by underlying in a joint declaration "that the Declarations attached to this Final Act cannot be interpreted or applied in a way contrary to the obligations of the Member States arising from the Treaty and Act of Accession".[18]

As we have seen (see also Fig. 3.1), EU primary law does not comprise the term ethics, but 'public morality'.[19] This notion is a public one, that is to say a collective one, as it is defined by public authorities, not by individuals. We have seen both implicit (in the context of abortion) and explicit reference to public morality.

Has this term been determined regarding its content in EU primary law? No, there are no explicit definitions, most likely because there seems to be, at least a minimum, consensus and the fact that the term of public morality has already been shaped regarding its content by the CJEU. If not defined, is it used in a way, which provides sufficient clarification (i.e. objective 1 of this book)? Due to the historic background and the context of abortion, this second question can be answered in the affirmative.

Nonetheless, the way in which this term of public morality is used cannot be qualified as very ambitious. Quite the opposite, this approach of the "Masters of the

---

[17] OJ 2007 C 306/1 (270), emphasis added.

[18] OJ 2003 L 236/1 (983); and noting "that the Commission subscribes fully to the above".

[19] The "spiritual and moral heritage" (recital 2 CFR) has already been mentioned. The CFR further mentions the "physical, mental, moral or social development" in the context of the prohibition of child labour and protection of young people at work (Art 32(2)). Finally, yet importantly, Art 165(2) TFEU refers to the "physical and moral integrity of sportsmen and sportswomen".

Treaties" can be qualified as an "umbrella philosophy", trying to establish a "principle of non-interference" of EU law with their nationally determined morality.[20] However, ethics and morality should definitely be more than a mere substitute for a kind of subsidiarity principle.

3.1.3 *Excursus: EU Values*

EU values[21] are not of relevance for our topic in terms of direct references to ethics or morality. However, Art 2 TEU, which enshrines the values of the EU, is of utmost importance for our topic in an indirect way. This provision has been inserted by the Lisbon Treaty, which entered into force on 1 December 2009, and reads as follows:

> The Union is founded on the values of respect for human dignity, freedom, democracy, equality, the rule of law and respect for human rights, including the rights of persons belonging to minorities.
>
> These values are common to the Member States in a society in which pluralism, non-discrimination, tolerance, justice, solidarity and equality between women and men prevail.

The first sentence states the values which according to the wording are pre-existing ("founded on"), however, does not further define them. The second sentence seems to have a different legal significance, as the wording does not refer to the EU, but to the MS, precisely their society. Perhaps one would expect a plural here, but the second sentence speaks of "a society". According to Pechstein, this formulation fluctuates between (desirably guided) description and prescription,[22] and can be seen as 'less', as it cannot trigger Art 7 TEU (sanctions in case of violations of values).[23]

Hermerén has emphasized that the common values are "one of several ways of keeping the member states of the European Union together by referring to values they have in common and by pointing out differences between these values and others".[24] These general common values of the EU have been applied to two areas (digitalization and non-financial reporting, partly in sports) and further specified in others (health and partly in sports), as can be seen below from Table 3.1.

In 2006, thus three years before the entry into force of the Lisbon Treaty, the EU health ministers declared the health values of "universality, access to good quality care, equity, and solidarity".[25] This example is not an application of the general values, but a concretization, resulting in mainly distinct values, where only solidarity

[20] Frischhut (2015, p. 544).

[21] For further details, see the various contributions in Sedmak (2010, 2012, 2013, 2014, 2015, 2016, 2017).

[22] Pechstein (2018, no. 1).

[23] Pechstein (2018, no. 8).

[24] Hermerén (2008, p. 375).

[25] Council conclusions on Common values and principles in European Union Health Systems, OJ 2006 C 146/1.

Table 3.1 EU common values applied and further specified

	Health	Non-financial reporting	Sports	Digitalization
Year	2006	2014	• 2017 • 2018	2018
Legal status	Soft-law (conclusions of health ministers)	Binding (amendment to EU directive)	Soft law: • EP resolution (2017) • Council conclusions (2018)	Soft-law (advisory opinion)
Application or distinct values	(Mainly) distinct values	(Mainly) application	• Promotion of EU values, plus distinct values • (Mostly) distinct values	(Mainly) application

is part of both the general and these specific values.[26] For this example of health values, we can again identify the EU's motto of 'united in diversity', as these Council conclusions of 2006 emphasize "that the practical ways in which these values and principles become a reality in the health systems of the EU *vary significantly* between Member States, and *will continue to do so*".[27] Unlike the general values, this document sheds further light on the content of these values. Equity, for instance, is determined in the sense that it "relates to equal access according to need, regardless of ethnicity, gender, age, social status or ability to pay". It is also worth mentioning that "[b]eneath [!] these overarching values, there is also a set of *operating principles*"[28], which cover quality, safety, care that is based on evidence and ethics, patient involvement, redress, privacy and confidentiality.

From health, let us now turn to corporate social responsibility (CSR). Based on the EU rules on non-financial reporting[29] for some large companies, the common good matrix, which lies at the heart of the Common Good Balance Sheet, is based on the values of "human dignity, solidarity and social justice, environmental sustainability, transparency and co-determination".[30] This is an example of values having a direct

[26]On solidarity, see Prainsack and Buyx (2017).

[27]See Footnote 25. emphases added.

[28]See Footnote 27

[29]Directive 2014/95/EU amending Directive 2013/34/EU as regards disclosure of non-financial and diversity information by certain large undertakings and groups, OJ 2014 L 330/1.

[30]Economy for the common good: https://www.ecogood.org/en/common-good-balance-sheet/common-good-matrix/.

impact on (large) companies, where we find an application of some of the EU's values, adding other 'principles' we know from EU law, such as sustainability[31] and transparency.[32]

An EP resolution on integrity, etc. in sports[33] took both the approach of promoting the general EU values ("such as pluralism, tolerance, justice, equality and solidarity"),[34] but also coined distinct values ("such as respect, friendship, tolerance and fair play"[35]; or "such as mutual respect, tolerance, compassion, leadership, equality of opportunity and the rule of law"[36]). Recently, the 2018 Council conclusions on promoting the common values of the EU through sport mainly refer to distinct values (printed in Italics), when they state that "sport can teach values such as *fairness*, *teambuilding*, democracy, tolerance, equality, *discipline*, *inclusion*, *perseverance* and *respect* that could help to promote and disseminate common values of the EU".[37] The same is true, when they state that "[v]alues such as *mutual respect*, *fair play*, *friendship*, solidarity, tolerance and equality should be natural to all those involved in sport".[38] As we can see, the majority of those values are not part of Art 2 TEU.

In digitalization, the Ethics Advisory Group established by the European Data Protection Supervisor has referred to dignity, freedom, autonomy, solidarity, equality, democracy, justice and truth, in order to leap from the EU's general common values to 'digital ethics'.[39] As we can see, the majority of values are those from Art 2 TEU (e.g. not comprising the rule of law, non-discrimination, tolerance), while also embracing autonomy, one of the principles from the 'principlism' of Beauchamp and Childress.

In terms of the legal status, no example except for the non-financial reporting directive, are legally binding (soft-law). Table 3.1 summarizes these four (non-exhaustive) examples of the EU's general common values in different specific fields.

These EU's general common values also have an external perspective. In its relations with the wider world, the EU "shall uphold and promote its *values* and interests and contribute to the protection of its citizens [...,] contribute to peace, security, the sustainable development of the Earth, *solidarity* and mutual respect among peoples, free and fair trade, eradication of poverty and the protection of *human rights*".[40]

---

[31] Art 3(3) and (5) TEU, etc.

[32] Art 11 TEU, Art 15(3) TFEU, etc.

[33] EP resolution of 2 February 2017 on an integrated approach to Sport Policy: good governance, accessibility and integrity, OJ 2018 C 252/2 [EP resolution sport & integrity].

[34] Ibid. pt. 45.

[35] Ibid. pt. 31.

[36] Ibid. pt. 44.

[37] Conclusions of the Council [etc.] on promoting the common values of the EU through sport, OJ 2018 C 196/23 (pt. 14).

[38] Ibid. pt. 17.

[39] Ethics Advisory Group (2018).

[40] Art 3(5) TEU; emphases added.

3.2 External Perspective: International Agreements, etc.

After the constitutional perspective (EU primary law), let us now turn to the external ethical perspective. Following the hierarchy of EU law,[41] the following chapter focuses on references to ethics and morality in international agreements (etc.),[42] before we will then turn to the internal perspective (EU secondary law, etc.) in the next chapter.

The documents identified have been researched in the EU's EUR-Lex database, searching for the terms 'ethi*' and 'mora*' (both, in title and text), and in the two subcategories of 'international agreements' and in 'EFTA documents'.[43] This research comprises both 'international agreements' according to Art 216 TFEU, as well as 'association agreements' in the sense of Art 217 TFEU. Moreover, 'resolutions', for instance of a Joint (Parliamentary) Assembly, which have been documented in EUR-Lex, have also been taken into account. On the other hand, irrelevant terms have been excluded.[44]

3.2.1 Status Quo of Ethics and Morality

Often, EU law refers to ethics and/or morality in different sensitive fields. This is also the case for one prominent example of an international agreement, the 'Comprehensive Economic and Trade Agreement' (CETA) between Canada, of the one part, and the EU and its Member States, of the other part.[45] In the heated debates, investment protection was one of the main issues. Hence, it is no surprise that the provision on the members of the multilateral investment tribunal is entitled 'ethics', emphasizing the importance of the independence of its members and the avoidance of both a direct or indirect conflict of interest.[46] In addition, the 'Joint Interpretative Instrument' stresses that "[s]trict [!] ethical rules for these individuals have been set to ensure their *independence* and *impartiality*, the *absence of conflict of interest*, *bias* or *appearance of* bias".[47]

This example of CETA investment protection referring to ethics concerns a very sensitive issue, which is key for the trust of citizens in order to alleviate fears of big companies being able to 'buy justice'. In terms of determination of content, it is quite

[41] According to Art 216(2) TFEU, the agreements concluded by the Union are binding upon the EU institutions and on the MS.

[42] The following chapter is based on the research of Gruber (2015); the author would also like to thank Mr Weinkogl (also MCI) for checking updates to this research.

[43] On EFTA see *infra* at note 85.

[44] See also Gruber (2015, pp. 19–22).

[45] OJ 2017 L11/1.

[46] Art 8.30 CETA.

[47] OJ 2017 L11/3 (4); emphases added. See also the Statement by the Commission and the Council on investment protection and the Investment Court System ('ICS'), on p. 20.

clear what the reference to ethics should stand for (independence and avoidance of conflict of interest). Apart from investment protection, we can also find a reference to ethics in the context of the recognition of professional qualifications.[48]

References in CETA to 'morality' follow a common pattern, which we have already seen in EU primary law (Art 36 TFEU: 'public morality'), where the concept of 'public morals' is one of the exceptions (or: 'reasons of justification'), besides 'public order' and 'public safety', to name but a few.

Another example comprising several references to ethics is the Korea agreement.[49] This agreement is also about trust based on ethics in a sensitive field. Here, 'ethical business practices' have to be set in place in order to avoid improper inducements by manufacturers and suppliers of pharmaceutical products or medical devices to health care professionals or institutions for the listing, purchasing or prescribing of pharmaceutical products and medical devices eligible for reimbursement under health care programmes.[50]

After those two representative examples of such international agreements referring to ethics, let us take a more detailed look at this issue and especially at the question of the determination of content (objective 1) of international agreements referring to ethics. Often we can find almost identical approaches in various agreements, as in some of the following examples referring to the Georgia agreement, the references could also have been indicated with regard to the Ukraine association agreement,[51] to name but one.

- In the context of trade and customs legislation, we can find the situation, not of ethics being determined by reference to other notions such as avoidance of conflicts of interest, independence, etc., but on the contrary the opposite situation. The association agreement with Georgia refers to the 'Blueprint on Customs ethics' in order to determine "the highest standards of *integrity*" in this regard.[52] In a similar way, the agreement with Indonesia refers to the 'World Tourism Organisation's Global Code of Ethics for Tourism' in order to "ensure balanced and sustainable development of tourism".[53]
- In the Georgia agreement, we can find one example, where the meaning of ethics can be traced in a systematic interpretation, when in the context of 'trade and investment promoting sustainable development', Art 231 refers to "voluntary sustainability assurance schemes such as fair and ethical trade schemes and eco-labels".

[48] OJ 2017 L11/306.

[49] Free trade Agreement between the EU and its MS, and the Republic of Korea, OJ 2011 L 127/6 [Agreement Korea].

[50] Ibid. Annex 2-D, Art 4(1).

[51] Association Agreement between the EU and the European Atomic Energy Community [EAEC] and their MS, and Ukraine, OJ 2014 L 161/3, as amended by OJ 2018 L 188/17 [Agreement Ukraine].

[52] Association Agreement between the EU and the EAEC and their MS, and Georgia, OJ 2014 L 261/4, as amended by OJ 2018 L 140/107 [Agreement Georgia], Art 67(2)(e); emphasis added.

[53] Framework Agreement on comprehensive partnership and cooperation between the European Community and its MS, and Indonesia, OJ 2014 L 125/17, Art 17(1).

Similar examples can be found in the context of tourism ("promote ethical standards in tourism by introducing a certified European Fair Trade Tourism label").[54]

- Another common field of 'ethicalization' are references to 'professional ethics' both in the private, as well as in the public field. Such rules can even apply after leaving the job.[55]
  - For lawyers providing legal services in respect of public international law and foreign law, the Georgia agreement refers to "compliance with *local* codes of ethics".[56] This approach makes sense, if the legal rules in this area are also located at national level.
  - Professional ethics in the public field can be found in the Moldova agreement.[57] This agreement foresees rules on cooperation, with the aim of fostering efficient and accountable public administration in Moldova, and to support the implementation of the rule of law. This cooperation shall, amongst others, also cover "the promotion of *ethical values* in the civil service".[58] It is interesting to see the link between ethics and values, although the detailed content remains somehow vague.
  - In another private field, the agreement with Central America states that cooperation on microcredit and microfinance shall also address the "exchange of experiences and expertise in the area of ethical banking".[59] The same statement with regard to the determination of ethics applies here.
  - Although training is an important element for ethical behaviour,[60] the following example is completely undetermined. This agreement states that elements of a training programme for port State inspectors should include, amongst others, "[E]thics".[61] Maybe this lacking determination is less of a problem, as 'ethics' here can be read in terms of the title of a subject of this training programme.
- In the field of healthcare, we have already seen the example of the Korea agreement, referring to ethical business practices of improper inducements by manufacturers and suppliers of pharmaceutical products or medical devices to health care professionals or institutions.[62]

---

[54]Resolution on the impact of tourism on the development of ACP countries, OJ 2006 C 330/15 [Resolution tourism], pt. 21.

[55]Decision No 2/92 of the ACP-EEC Committee of Ambassadors of 22 December 1992 laying down the Staff Regulations of the Technical Centre for Agricultural and Rural Cooperation under the Fourth ACP-EEC Convention, OJ 1993 L 53/33, Art 16.

[56]Ibid. Annex XIV-B; emphasis added.

[57]Association Agreement between the EU and the EAEC and their MS, and Moldova, OJ 2014 L 260/4, as amended by OJ 2018 L 176/21.

[58]Ibid. Art 22(e); emphasis added.

[59]Agreement establishing an Association between the EU and its MS, and Central America, OJ 2012 L 346/3, as amended by OJ 2015 L 196/59, Art 71.

[60]Frischhut (2015, p. 572).

[61]Agreement on Port State Measures to Prevent, Deter and Eliminate Illegal, Unreported and Unregulated Fishing, OJ 2011 L 191/3, Annex E.

[62]*Supra*, note 50.

– Another provision of the same Annex on pharmaceutical products and medical devices confirms the shared principles of the contracting parties with regard to "*ethical practices* by manufacturers and suppliers of pharmaceutical products and medical devices and by health care providers on a global basis *in order to* achieve *open*, *transparent*, *accountable* and *non-discriminatory* health care decision-making".[63] As the *telos*[64] is clearly stated, we have a strong guidance towards the determination of the meaning of ethics in this regard. This example is reminiscent of consequentialism ('in order to'), however, at the same time exhibits some elements of principlism[65] (transparency, non-discrimination, etc.).
– Another example in cross-border healthcare deals with a kind of 'circumvention tourism'.[66] This resolution "[c]alls on all States to ensure the ethics of transplantation by adopting measures to eliminate 'transplant tourism'".[67] Here, too, we have a strong guidance with regard to the determination of the content of ethics, as the *telos* is clearly stated.

- In another field, which we can entitle with 'ethics and society', we find a reference to "the ethical, cultural and social values of the society" to which children belong and which shall not prejudice the right of the child to a loving family.[68] Although ethics is not determined in this document itself, we can read it as a reference to the national or regional level of the relevant society.

After ethics, let us now turn to references to morality. The introductory example of CETA is representative in the sense that in the majority of cases, 'public morality'[69] is used as an exception clause.[70] Besides public security or public order, 'public morals' can be such a reason of justification ('exception'), provided that such measures are not applied in a manner which would constitute a means of "arbitrary or unjustifiable *discrimination* between countries where like conditions prevail, or a *disguised restriction* on establishment or cross-border supply of services".[71] This is an approach, which we already know from inside of the internal market.

A slightly different version of an exception clause can be found in the Ukraine Agreement, where one of the grounds for refusal or invalidity of a trademark registration are trademarks, which are contrary to 'public policy' or "to accepted principles

---

63 OJ 2011 L 127/1154, Annex 2-D, Art 1(e); emphases added.

64 On the replacement of the term 'teleological' by ' consequentialist', see Louden (2012, p. 503).

65 The notion of 'principlism' can refer to the above-mentioned four principle-approach of Beauchamp and Childress. However, it can also be seen in a broader sense, referring to any ethical approach, basing its deliberations on principles. The author would like to thank Göran Hermerén (Lund University | 2002–2011 EGE president/chairperson) for valuable feedback in this regard.

66 Cohen (2012).

67 Resolution tourism, pt. 33.

68 Resolution on children's rights and child soldiers in particular, OJ 2004 C 26/17, recital D.

69 E.g. Trade Agreement between the EU and its Member States, and Colombia and Peru, OJ 2012 L 354/3, as amended by OJ 2018 L 1/1, Art 106(1)(a).

70 Gruber (2015, p. 28).

71 Agreement Georgia, Art 134(2)(a); emphases added.

of morality".[72] While this concept is undetermined, a similar provision on patents (protection of biotechnological inventions) is more precise, as it states examples of what is considered un-patentable: processes for cloning human beings, or modifying their germ line genetic identity, as well as uses of human embryos for industrial or commercial purposes.[73]

In the field of development aid, we find examples of morality used as an argument supporting a certain position. A resolution on climate change states that industrialised countries "have a *historical responsibility* for climate change and are *morally obliged* to assist ACP countries".[74] Another one notes the "*moral* and sovereign *rights* of affected Southern African states to accept or reject GMOs coming as food aid",[75] as well as the "eradication of poverty to be a moral and political imperative".[76] This phenomenon causes no major challenges, if a legal provision 'only' refers to moral (or ethical) considerations as a supporting argument.[77]

This is more difficult with the following example, as it is not quite clear, what is meant by the "*moral*, political and economic *support* [that] should be offered to the Burundian people".[78] *How* does a moral support look like, is there a right to moral support, etc.?

- An interesting example can be found in the following resolution on embargoes: "Points out that, whilst the overt reason for imposing sanctions is normally to bring about a change of regime in a particular country, or at least a major change in the policy of that country's government, their imposition may also serve simply as an expression of moral condemnation".[79] While besides other hard-facts morality also seems to be important, we can see this as a minimum approach ('at least' moral support).
- The wording "every child has a right to a standard of living adequate for the child's physical, mental, spiritual, moral and social development"[80] is reminiscent of Art 32 CFR, which addresses the "physical, mental, moral or social development" of young people at work.
- The following example concerning the appointment of arbitrators reminds us of the members of the multilateral investment tribunal in CETA: "appointment of an

[72]Art 193(2)(f); for a similar provision on designs see Art 217(5).

[73]Art 221(5); see also (d) on animals. On the similarity with an EU directive (note 113), see *infra* Sect. 4.1.

[74]Resolution on the social and environmental consequences of climate change in the ACP countries, OJ 2009 C 221/31, recital O; emphases added.

[75]Resolution on the situation in Southern Africa, OJ 2003 C 231/53, recital F.

[76]Resolution on the future of ACP-EU relations, OJ 1999 C 271/35, pt. 4.

[77]Frischhut (2015, p. 561).

[78]Resolution on support for the peace process in Burundi, OJ 1999 C 271/49, recital B; emphasis added.

[79]Resolution on the impact of sanctions and, in particular, of embargoes on the people of the countries on which such measures are imposed, OJ 2002 C 78/32 [Resolution embargoes], pt. 2.

[80]Convention on the International Recovery of Child Support and Other Forms of Family Maintenance, OJ 2011 L 192/51, recital 5(2).

independent and impartial arbitrator of a nationality other than the nationalities of the parties, and of high moral standing."[81] The content of this moral standing remains undetermined.

- The same applies for the last example in this regard: "The salary and social contributions of observers shall be borne by the competent authorities of the Gabonese Republic. Captains shall do everything in their power to ensure the physical and moral safety of observers carrying out their duties."[82]

Finally, we do not only find examples relating to human beings, in the context of animal transport, the preamble of this Convention holds that "every person has a *moral obligation* to respect all animals and to have due consideration for their capacity for suffering",[83] and another one with a similar wording referring to "their capacity for suffering and memory".[84] Hence, two references to moral obligations, which can be seen as supporting arguments.

After international agreements, let us now turn to documents of the 'European Free Trade Area' (EFTA), which are displayed here in a separate way due to three reasons. First, because of the significance of this agreement, second, because they are also separately documented in the EUR-Lex database, and finally, because they occur in a different context. EFTA comprises Norway, Iceland, Liechtenstein and Switzerland, where all of these countries, except for Switzerland, are linked to the EU via the European Economic Area (EEA).[85]

There are two examples of EFTA documents referring to ethics, both from the EFTA Surveillance Authority (ESA), which is the equivalent to the EC in terms of monitoring and enforcing the relevant rules. In the context of the financial crisis, a global reduction in liquidity, and various other complex reasons led to the collapse of the three main Islandic banks. An essential part of the Icelandic financial sector "was the restructuring of household and corporate debt", which was qualified to be "a complex and sensitive issue with a number of financial, economic and *ethical* considerations".[86] Some of the "most relevant changes" addressed in terms of restructuring aid granted to the *Landsbankinn* banks was "revised risk manage-

[81] Decision No 3/90 of the ACP-EEC Council of Ministers of 29 March 1990 adopting the general regulations, general conditions and procedural rules on conciliation and arbitration for works, supply and service contracts financed by the European Development Fund (EDF) and concerning their application, OJ 1990 L 382/1, Annex V, Art 10(3)(a).

[82] Protocol setting out the fishing opportunities and the financial contribution provided for by the Agreement between the European Community and the Gabonese Republic on fishing off the coast of Gabon for the period 3 December 2001 to 2 December 2005, OJ 2002 L 73/19, Annex, pt. 7.

[83] European Convention for the Protection of Animals during International Transport (revised), OJ 2004 L 241/22 [Convention animal transport], recital 2; emphasis added.

[84] European Convention for the protection of vertebrate animals used for experimental and other scientific purposes, OJ 1999 L 222/31, as amended by OJ 2003 L 198/11 [Convention animal experiments], recital 2.

[85] Agreement on the European Economic Area, OJ 1994 L1/3, as amended by OJ 2016 L 141/3.

[86] ESA Decision No 291/12/COL of 11 July 2012 on restructuring aid to Arion Bank (Iceland), OJ 2014 L 144/169, recital 123; emphasis added.

ment and a greater significance of corporate responsibility and compliance with *high ethical* standards".[87]

What we can see here is another example of referring to ethics in a sensitive field. The first example exhibits a general awareness for ethics,[88] while the second is not determined regarding its content. How should those standards look like, where could they be found? Such ethical rules should be further determined, especially in the banking sector.

Both ESA decisions also address the issue of 'moral hazard', which is a term of microeconomics. "In general, moral hazard occurs when a party whose actions are unobserved affects the probability or magnitude of a payment".[89] This can occur in case "of workers who perform below their capabilities when employers cannot monitor their behavior ('job shirking')",[90] or in case of banks shifting risk to the general tax-paying public. Both decisions address moral hazard in the context of burden sharing in the sense that "aid should be limited to the minimum necessary and an appropriate own contribution to restructuring costs should be provided by the aid beneficiary".[91] These examples of referring to a non-legal term are less of a problem. First, we deal with a reference to a determined concept (here not of practical philosophy, but of economics), and the consequences are clearly stated. Hence, we could qualify this reference as a supporting argument, as we have already seen.[92]

In terms of morality, we can find an example of referring to moral obligations in a situation, where no legal obligation exists. In the discussion of adjusting the EEA agreement in terms of higher contributions in the context of the EU enlargement, one argument used was "the EEA EFTA States' obligation to provide (moral) support in connection with the enlargement of the EU". This was stated, because under the EEA Agreement, "the EU has no legal entitlement to demand a sharp increase in the previous level of payments".[93]

3.2.2 Conclusion

As of 1993, we can trace the first references to ethics in international agreements, with the majority of relevant documents since the turn of the millennium.[94] This

[87]ESA Decision No 290/12/COL of 11 July 2012 on restructuring aid granted to Landsbankinn (Iceland), OJ 2014 L 144/121, recital 104; emphasis added.

[88]Gruber (2015, p. 40).

[89]Pindyck and Rubinfeld (2018, p. 658); no emphasis added.

[90]Pindyck and Rubinfeld (2018, p. 658).

[91]ESA Decision No 291/12/COL, recital 204; ESA Decision No 290/12/COL, recital 207; et passim.

[92]*Supra* note 77.

[93]Resolution on the "Enlargement of the European Economic Area (EEA)—institutional and legal issues", OJ 2003 C 308/16, pt. 4.5.

[94]Gruber (2015, pp. 22–23).

roughly corresponds with the general 'ethicalization' in terms of the founding of ethics advisory bodies at EU level in 1991 and 1997 respectively.[95]

We have seen references to ethics in several sensitive fields, such as investment tribunals, influence of the pharma industry on doctors, etc., or the supporting of private banks with taxpayers' money. What these examples have in common is the fact that ethics is always a means of strengthening citizens' trust in these areas.

Often we have seen similar approaches in different agreements, as well as a link between concepts such as integrity and ethics. The key question, which is the determination of content of both ethics and morality (i.e. objective 1) has to be answered in a differentiated way: sometimes, it was possible to trace the meaning of these references to ethics and morality, but at times, this was not the case. In some of the numerous references in the context of professional ethics, the task of determining the content was one of the national level, as this level was also in charge of the legal perspective. The notion of morality has mainly been used as an exception clause, besides self-standing notions such as 'moral hazard'. The beneficiaries of ethical behaviour have mainly been humans, but some examples also covered animals. Some of these documents also referred to related concepts such as values.[96] This is true for CETA, which "reflects the strength and depth of the EU-Canada relationship, as well as the fundamental values that we cherish".[97] No references to ethics or morality can be found in the recent EU Japan agreement published in July 2018.[98]

3.3 Internal Law Making Perspective

3.3.1 A 'Gouvernement Des Juges'?

EU law also comprises case-law and the CJEU case-law has played a paramount role in shaping the EU *acquis*. Therefore, let us now turn to ethics and morality in case-law and analyse the CJEU's approach in this field. In EU integration in general, the CJEU has often been criticized for its pro-active role.[99] As already mentioned, this chapter shall answer the question, if we can observe a '*gouvernement des juges*', or if the CJEU rather takes a more reluctant approach, a so-called 'judicial self-restraint' (i.e. objective 3)?

---

[95]See *infra* Sect. 4.2.1.

[96]For further details see Gruber (2015, pp. 34–37).

[97]CETA Joint Interpretative Instrument, recital 1(c).

[98]Strategic Partnership Agreement between the EU and its MS, and Japan, OJ 2018 L 216/4.

[99]On this issue see Dawson et al. (2013), Horsley (2013), Lienbacher (2013), Martinsen (2015).

3.3.1.1 The CJEU's Judicial Self-restraint

Analysing the case-law of the CJEU, one has to be aware of cases where the judgment merely quotes EU legislation (as this will be covered separately[100]), international or national law. In addition, ethics and morality used as arguments of the parties of a case (EC, other EU institutions, or MS) have to be seen in a different light, the same applies for questions of a national court in a preliminary ruling procedure. Finally, one has to separate arguments of an Advocate General, and the binding judgment of the Court of Justice.

EU law affects almost every aspect of national law, thus also some very sensitive areas. As the Court has held, there are areas "in which there are significant *moral*, religious and cultural *differences* between the Member States. In the absence of [EU] harmonisation in the field, *it is for each Member State* to determine in those areas, *in accordance with its own* scale of *values*, what is required in order to ensure that the interests in question are protected".[101] This is the case in the following fields: various games of chance,[102] the import of "articles having an indecent or obscene character",[103] protection of children from immoral media,[104] prostitution,[105] or abortion.[106]

We have already seen the notion of 'public morality', as one of the reasons of justification in the context of the fundamental freedoms of the internal market, where a similar approach was taken in international agreements. Interpreting this reason of justification, the Court held that "in principle it is for *each Member State* to determine in accordance with its own scale of *values* and in the form selected by it the requirements of public morality in its *territory*".[107] Hence, it is not the EU to determine this notion, nor a majority of MS, but each single MS. Reference is also made to the national values, although one should take into account that this statement (1986) was given roughly 20 years before the Lisbon Treaty inserted Art 2 TEU on the common values.[108] The limitation stated in this case was the one of 'double morality', where goods legal in the home country cannot be qualified as obscene, if imported from another MS.[109]

---

[100] See *infra* Sect. 3.3.3.

[101] CJEU judgment of 8 September 2009, *Liga Portuguesa*, C-42/07, EU:C:2009:519, para 57; emphases added.

[102] Ibid (games of chance via the internet); CJEU judgment of 24 March 1994, *Schindler*, C-275/92, EU:C:1994:119, para 32 (lotteries); CJEU judgment of 6 March 2007, *Placanica*, joined cases C-338/04, C-359/04 and C-360/04, EU:C:2007:133, para 47 (betting and gaming).

[103] CJEU judgment of 14 December 1979, *Henn and Darby*, C-34/79, EU:C:1979:295, para 15; CJEU *Conegate,* 121/85, para 14; emphases added.

[104] CJEU judgment of 14 February 2008, *Dynamic Medien*, C-244/06, EU:C:2008:85, para 44.

[105] CJEU judgment of 20 November 2001, *Jany*, C-268/99, EU:C:2001:616, para 56.

[106] CJEU *SPUC*, C-159/90, para 20.

[107] CJEU *Conegate,* 121/85, para 14; emphases added.

[108] On the "ethical values in sport", see CJEU judgment of 18 July 2006, *Meca-Medina*, C-519/04 P, EU:C:2006:492, para 43.

[109] CJEU *Conegate,* 121/85, para 20.

'Ethics' was an issue for instance in an Austrian case on the protection of pregnant workers against dismissal from work.[110] The question was on the beginning of pregnancy in case of in vitro fertilisation (IVF): either already at the time of fertilization of her ova by her partner's sperm cells, or at the time of transfer into her uterus. Before providing an answer on the details of this case, the Court gave a very important general statement:

> artificial fertilisation and viable cells treatment is a *very sensitive social* issue in many Member States, marked by their *multiple traditions and value systems*, the Court is *not* called upon, by the present order for reference, to broach *questions of a medical or ethical nature*, but must *restrict itself* to a *legal* interpretation of the relevant provisions of [EU law].[111]

At the time of this judgment, the Lisbon Treaty had already been signed (2007), although not yet entered into force (2009). Still, the Court referred to the "multiple traditions and value systems". This Grand Chamber judgment clearly demonstrates the Court's judicial self-restraint, comprising various dimensions: a vertical one, whereas these questions have to be determined at a national level, as well as a horizontal one, according to which it is for the legislature and not for the courts, to decide on these "sensitive social issue[s]". As the Court has held in other cases concerning 'morality', "[e]ven if the morality of lotteries is at least questionable, it is not for the Court to substitute its assessment for that of the legislatures of the Member States".[112] Even if the Court, in the following, decides this IVF case solely by interpreting the relevant provisions of EU law (i.e. beginning of pregnancy only as of transfer into uterus), in the end this legal interpretation of legal norms will have an indirect impact on the ethical nature of this topic. Moreover, although it is for the MS to take these decisions, the legal interpretation takes place at EU level. Based on this analysis, it is also not really a necessity for the CJEU to determine the content of the concept of 'ethics', as this perspective has been clearly excluded for the procedure of solving this case.

Three years later, the Court (again, Grand Chamber) had to decide another case in the field of bioethics, namely on the patentability of neural precursor cells and the processes for their production from embryonic stem cells. This case was about the Directive on biotechnological inventions, which, amongst others, excludes the patentability of "uses of human embryos for industrial or commercial purposes".[113] The key challenge, thus, centred on the interpretation of the notion of 'human embryo'. The Court confirmed its statement in *Mayr*, not to decide questions of ethical nature in very sensitive fields, which are marked by MS's "multiple traditions and value systems",

---

[110] On additional challenges in case of cross-border reproductive care, see Frischhut (2017).

[111] CJEU judgment of 26 February 2008, *Mayr*, C-506/06, EU:C:2008:119, para 38; emphases added.

[112] CJEU *SPUC*, C-159/90, para 20; CJEU *Schindler*, C-275/92, para 32.

[113] Directive 98/44/EC of 6 July 1998 on the legal protection of biotechnological inventions, OJ 1998 L 213/13 [Directive Biotech], Art 6(2)(c). On this directive, see also *infra* Sect. 3.3.3.1.

such as the definition of human embryo.[114] However, it took a different approach, as this statement would suggest. The Court lifted the interpretation of this notion form the MS level at EU level, when stating that the notion of 'human embryo' is "an *autonomous* concept of European Union law which must be interpreted in a *uniform* manner throughout the territory of the Union".[115] While there are good reasons that notions, which are decisive for the internal market are defined at EU level,[116] a consistent application of the 'multiple value systems' approach should have led to a definition at national level, only constrained by the limitation of 'double morality'.[117]

Based on the concept of 'human dignity', which was mentioned in the Directive as a reason to exclude patentability,[118] the Court held "that the concept of 'human embryo' within the meaning of Article 6(2)(c) of the Directive must be understood in a *wide sense*"[119] and came to the following solution for fertilised and non-fertilised ova.

> Accordingly, any human ovum must, as soon as fertilised, be regarded as a 'human embryo' within the meaning and for the purposes of the application of Article 6(2)(c) of the Directive, since that fertilisation is such as to *commence the process of development of a human being*.[120]
>
> That classification must also apply to a non-fertilised human ovum into which the cell nucleus from a mature human cell has been transplanted and a non-fertilised human ovum whose division and further development have been *stimulated by parthenogenesis*. Although those organisms have not, strictly speaking, been the object of fertilisation, due to the effect of the technique used to obtain them they are, *as is apparent from the written observations presented to the Court*, capable of *commencing the process of development of a human being just as* an embryo created by fertilisation of an ovum can do so.[121]

It is important to stress, from where the Court got this 'natural science' related information. Here, in *Brüstle*, the Court relied on information presented by the parties of this case, in *Mayr*[122] the relevant information was provided by the Commission.

Three years later, in another Grand Chamber judgment, the Court partly had to revoke the approach it took in *Brüstle*, when interpreting the same legal provision. This case was about unfertilised human ovum (second quotation mentioned above) whose division and development to a certain stage have been stimulated by parthenogenesis. Although in this case the Court itself did not refer to the terms ethics or morality, this judgment is highly relevant to our issue. The Court emphasized that

---

[114]CJEU judgment of 18 October 2011, *Brüstle*, C-34/10, EU:C:2011:669, para 30; referring to CJEU *Mayr*, C-506/06, para 38.

[115]CJEU *Brüstle*, C-34/10, para 26; emphases added.

[116]CJEU *Brüstle*, C-34/10, para 27.

[117]On proportionality see *infra* at note 135.

[118]Directive Biotech, recitals 16 and 38.

[119]CJEU *Brüstle*, C-34/10, para 34; emphasis added.

[120]CJEU *Brüstle*, C-34/10, para 35; emphases added.

[121]CJEU *Brüstle*, C-34/10, para 36; emphases added.

[122]CJEU *Mayr*, C-506/06, para 30.

the legal solution in *Brüstle* had been based on "the written observations presented to the Court".[123]

> However, in the present case, the *referring [N.B. national] court* [...] stated in essence that, according to *current scientific knowledge*, a human parthenote, due to the effect of the technique used to obtain it, is *not* as such capable of commencing the process of development which leads to a human being. That assessment is *shared by all of the interested parties* who submitted written observations to the Court.[124]

In the following, the Court did not take the final decision itself, but left it to the national court "to determine whether or not, in the light of knowledge which is *sufficiently tried and tested by international medical science* [...], human parthenotes, such as those which are the subject of the applications for registration in the case in the main proceedings, have the *inherent capacity of developing into a human being*".[125]

What we can take away from this case is the fact that the Court's approach in *Brüstle*, to shift the solution of a "very sensitive" issue at EU level, was a 'flash in the pan'. It is difficult to verify or falsify the statement that the CJEU's interpretation of human dignity in *Brüstle* was "motivated by (covert) religious motives".[126] However, we can clearly state that nowadays it is more likely that the CJEU would decide a case such as *Brüstle* in a more reluctant way, that is to say, not to lift such interpretations of key terms (such as 'human embryo') to EU level. The Court also made clear that its statements are "limited to the patentability of biotechnological inventions".[127] In other words, the CJEU did not want to decide the issue of the beginning of human life in general. This sectoral approach is also important insofar as otherwise we would have a contradiction between *Mayr* (transfer into uterus) on the one hand, and *Brüstle* (human embryo, as soon as fertilised) as well as *ISC* ("capacity to develop into a human being"[128]), on the other.

Another example of the Court's more reluctant approach in a sensitive field is 'surrogacy', a phenomenon, which, according to the EP, "undermines the *human dignity* of the woman since her body and its reproductive functions are used as a *commodity*".[129,130] In two judgments, both given nine month before the *ISC* case, the Court had to decide technical questions of non-discrimination based on gender[131] and disability.[132] Although surrogacy can easily be qualified as a "very sensitive social

[123]CJEU judgment of 18 December 2014, *International Stem Cell [ISC]*, C-364/13, EU:C:2014:2451, paras 31–32.

[124]CJEU *ISC*, C-364/13, para 33; emphases added.

[125]CJEU *ISC*, C-364/13, para 36; emphases added.

[126]Plomer (2018, 36).

[127]CJEU *ISC*, C-364/13, para 22.

[128]CJEU *ISC*, C-364/13, para 31.

[129]EP annual report on human rights and democracy in the world 2014 and the EU policy on the matter, P8_TA(2015)0470 [EP report human rights], para 114; emphases added.

[130]On the topic of commodification, see Sandel (2012).

[131]CJEU judgment of 18 March 2014, *D*, C-167/12, EU:C:2014:169.

[132]CJEU judgment of 18 March 2014, *Z*, C-363/12, EU:C:2014:159.

issue" as stated in *Mayr*[133] and *Brüstle,*[134] the Court (again, Grand Chamber) neither referred to ethics nor morality, and solved this case at a legal level in a very technical way. One explanation could be that the relevant provisions of EU law did not refer to these terms of 'ethics' or 'morality', which is why the Court saw no necessity to 'leave the legal turf'.

After these examples related to different EU directives, let us turn back to the fundamental freedoms. Here we have seen the Court's reluctant approach, leaving more discretion to the MS, which corresponds with the 'post-*Brüstle* approach'. The key limitation we have seen there was a prohibition of 'double morality'.[135] Apart from this, the CJEU has developed another very acceptable solution to deal with ethically sensitive issues, which is a 'more generous' proportionality[136] review. This has been qualified as a "procedural" review by de Witte in his seminal paper "Sex, drugs & EU law",[137] or as a "minimal proportionality control" by Hatzopoulos.[138] This can be seen as a 'golden mean' between either deciding these questions at national level in terms of diversity of moral and ethical choices (argument from self-determination[139]), and the decision of such issues at EU level by "the transnational judiciary" (argument from containment[140]). This means that the CJEU intervenes less substantively in the national regulation by means of the proportionality test, or as de Witte puts it:

> It is argued that a *procedural* proportionality test that respects the substance of national moral and ethical choices, and that instead focuses on teasing out discriminatory or protectionist biases, must only assess the *normative coherence of national policies*, the *consistent application of sanctions, and legislative transparency*.[141]

The CJEC would therefore not require a Member State to follow the approach of another Member State. As long as the Member State concerned does not act in contradictory ways within its own legal system, the CJEC will not 'interfere'. This approach also entails the prohibition of 'double morality', as mentioned above.

In this context, the CJEU has also made an important clarification in the famous *Omega* case. The question centred on the number of MS that have to adopt a certain position based on ethical or moral grounds. In an earlier judgment on gambling, the Court has held as follows:

> First of all, it is not possible to disregard the *moral*, religious or cultural aspects of lotteries, like other types of gambling, in *all* the Member States. The *general tendency of the Member*

[133]CJEU *Mayr*, C-506/06, para 38.

[134]CJEU *Brüstle*, C-34/10, para 30.

[135]*Supra* at note 109.

[136]On proportionality, see also Hermerén (2012).

[137]de Witte (2013, p. 1573).

[138]Hatzopoulos (2012, p. 159).

[139]de Witte (2013, p. 1551).

[140]de Witte (2013, p. 1552).

[141]de Witte (2013, p. 1573); no emphasis added.

> *States* is to restrict, or even prohibit, the practice of gambling and to prevent it from being a source of private profit. [...][142]

The necessary number of MS having to share a similar view was clarified as follows:

> It is *not indispensable* in that respect for the restrictive measure issued by the authorities of a Member State to correspond to a conception *shared by all* Member States as regards the precise way in which the fundamental right or legitimate interest in question is to be protected. Although, in paragraph 60 of Schindler [N.B. see *supra*], the Court referred to moral, religious or cultural considerations which lead all Member States to make the organisation of lotteries and other games with money subject to restrictions, it was *not* its *intention*, by mentioning that common conception, *to formulate a general criterion* for assessing the proportionality of any national measure which restricts the exercise of an economic activity.[143]

Omega was not only an important case in terms of the extent of a consensus between MS, it can also be seen as a landmark case in terms of addressing values,[144] three years before the signing of the Lisbon Treaty. This case was about the possibility to restrict the fundamental freedoms based on "a *fundamental value* enshrined in the national [i.e. German] constitution, namely human dignity".[145] The Court allowed this national value, now an EU value, to enter the fundamental freedoms via the notion of 'public order', despite the high requirements in this context: first, 'public policy' "must be interpreted strictly" and, second, there has to be a "genuine and sufficiently serious threat to a fundamental interest of society".[146] The strong content-related link between 'public policy' as a legal reason of justification and morality also becomes obvious, when the Court states that "the concept of public policy may vary from one country to another and from one era to another"[147]; thus, also the regional and evolutionary character, we have already seen for 'public morality'.

Another sensitive area is genetically modified organisms ('GMOs'). In this context, a directive emphasizes the importance of "ethical principles recognised in a Member State", which allows them to "take into consideration ethical aspects when GMOs are deliberately released or placed on the market as or in products".[148] This might have inspired Poland to argue with ethical principles for defending non-compliance with this Directive, precisely the argument that "the adoption of the contested national provisions was inspired by the Christian and Humanist ethical

---

[142]CJEU *Schindler*, C-275/92, para 60; emphases added.

[143]CJEU judgment of 14 October 2004, *Omega*, C-36/02, EU:C:2004:614, para 37; emphases added.

[144]This book is based on a more narrow understanding of values (see Sect. 3.1.3), than the broad approach (of five categories) by Saurugger and Terpan (2018) (internal market, social values, human rights, EU governance, as well as fostering European integration and protecting the autonomy of European legal order).

[145]CJEU *Omega*, C-36/02, para 32; emphases added.

[146]CJEU *Omega*, C-36/02, paras 28 and 30.

[147]CJEU *Omega*, C-36/02, paras 31.

[148]Directive 2001/18/EC of 12 March 2001 on the deliberate release into the environment of genetically modified organisms [...], OJ 2001 L 106/1, as amended by OJ 2018 L 67/30 [Directive GMOs], recital 9.

principles adhered to by the majority of the Polish people".[149] In this regard, Poland put forward the following arguments:

> a *Christian* conception of life which is opposed to the manipulation and transformation of living organisms created by *God* into material objects which are the subject of intellectual property rights; a *Christian and Humanist* conception of progress and development which urges *respect for creation* and a quest for *harmony between Man and Nature*; and, lastly, *Christian and Humanist* social principles, the reduction of living organisms to the level of products for *purely commercial ends* being likely, inter alia, to undermine the foundations of society.[150]

This case would have allowed the CJEU to broach intriguing questions of the relationship of EU law and ethics. However, the Court did not enter into a substantive analysis. By stating that Poland, "upon which the *burden of proof* lies in such a case, has *failed*, in any event, to establish that the true *purpose* of the contested national provisions was in fact to pursue the *religious and ethical* objectives relied upon",[151] it is consequently "not necessary to rule on the question *whether*—and, if so, *to what extent* and *under which possible circumstances*—the Member States retain an option to rely on *ethical or religious* arguments in order to justify the adoption of internal measures which [...] derogate from [EU law]".[152] While it is not surprising that the Court did not allow a MS to deviate from legal obligations of an EU Directive, this statement at least leaves open the possibility of a MS, which is able to comply with this burden of proof, to rely on ethical grounds. This case is also interesting because it does not only address the relationship of EU law and ethics, but also of ethics and religion, precisely, one religion (Christianity), and of humanism.

It is also worth mentioning that Poland has positioned ethics as an argument at different levels, in order to defend its position. Poland referred to both the Polish society which "attaches great importance to Christian and Roman Catholic values", as well as to the members of the Polish parliament.[153] It is no surprise, that the Court clearly rejected this possibility by stating "a Member State cannot rely in that manner on the views of a section of public opinion in order unilaterally to challenge a harmonising measure adopted by the [EU] institutions".[154]

3.3.1.2 Conclusion

Based on the analysis of this case-law the above-mentioned question can clearly be addressed in the sense of a judicial self-restraint. This is true both with regard

---

[149]CJEU judgment of 16 July 2009, *Commission versus Poland (GMOs)*, C-165/08, EU:C:2009:473, para 30.

[150]CJEU *EC versus Poland (GMOs)*, C-165/08, para 31; emphases added.

[151]CJEU *EC versus Poland (GMOs)*, C-165/08, para 52; emphases added.

[152]CJEU *EC versus Poland (GMOs)*, C-165/08, para 51; emphases added.

[153]CJEU *EC versus Poland (GMOs)*, C-165/08, para 58.

[154]CJEU *EC versus Poland (GMOs)*, C-165/08, para 56. In this case, the Court also did not refer to 'public morality' as a separate reason of justification, besides protection of human health and of the environment (para 55).

to ethics and morality, thus in either case, the Court saw no necessity to determine the content of these concepts, as this decision was left to the MS, acting according to their values. This holds true for the above-mentioned sensitive fields, where the Court has observed "significant moral, religious and cultural differences". However, on a timeline, today, one would have to add the EU's common values. As stated in *Omega*, a consensus amongst the MS is no necessity and the Court accepts aspects that are specifically important for a country, such as human dignity for Germany, or for Italy, rejecting the mafia. In the latter situation, the General Court recently has accepted the non-registration of a figurative trademark "La Mafia" emphasizing "accepted principles of morality are not the same in all Member States, inter alia for linguistic, historic, social and cultural reasons".[155]

The Court's technical legal approach can be welcomed as it leaves these decisions to the national level and to the citizens' representatives. However, one should not disregard the fact that in an indirect way also the legal approach will determine a medically or ethically sensitive topic. Due to this judicial self-restraint, the Court only provides sectoral solutions, thus no general statement with regard to the beginning of life.[156]

The limitations to this national discretion are the prohibition of double morality and the requirements of coherence and legislative transparency, or in other terms, a reduced (or 'procedural') proportionality review.

The relationship between law and ethics concerns similar issues, as the one of law and religion. In this context, there would have been very interesting topics in this GMO case, which in the end have not been answered, since Poland has not been able to prove its point of view.

After this qualitative analysis, let us have a brief look at some quantitative findings of analysing the terms of 'ethics' and 'morality' in CJEU case-law from 1961–2015.[157] Focusing on those cases, where the Court itself has refereed to these terms (thus, excluding quotations of EU law or mere statements of parties, referring to these key terms), this research has revealed that more than 70% of cases have been decided since 1998,[158] with 29% references to ethics, 67% to morality, and 4% to both terms.[159] This roughly corresponds with general 'ethicalization' since the 1990s.

---

[155] GC judgment of 15 March 2018, *La Mafia Franchises*, T-1/17, EU:T:2018:146, para 28. On the (new) regulation, see *infra* at note 369.

[156] *Mayr*: transfer into uterus, *Brüstle*: fertilization, *ISC*: capacity to develop into a human being.

[157] The following empirical analysis is based on the research of Rudigier (2015).

[158] 1998–2003: 23%; 2004–2009: 15%; 2010–2015: 33%.

[159] Rudigier (2015, p. 29).

3.3.2 Ethics in Law Making: Ethics Rules on Lobbying

After EU primary law (the constitutional perspective) and international agreements (the external perspective), before turning to EU secondary (and tertiary) law (the internal legislative perspective, in terms of the output), we need to shed some light on the decision-making procedure itself. Lobbying is a much-contested topic, especially because of asymmetries regarding information, but also regarding resources in general. A lack of transparency often leads to mistrust, as we have seen in case of CETA. Similar to CETA and the fear of the possibility to 'buy justice' in the context of investment protection tribunals, lobbying is very much about the fear of citizens that large companies can simply 'buy legislation'.

None of the three decision-making powers of the EU, the EC, the EP nor the Council of the EU, mention either ethics or morality in their Rules of Procedure,[160] and the same is true for the EU staff regulations.[161] Thus, as mentioned above,[162] for this chapter also implicit references will be taken into account, as there is no explicit mentioning of 'ethics' or 'morality'. Tracing these implicit references shall make it possible to answer the question, if the EU provides for 'ethical lobbying', and how the determination takes place.[163]

These implicit references occur in terms of principles such as integrity, diligence, honesty and accountability, which can refer either to the targets, or to the actors of lobbying. The majority of documents of this '*acquis légal & éthique*' concerns targets.[164] Hence, we will start analysing the rules on these targets (comprising both political actors, as well as administrative staff), before moving to the actors, i.e. consultants and lobbyists, as well as experts.

---

[160] Frischhut (2015, pp. 539–541).

[161] Regulation No 31 (EEC), 11 (EAEC), laying down the Staff Regulations of Officials and the Conditions of Employment of Other Servants of the European Economic Community and the European Atomic Energy Community, OJ 1962 45/1385, as amended by OJ 2017 C 429/9 [Regulation staff].

[162] Note 54.

[163] The following chapter is based on Grad and Frischhut (2019), comprising further details on this topic.

[164] For an overview of the different documents see Grad and Frischhut (2019, pp. 309–310).

3.3.2.1 Rules on Targets

Besides a general negative conception of lobbying[165] and information asymmetries,[166] the most common challenges with regard to targets of lobbying are conflicts of interest, acceptance of gifts and corruption,[167] and finally the revolving doors phenomenon. They can be overcome by transparency, other general 'guiding principles' on 'ethical behaviour', rules on independence and accountability towards citizens and one's institution, and finally rules on post term-of-office.

Transparency plays a key role for lobbying and can contribute to more ethical lobbying in manifold ways.[168] For instance, it can help to overcome information asymmetries, by enabling more equal access to information. At the same time, it can improve the quality of decisions taken, if these decisions (plus corresponding background information) can be known by others, and therefore be challenged. Transparency is an important principle of EU law, which is enshrined in Art 1 TEU and 10 TEU and in Art 15 TFEU. According to the CJEU, it "enables citizens to *participate* more closely in the decision-making process and guarantees that the administration enjoys greater *legitimacy* and is more effective and more *accountable* to the citizen in a democratic system".[169]

In terms of 'guiding principles', the EP provides most principles in its Code of Conduct (EP CoC)[170]; these are: "disinterest, integrity, openness, diligence, honesty, accountability and respect for Parliament's reputation".[171] Integrity is also the principle that plays a key role for the independence of the Commission, whereas its members shall "behave with integrity and discretion"[172] with regard to appointments or benefits, after they have ceased to hold office. In literature, integrity has been defined as "the quality of being honest and morally upright".[173] In January 2018, the EC adopted a new Code of Conduct (EC CoC), which requires members to "behave

[165] This comprises activities "carried out with the objective of directly or indirectly influencing the formulation or implementation of policy and the decision-making processes of the EU institutions, irrespective of where they are undertaken and of the channel or medium of communication used"; Agreement between the EP and the EC on the transparency register for organisations and self-employed individuals engaged in EU policy-making and policy implementation, OJ 2014 L 277/11 [Agreement transparency register], Art 7(1).

[166] James (2008).

[167] While lobbying can be seen to play a certain legitimate role in a democracy, corruption is part of the criminal sphere.

[168] Transparency has even been referred to as "a transversal value" and "might even become itself a virtue"; Hamm (2018, 119).

[169] CJEU judgment of 9 November 2010, *Schecke*, C-92/09, EU:C:2010:662, para 68; emphases added.

[170] EP Code of Conduct for Members of the European Parliament with respect to financial interests and conflicts of interest, http://www.europarl.europa.eu/sides/getDoc.do?pubRef=-//EP//TEXT+RULES-EP+20180731+ANN-01+DOC+XML+V0//EN&language=EN&navigationBar=YES [EP CoC].

[171] Art 1(a) EP CoC.

[172] Art 245(2) TFEU.

[173] Petrick (2008, p. 1141).

and perform their duties with complete independence, integrity, dignity, with loyalty and discretion", as well as to "observe the highest standards of ethical conduct".[174] The fact that these 'ethical standards' are not directly determined is less of a problem, as the principles mentioned before will very much contribute to the determination of these ethical standards. Integrity seems to be an important principle in this regard, as it is further determined in Art 6 CoC. This includes the requirement to manage the material resources of the EC in a "responsible manner", reluctance in the context of free travel offered by third parties and hospitality, not to accept gifts worth more than € 150,[175] as well as notification of any decoration, prize or honour awarded to them. For 'officials of the Union', i.e. the staff of EU institutions, several principles are addressed. These comprise objectivity, impartiality and loyalty to the EU,[176] independence and avoidance of "actual or potential conflict of interest",[177] "integrity and discretion" after leaving the service,[178] as well as requirements for recruitment, "highest standard of ability, efficiency and integrity".[179] In addition, for the Commission's staff the relevant document also mentions objectivity and impartiality as key principles, besides the 'general principles' of lawfulness, non-discrimination and equal treatment, proportionality and consistency.[180] Although not a target of lobbying, also the CJEU in its recent code of conduct does not refer to ethics or morality as such, but operates based on principles, such as independence, integrity, dignity, impartiality, loyalty, discretion, and avoidance of a conflict of interest.[181]

Regarding its content, unethical behaviour very often can be explained in terms of a conflict of interest, which occurs in situations, where a person is faced with a clash of a personal interest and the public interest, this person has to represent. According to the EC Code of conduct, "[a] conflict of interest arises where a personal interest may influence the independent performance of their duties", or negatively defined, a conflict of interest does not exist if a member is only concerned as a member of the general public or of a broad class of persons.[182] Transparency also plays a role here, in the avoidance of conflicts of interest, by means of disclosure obligations with regard to certain financial interests (occupation, board membership, company holdings, etc.).[183]

---

[174] EC decision of 31 January 2018 on a Code of Conduct for the Members of the EC, OJ 2018 C 65/7 [EC CoC].

[175] Same threshold in Art 5(1) EP CoC.

[176] Art 11(1) Regulation staff.

[177] Art 11(3) Regulation staff.

[178] Art 16(1) Regulation staff.

[179] Art 12(1) and Art 27(1) Regulation staff.

[180] EC Rules of Procedure of the Commission (C(2000) 3614), OJ 2000 L 308/26, as amended by OJ 2011 L 296/58, Annex I, Code of good administrative behaviour for staff of the EC in their relations with the public.

[181] CJEU Code of Conduct for Members and former Members of the Court of Justice of the European Union, OJ 2016 C 483/1; according to Art 9, integrity, dignity, loyalty and discretion apply after their office as well.

[182] Art 2(6) EC CoC. In a very similar way: Art 3(1) EP CoC.

[183] Art 3 EC CoC; Art 4 EP CoC.

The phenomenon of 'revolving doors' refers to situations, where former public officials start working in the private sector in jobs which target their former field of profession, or where individuals join an EU institution from the private sector.[184] This can result in privileged access of certain interest groups to decision makers. According to the European Ombudsman, implementing rules on this phenomenon "is central to maintaining high ethical standards in public administrations".[185] Based on recent scandals (e.g. 'Barrosogate'[186]), the EC CoC has strengthened the rules on 'post term of office activities', whereby the members continue to be bound by their duty of integrity and discretion ('cooling-off period').[187] This comprises, amongst others, the prohibition for former Commissioners to lobby members or their staff "on matters for which they were responsible within their portfolio for a period of two years after ceasing to hold office".[188] In case of the president, this period is even three years.[189] The EP has softer rules on lobbying, as former members of the EP (MEPs) just have to inform the EP and may not benefit from facilities granted to former MEPs, but lobbying as such is not prohibited.[190] While the only possible argument could be seen in the bigger number of former MEPs, this topic is clearly a possibility for the EP to increase citizens' trust by strengthening these post-term rules. In terms of EU staff, "appointing authority shall, in principle, prohibit them, during the 12 months after leaving the service, from engaging in lobbying or advocacy vis-à-vis staff of their former institution".[191]

All these substantive rules have to be accompanied by procedural safeguards. The EP has established an Advisory Committee on the Conduct of Members ('the Advisory Committee'), which shall make recommendations in the event of possible breaches of the EP's code of conduct.[192] The requirements for qualification of its five members[193] are not very ambitious, since it only requires "taking due account of the Members' experience and of political balance".[194] Requested by the president of the EP, the Advisory Committee shall examine the circumstances of the alleged breach, and may hear the MEP concerned. Based on its findings, the Advisory Committee makes a recommendation to the EP president concerning a possible decision.[195] The Committee also has an important preventive function. If a possible conflict of

---

[184] Tansey (2014, p. 257).

[185] European Ombudsman (2018, p. 15).

[186] Grad and Frischhut (2019).

[187] Art 11(1) EC CoC.

[188] Art 11(4) EC CoC.

[189] Art 11(5) EC CoC.

[190] Art 6 EP CoC.

[191] Art 16(3) Regulation staff.

[192] Art 8 EP CoC.

[193] MEP from the 'Committee on Constitutional Affairs' and the 'Committee on Legal Affairs'; Art 7(2) EP CoC.

[194] Art 7(2) EP CoC.

[195] Art 8(2) EP CoC.

interest occurs, in case of ambiguity a MEP may seek advice in confidence from the Committee.[196]

The Commission clearly has set higher demands for the members of its ethics committee. The requirements for becoming a member of the 'Independent Ethical Committee' (IEC) are "competence, experience, independence and professional qualities", in addition to "an impeccable record of professional behaviour as well as experience in high-level functions in European, national or international institutions"; moreover, they have to sign a declaration on the absence of conflicts of interest.[197] The IEC shall advise the EC on "any ethical question" related to the EC CoC and provide general recommendations to the Commission on ethical issues in this regard.[198] Unlike the EP's committee, the IEC can also include a "dissenting point of view" in its opinion.[199] In case of the EC and a possible conflict of interest, it is not a member (as in case of the EP), but the EC president, who can consult the IEC,[200] in a similar way as in cases of post term of office activities,[201] with the possibility to make public the IEC opinion.[202]

3.3.2.2 Rules on Actors

As the EC nowadays often relies on outside expertise, rules on experts play an important role for ethical lobbying and can be positioned at the interface of targets and actors of lobbying. In fact, nowadays, it is a huge challenge to determine if in the context of decision-making, information is provided from a true expert, or from a 'disguised lobbyist'. That is why the EC has established horizontal rules on the creation and operation of EC expert groups, which strive for a balanced composition of expert groups and comprise rules on conflict of interest, in order to "ensure the highest level of integrity of experts".[203]

The EP and the EC have set up a transparency register and a code of conduct for lobbyists, which, unfortunately, is only voluntary.[204,205] The European Council and the Council of the EU have been invited to join the register, but have not done so far. This code of conduct is more concrete and foresees 14 quite detailed obligations for lobbyists, addressing lobbyists' behaviour with regard to the EU institutions, their

---

196 Art 3(2) EP CoC.

197 Art 12(4) EC CoC.

198 Art 12(1) EC CoC.

199 Art 12(7) EC CoC.

200 Art 4(4) EC CoC.

201 Art 11(3) EC CoC.

202 Art 11(7) EC CoC.

203 EC decision establishing horizontal rules on the creation and operation of Commission expert groups, C(2016) 3301 final 30.5.2016 [EC decision experts], recital 3, Art 2(4), Art 11.

204 The worst that can happen to a lobbyist who is in the register and does not comply, is a removal from the register and a loss of incentives provided by the register, like an access badge to the EP.

205 Annex III of Agreement transparency register (OJ 2014 L 277/21).

members, officials and other staff. It also entails transparency, operates less based on principles for ethical behaviour, and just mentions 'honesty' in the context of how information or decisions are obtained.

3.3.2.3 Conclusion

The overall approach in the context of decision-making is not one as we have seen it so far, i.e. referring to terms of ethics and morality. Rather, the relevant documents refer to certain principles, which are important to attain the same objective, that is to say ethical behaviour of either side, of both actors and targets of lobbying, as well as of 'true' experts. One key principle is also to avoid a situation of an actual or potential conflict of interest. Other principles comprise accountability, dignity, diligence, discretion, disinterest, honesty, impartiality, independence, integrity, loyalty, objectivity, openness, responsibility, and transparency. These principles (among which especially transparency) are of utmost importance to (re-)gain citizens' trust. Intransparent decision-making as well as unethical behaviour will further widen the gap between the EU and its citizens. The already mentioned CETA agreement was a clear example of decreasing trust by not providing sufficient transparency. The Commission seemed to have learned from this example, as the Brexit negotiations are more open and documents more easily accessible.

These principles have to apply both during, and partially also after holding a certain office. Moreover, these substantive rules have to be accompanied by procedural rules, as is the case for the two committees of the EP and the EC. These committees not only play an important role in a concrete situation, but also have an important preventive function. Comparing these two committees, the EC's IEC is clearly more ambitious with regard to the requirements of becoming a member, and allows for dissenting opinions, where an opinion is not adopted unanimously. Beside this, every ethics or expert committee ideally should strive for a balanced composition of its qualified members. With regard to the legal quality of these documents, we have seen both examples of hard law (e.g. the regulation on EU staff), as well as soft-law documents.

3.3.3 Ethics and Morality in EU Secondary (and Tertiary) Law

Following the vertical hierarchy of EU law, we now turn to EU secondary law, mainly enacted by the EP and the Council, as well as some examples of tertiary EU law, enacted based on the former. Not surprisingly due to the number of EU legal documents in this field, also the largest number of documents referring to ethics and/or morality can be found here. As it has been mentioned in the introduction, the objective of this book is not to create an inventory of all the examples of EU law, which refer to ethics and/or morality. Hence, in the following, the essence of this research conducted in two waves will be presented by means of some noteworthy examples.[206]

This chapter starts with some examples of consequences of unethical behaviour, remarks concerning the requirement of legal certainty (Sect. 3.3.3.1). This research was mainly conducted in English, also taking into account other languages. That is why in a next step, some language inconsistencies will be highlighted (Sect. 3.3.3.2), before turning to the main part of categorizing the way how ethics and morality are determined regarding their content in EU secondary (and tertiary) law (Sect. 3.3.3.3).

3.3.3.1 Consequences of Unethical Behaviour, as Well as Legal Certainty (Continued)

The consequences of (non-)compliance with ethics, if mentioned in an EU legal document, can be seen from various examples. EU rules on authorisation and supervision of genetically modified food and feed require, amongst others "a reasoned statement that the food does not give rise to ethical or religious concerns".[207] In addition, the EU regulation on clinical trials requires prior authorisation, whereby a "clinical trial shall be subject to scientific and ethical review".[208]

Moreover, we can see the consequences of unethical behaviour in the context of Horizon 2020, where "[r]esearch and innovation activities supported by Horizon 2020 should respect fundamental ethical principles".[209] A "proposal which contravenes ethical principles […] may be excluded from the evaluation, selection and award procedures at any time"[210]; in addition the Commission "shall systematically carry out ethics reviews for proposals raising ethical issues",[211] and the grant agreement has to acknowledge "the right of the Commission to carry out an ethics audit by independent experts".[212] Based on what we have seen in the chapter on the CJEU's case-law on stem cell patentability,[213] it is no surprise that "[t]he use, if any, of human stem cells, be they adult or embryonic, […] is subject to *stringent* ethics review".[214]

---

[206]The following chapter is based on the research by Frischhut (2015) (also entailing further examples); this research has been updated by the author.

[207]Regulation (EC) No 1829/2003 of 22 September 2003 on genetically modified food and feed, OJ 2003 L 268/1, as amended by OJ 2015 L 327/1 [Regulation GM food], Art 5(3)(g).

[208]Regulation clinical trials, Art 5.

[209]Regulation (EU) No 1291/2013 of 11 December 2013 establishing Horizon 2020—the Framework Programme for Research and Innovation (2014–2020) […], OJ 2013 L 347/104, as amended by OJ 2015 L 169/1 [Regulation establishing Horizon 2020], recital 29.

[210]Regulation (EU) No 1290/2013 of 11 December 2013 laying down the rules for participation and dissemination in "Horizon 2020—the Framework Programme for Research and Innovation (2014–2020)" […], OJ 2013 L 347/81, as amended by OJ 2014 L 174/14 [Regulation participation Horizon 2020], Art 13(3).

[211]Regulation participation Horizon 2020, Art 14(1).

[212]Regulation participation Horizon 2020, Art 18(6).

[213]*Supra* Sect. 3.3.1.1.

[214]Regulation establishing Horizon (2020), recital 31; emphasis added.

Although only soft-law, the 'European Charter for Researchers' states that "[r]esearchers need to be aware that they are accountable towards their employers, funders or other related public or private bodies as well as, on more ethical grounds, towards society as a whole."[215] In the context of fishery, we find a responsibility for the "correct and appropriate use of the data with regard to scientific ethics".[216]

In cross-border healthcare, EU patient mobility rights are limited according to the corresponding directive insofar as these rights may not be used in a way which "undermin[es] the fundamental ethical choices of Member States".[217] Nevertheless, which kind of medical, health, or related treatment[218] should be qualified as unethical?[219] These are only some examples that raise a number of important questions: Is there a definition or at least a certain form of understanding as to what has to be understood by 'ethical'?

As mentioned above, as part of EU's common values,[220] the 'the rule of law',[221] according to the EC's recent communication,[222] also entails legal certainty. According to the CJEU, this requires that "legislation must be clear and predictable for those who are subject to it".[223] Thus, one might wonder, if EU legislation referring to ethics and morality is clear and predictable and "formulated with sufficient precision to enable the individual to regulate his or her conduct",[224] or whether it remains undetermined in the end?

This might be less of a problem, if legal documents refer to "minor's physical, mental, spiritual, moral and social development",[225] the "physical, mental and moral

---

[215]EC recommendation 2005/251/EC of 11 March 2005 on the European Charter for Researchers and on a Code of Conduct for the Recruitment of Researchers, OJ 2005 L 75/67 [EC Charter researchers], Annex, Section 1.

[216]Regulation (EU) 2017/1004 of 17 May 2017 on the establishment of a Union framework for the collection, management and use of data in the fisheries sector and support for scientific advice regarding the common fisheries policy [...], OJ 2017 L 157/1 [Regulation data fisheries], Art 20(1)(c).

[217]Directive 2011/24/EU of 9 March 2011 on the application of patients' rights in cross-border healthcare, OJ 2011 L 88/45, as amended by OJ 2013 L 353/8 [Directive patient mobility], recital 7.

[218]For a visualized overview see Hall (2013, p. 12).

[219]See *infra* at note 351.

[220]*Supra* Sect. 3.1.3.

[221]Cf. Bogdandy and Ioannidis (2014, 62–63), Bogdandy, Bogdanowicz, Canor, Taborowski, and Schmidt (2018).

[222]COM (2014) 158 final 11.3.2014, p. 4 and Annex 1.

[223]CJEU *Meridionale Industria Salumi*, 212 to 217/80, para 10.

[224]Venice Commission, Report on the Rule of Law, CDLAD(2011)003rev, 10.

[225]Directive 2013/33/EU of 26 June 2013 laying down standards for the reception of applicants for international protection, OJ 2013 L 180/96, Art 23(1).

integrity"[226] of victims of crime, or the "morals of young persons".[227] In the other cases mentioned above, the missing determination of unethical behaviour can have important consequences.

However, before we turn to the determination of content, let us take a closer look at the different language versions of EU documents referring to ethics and morality.

3.3.3.2 Language Inconsistencies

In the context of a Union with 24 different languages,[228] it is important to follow a linguistically holistic[229] approach. As we have just seen, ethics and morality, in theory, have a different meaning and therefore it is astonishing that they are used differently in different language versions. What reads "[c]onsumers in the [EU] would [...] find it *morally* unacceptable that their increased use of biofuels could have the effect of destroying biodiverse lands"[230] in the English version,[231] refers to ethics ("*ethisch inakzeptabel*") in the German version.[232] However, as those terms are generally distinguished, we can assume that this wording is based on imprecise translation and without further significance.

The same might hold true for the case of the already mentioned Directive Biotech,[233] which refers to the "ethical or moral principles recognised in a [sic!] Member State",[234] whereas the German version uses the plural ("*in den Mitgliedstaaten*").[235] As mentioned above in the context of human dignity, the number of

226Directive 2012/29/EU of 25 October 2012 establishing minimum standards on the rights, support and protection of victims of crime, and replacing Council Framework Decision 2001/220/JHA, OJ 2012 L 315/57, recital 9.

227Council Directive (EU) 2017/159 of 19 December 2016 implementing the Agreement concerning the implementation of the Work in Fishing Convention, 2007 of the International Labour Organisation [...], OJ 2017 L 25/12, Art 6.

228According to Art 55(1) TEU and Art 358 TFEU, the Treaties (Primary law) are "equally authentic" in each of these 24 languages. The same is true for Secondary law, comprising 24 "official languages and the working languages of the institutions of the Union"; Council Regulation No 1 Determining the Languages to be Used by the European Economic Community, OJ 1958 P 17/385, as amended by OJ 2013 L 158/1, 71. According to Art 4, "[r]egulations and other documents of general application shall be drafted in the official languages".

229As a limitation it has to be stated, that beside English (EN), these will be the languages spoken (German, DE; French, FR; Spanish, ES) or at least passively understood (Italian, IT) by the author.

230Directive 2009/30/EC of 23 April 2009 [amending certain other directives], OJ 2009 L 140/88 [Directive greenhouse gas emissions], recital 11; emphasis added.

231Similar in FR, ES, IT.

232For a similar example see also CJEU judgment of 5 December 1996, *Merck*, C-267/95, EU:C:1996:468, para 53 ("ethical obligations" versus "*moralische Verpflichtungen*").

233Recital 39.

234Similar in FR, ES, IT.

235According to de Witte (2013, p. 1558), "the preamble to Directive 98/44 speaks of the respect for the ethical or moral principles recognized in *a* Member State, [...] and the European Parliament long halted the decision-making process by referring to the irreconcilable differences of opinion

MS sharing a certain conception can play an important role in case of authorities of a MS issuing a restrictive measure.[236]

Although this will be the compelling solution, it might sound funny if only the English version of a code of conduct (relating to transactions in transferable securities) declares the code's objective as "to establish standards of ethical behaviour on a Community-wide basis", whereas the other language version examined only refer to loyal behaviour (for example, FR: "*comportement loyal*"[237]).[238]

There are other examples of differences in translation which can be clustered into a less problematic category, where the term 'ethical' is just explicitly missing—but to some degree implicitly included—in another language version.

A first example refers to the degree to which substances can be tested on animals.[239] Here, only the German version refers to ethics,[240] whereas a similar idea is worded in different ways in English ("can humanely be allowed" similarly in ES), and the French (and IT) version referring to the degree of pain suffered by the animal (FR: "*sans que cela fasse trop souffrir l'animal*").

A second example refers to doping, where the use of drugs in sport is denounced as "unsporting behaviour" in the English version, whereas all the other examined versions refer to the ethics of the sport (for example, ES: "*contrario a la ética deportiva*").[241] Therefore, in both cases, the result might be the same, but the wording is different.

The same is true, if the term code of conduct ("*Verhaltenskodex*") is used in one version (DE), whereas the other languages examined use the term code of ethics, and so on.[242] In a similar way, concerning ethical rules of a professional nature, one has to be aware of the fact that often professional rules[243] in one language version (DE:

---

between the Member States, highlighting that it should be for States and their citizens to make their own assessments of these divisive moral questions"; no emphasis added.

[236] See *supra* at note 142.

[237] EC recommendation 77/534/EEC of 25 July 1977 concerning a European code of conduct relating to transactions in transferable securities, OJ 1977 L 212/37 [EC recommendation securities], Annex.

[238] For further examples, see Frischhut (2015, p. 538).

[239] Council Regulation (EC) No 440/2008 of 30 May 2008 laying down test methods pursuant to Regulation (EC) No 1907/2006 on the Registration, Evaluation, Authorisation and Restriction of Chemicals (REACH), OJ 2008 L 142/1, as amended by OJ 2017 L 112/1, Annex, Part B.4, 1.4.2.3.

[240] DE: "*ethisch verantwortbar*".

[241] Resolution of the Council [etc.] of 3 December 1990 on Community action to combat the use of drugs, including the abuse of medicinal products, particularly in sport, OJ 1990 C 329/4, Annex I.

[242] Council Decision 2008/210/EC of 18 February 2008 on the principles, priorities and conditions contained in the European Partnership with Albania [etc.], OJ 2008 L 80/1 [Council decision Albania], Annex, pt. 3.1; FR: "*code de déontologie*", ES: "*el código deontológico*", IT: "*codice ético*".

[243] Directive 2005/36/EC of 7 September 2005 on the recognition of professional qualifications, OJ 2005 L 255/22, as amended by OJ 2017 L 317/119 [Directive recognition qualifications].

"*standesrechtlichen Regeln*") correspond to "rules of professional ethics" in other versions.[244]

To sum it up, we can say that the general EU rule to take into account not only one language version of course also helps in case of the language inconsistencies in our context. However, in case of fundamental concepts like 'ethics' or 'morality', more "clarity and consistency"[245] would be desirable. Still, it can also rest unclear if the language versions that are 'united in diversity' are due to imprecise translations (for example, somewhere in a very comprehensive annex), or are the result of debates on principles.

3.3.3.3 Status Quo of Ethics and Morality

In EU primary law, we have seen 'morality' used as an umbrella to protect MS from EU interference in sensitive fields.[246] We can find a similar [1.] 'protection shield'-approach in EU secondary law. As we have already seen in the context of Horizon 2020, the use of human stem cells is "subject to stringent ethics review"; this provision continues by stating that "[n]o project involving the use of human embryonic stem cells should be funded that does not obtain the necessary approvals from the Member States".[247]

The wording is even stronger in case of genetically modified food and organisms, where reference is made to "competence [sic] of Member States as regards ethical issues."[248]

The example of EU patient mobility has already been mentioned in terms of consequences of unethical behaviour. According to this directive, patients' rights are limited insofar as these rights may not be used in a way which "undermin[es] the fundamental ethical choices of Member States".[249] This reference to the term 'ethics' in this EU legal document is clearly motivated by the fear that a broad interpretation of the term "health services" could entitle EU citizens to use certain

244 Directive 2006/123/EC of 12 December 2006 on services in the internal market, OJ 2006 L 376/36 [Directive services], recital 99 (et passim); EN: "ethical rules laid down by professional bodies"; DE: "*von den Berufsverbänden festgelegten Standesregeln*".

245 In that context, according to the Interinstitutional Agreement [EP, Council, EC] on Better Law-Making, OJ 2016 L 123/1 [IIA Better Law-Making], pt. 2, these institutions "agree to promote simplicity, *clarity and consistency* in the drafting of Union legislation"; emphasis added. According to the Joint Declaration [of the same three institutions] on practical arrangements for the co-decision procedure [...], OJ 2007 C 145/5, "[n]o changes shall be made to any agreed texts without the explicit agreement, at the appropriate level, of both the [EP] and the Council" (pt. 41), after "the agreed text [has been] finalised by the legal-linguistic services of the [EP] and of the Council acting in close cooperation and by mutual agreement" (pt. 40).

246 *Supra* Sect. 3.1.2.

247 Regulation establishing Horizon 2020, recital 31; emphasis added.

248 Regulation GM food, recital 42.

249 Directive patient mobility, recital 7.

sensitive health services abroad.[250] Thus, ethics, again, serves as a protection shield against EU interference.

Moreover, we have also already seen the example of Directive Biotech, which, amongst others, excludes the patentability of "uses of human embryos for industrial or commercial purposes".[251] The TRIPs Agreement foresees the possibility to exclude inventions from patentability, if they are against *ordre public* or morality.[252] When making use of this possibility, the directive makes clear that "*ordre public* and morality correspond in particular to ethical or moral principles recognised in a Member State"[253]; hence, not at EU level. Further examples of referring to the national level for the determination of ethics can be found in the field of research.[254]

After this category of ethics being used as a 'protection shield', we find another category, where ethics (or morality[255]) is used as [2.] a supportive argument for a certain legal solution. Here, it is less of a problem, if the content of ethics is not determined, as the legal solution itself might fulfil the requirements of legal certainty. This is the case for the statement that consumers in the EU would "find it morally unacceptable that their increased use of biofuels could have the effect of destroying biodiverse lands",[256] or that "[c]onsumers' choices can be influenced by, inter alia, health, economic, environmental, social and ethical considerations".[257] In another example, the killing of seals is qualified as morally problematic as such, beside commercial killing being qualified as more problematic than traditional hunting by Inuit.[258]

---

[250]See *infra* at note 351.

[251]Art 6(2)(c).

[252]Recital 36.

[253]Recital 39.

[254]Council Decision (EU) 2017/955 of 29 May 2017 amending Decision 2008/376/EC on the adoption of the Research Programme of the Research Fund for Coal and Steel and on the multiannual technical guidelines for this programme, OJ 2017 L 144/17 [Council Decision Research Coal and Steel], Art 29a(6): "Participants shall comply with national legislation, regulations and ethical rules in the countries where the action is carried out"; EC Charter researchers, Annex, Section 1: "Researchers should adhere to the recognised ethical practices and fundamental ethical principles appropriate to their discipline(s) as well as to ethical standards as documented in the different national, sectoral or institutional codes of ethics."

[255]Council Regulation (EU) 2016/369 of 15 March 2016 on the provision of emergency support within the Union, OJ 2016 L 70/1, recital 1: "Mutual assistance and support in the face of disasters is both a fundamental expression of the universal value of solidarity between people and a moral imperative, as such disasters may lead to a significant number of people being unable to meet their basic needs, with potential severe adverse effects on their health and lives".

[256]Directive greenhouse gas emissions, recital 11.

[257]Regulation (EU) No 1169/2011 of 25 October 2011 on the provision of food information to consumers, OJ 2011 L 304/18, as amended by OJ 2015 L 327/1, recital 3, see also Art 3(1).

[258]Regulation (EU) 2015/1775 of 6 October 2015 amending Regulation (EC) No 1007/2009 on trade in seal products [...], OJ 2015 L 262/1 [Regulation seal products]: "[...] public moral concerns about the animal welfare aspects of the killing of seals and the possible presence on the Union market of products obtained from seals killed in a way that causes excessive pain, distress, fear and other forms of suffering" (recital 1); "For those reasons, seal hunts traditionally conducted by Inuit and

In context of 'novel food', we find a supportive argument to contribute to animal welfare and ethics: "[...] tests on animals should be replaced, reduced or refined. Therefore, [...] duplication of animal testing should be avoided, where possible. Pursuing this *goal* could reduce possible *animal welfare and ethical concerns* with regard to novel food applications".[259]

Apart from ethics used as a supportive argument, we can further identify references in order to create [3.] a parallel ethical assessment beside the legal one. In this category, we can identify coexistence of law and ethics (that is to say, a parallel system), with Directive Biotech stating that "substantive patent *law cannot* serve to *replace* or render superfluous [...] compliance with certain *ethical* standards"[260] and that "*ethical or moral* principles *supplement* the standard *legal* examinations under patent law".[261] The same holds true in the field of protection of the EUs financial interests, where the definition of 'professional misconduct' "means violation of *laws* or regulations *or* of *ethical standards* of the profession to which the person belongs".[262]

In the field of transferable securities, we find a noteworthy statement of the European Commission concerning the relationship of EU harmonization and ethics. "This code of conduct, to be issued in the form of a Commission recommendation, must be seen separately from the Commission's other harmonization work in this sector [...] because the *ethical approach has been given priority over the legislative approach*".[263]

A similar parallelism can be found in case of staff responsibility (of the EU Institute for Security Studies): "Employees shall abstain from any public action or statement or publication if such action, statement or publication is incompatible with the duties or obligations of an international civil servant or liable to involve the moral or material responsibility of the Institute."[264]

In addition to the parallelism of law and ethics, a similar relation can be addressed between science and ethics. In the context of Registration, Evaluation, Authorisation

---

other indigenous communities do not raise the same public moral concerns as seal hunts conducted primarily for commercial reasons" (recital 2).

[259] Regulation (EU) 2015/2283 of 25 November 2015 on novel foods [...], OJ 2015 L 327/1 [Regulation novel foods], recital 32; emphases added.

[260] Recital 14, emphases added. See also CJEU judgment of 9 October 2001, *Netherlands versus EP and Council*, C-377/98, EU:C:2001:523, para 80.

[261] Recital 39, emphases added. See also Presidency Conclusions, Stockholm European Council (23./24.3.2001), part I, VI. 44.

[262] EC decision 2014/792/EU of 13 November 2014 on the Early Warning System to be used by authorising officers of the EC and by the executive agencies, OJ 2014 L 329/68, Art 2(g); emphases added. See also Regulation (EU, Euratom) 2018/1046 of 18 July 2018 on the financial rules applicable to the general budget of the Union, OJ 2018 L 193/1 [Regulation financial rules], Art 136(1)(c).

[263] EC recommendation securities, pt. 5.

[264] Council Decision (CFSP) 2016/1182 of 18 July 2016 concerning the Staff Regulations of the European Union Institute for Security Studies, OJ 2016 L 195/31, Annex, Art 2(7)(c).

and Restriction of Chemicals (REACH), we find several references to the requirement of being both "scientifically and ethically justified".[265,266]

These parallel situations are extended to a more holistic view in case of the EC proposal on health technology assessment (HTA), which refers to economic, medical, organisational, social, legal and ethical issues.[267]

After ethics only serving as a 'protection shield', or being used as a 'supportive argument', we have now seen ethics in terms of a parallel assessment of legal as well as ethical requirements. Already the last category requires a substantive determination, of what is meant by (un-)ethical behaviour. This leads us to our next (and very important) category, of [4.] ethics being determined by 'ethics committees'. There are committees, which focus exclusively on ethics, or others, where ethics is one of the aspects to be covered.[268] These committees can be installed either at [a.] EU or at [b.] national level and can take various forms. The underlying idea of all these committees is to outsource this ethical assessment, in order to achieve independent, objective and good quality opinions.

However, there are also examples where the EC[269] itself is tasked with the assessment at [4.a.] EU level. In Horizon 2020 the EC "shall systematically carry out ethics reviews for proposals raising ethical issues" by verifying "the respect of ethical principles and legislation".[270] From a procedural perspective, this "process of the ethics review [has to be] as transparent as possible and [...] carried out in a timely manner".[271] The "grant agreement shall, where appropriate, contain provisions ensuring the respect of *ethical principles*, including the establishment of an *independent ethics*

---

265 EC Regulation (EU) 2017/735 of 14 February 2017 amending, for the purpose of its adaptation to technical progress, the Annex to Regulation (EC) No 440/2008 laying down test methods pursuant to Regulation (EC) No 1907/2006 on the Registration, Evaluation, Authorisation and Restriction of Chemicals (REACH), OJ 2017 L 112/1, Annex, passim.

266 See also Regulation clinical trials, Art 2(2)(30): "'Good clinical practice' means a set of detailed *ethical and scientific* quality requirements [...]"; emphasis added; and Regulation medical devices, recital 71.

267 EC proposal for a regulation on HTA and amending [Directive patient mobility], COM(2018) 51 final 31.1.2018, recital 3 (et passim).

268 Regulation (EC) No 1394/2007 of 13 November 2007 on advanced therapy medicinal products [...], OJ 2007 L 324/121, as amended by OJ 2010 L 348/1 [Regulation advanced therapy], Art 21(2) provides for a 'Committee for Advanced Therapies' and requires a "balanced coverage of the scientific areas relevant to advanced therapies, including medical devices, tissue engineering, gene therapy, cell therapy, biotechnology, surgery, pharmacovigilance, risk management and ethics".

269 I will not further elaborate on examples of 'comitology', where the EC takes implementing measures on professional ethics, as for example, in Directive 2006/43/EC of 17 May 2006 on statutory audits of annual accounts and consolidated accounts [...], OJ 2006 L 157/87, as amended by OJ 2014 L 158/196 [Directive statutory audits], recital 9.

270 Regulation participation Horizon 2020, Art 14(1).

271 Regulation participation Horizon 2020, Art 14(2).

board and the right of the Commission to carry out *an ethics audit* by independent experts".[272,273]

Due to its importance for our topic, the already mentioned EGE will be covered in a distinct chapter.[274] However, it has also been tasked by different legal documents with ethical assessments. One year after the EGE's establishment in 1997, Directive Biotech provided that the EGE "evaluates all [sic!] ethical aspects of biotechnology".[275] In the field of GMOs, the already mentioned Directive on the deliberate release into the environment,[276] provides that "the Commission shall, on its own initiative or at the request of the [EP] or the Council, consult *any* committee it has created with a view to obtaining its advice on the *ethical* implications of *biotechnology*, *such as* [EGE], on ethical issues of a general nature".[277] Such consultation has to be "conducted under clear rules of openness, transparency and public accessibility".[278] Always keeping in mind the fact that EGEs opinions are not legally binding, the wording in 'Regulation GM food' is alleviated, as the "Commission, on its own initiative or at the request of a Member State, *may* consult [EGE] or any other appropriate body".[279] Not as regards the procedure (consultation), but to the output, it is stated that the opinions have to be made "available to the public".[280]

Apart from the EGE, there are several other institutional ethics committees, notably in the financial field. The European Investment Bank (EIB) follows a combined institutional and substantive approach, by having established an 'Ethics and Compliance Committee', which "shall rule on any potential conflict of interest" based on legal—not ethical—provisions.[281] Recently, the EIB has strengthened the role of this Committee "by introducing the possibility for this Committee to provide opinions on *any* ethical matter concerning a member of the Management Committee or of the Board of Directors".[282] In addition, the European Central Bank (ECB) follows a combined approach for the TARGET2-Securities Board, consisting of a code

[272]Regulation participation Horizon 2020, Art 18(6); emphases added.

[273]Further details implementing this legal requirement can be found on the EC's website: http://ec.europa.eu/research/participants/docs/h2020-funding-guide/cross-cutting-issues/ethics_en.htm.

[274]See *infra* Sect. 4.2.

[275]Recital 44 and Art 7.

[276]At notes 75 and 148.

[277]Art 29(1) Directive GMOs; emphases added.

[278]Art 29(2) Directive GMOs.

[279]Art 33(1) Regulation GM food.

[280]Art 33(2) Regulation GM food.

[281]Decision of the Board of Governors of 12 May 2010 on the amendment of the Rules of Procedure of the European Investment Bank to reflect the entry into force of the Treaty of Lisbon and of the new Statute of the Bank, OJ 2011 L 266/1, Art 11(4).

[282]Decision of the Board of Governors of 20 January 2016 on the Amendments to the Rules of Procedure of the EIB to reflect the Strengthening of the EIB Governance [2016/772], OJ 2016 L 127/55, recital 2; emphasis added.

of conduct[283] and an 'Ethics Officer'.[284] Members can contact the Ethics Officer in order to seek advice on an ad hoc basis.[285] The ECB[286] itself has established an 'Ethics Committee', due to the "increased level of *public awareness* and scrutiny [which] requires the ECB to have in place, and strictly adhere to, *state-of-the-art ethics rules* in order to safeguard the ECB's *integrity* and avoid reputational risks"[287]; it shall provide advice on questions of ethics based on individual requests.[288]

Finally, in a similar way as the EGE advises the EC, the 'European Data Protection Supervisor' has appointed an 'Ethics Advisory Group' as an "external advisory group on the ethical dimensions of data protection".[289] One reason for the establishment of this Body is technological advancement (big data computing and machine learning), which allows for the collection and usage of personal data "in increasingly *opaque and complex* ways, thus posing significant threats to *privacy* and *human dignity*".[290]

Apart from ethics committees at EU level, there are also examples of ethics committees at [4.b.] national level.

A combined approach of both EU (the role of the EC has already been described) and national ethical scrutiny can be found in Horizon 2020. There participants are not only obliged to "comply with national legislation, regulations and ethical rules in the countries where the action will be carried out", but also "[w]here appropriate, [to] seek the approval of the relevant national or local ethics committees prior to the start of the action".[291]

Also in the field of the research fund for coal and steel, participants shall, where appropriate, "seek the approval of the relevant national or local ethics committees prior to the start of the action".[292]

---

[283] The code of conduct contains well-known principles such as avoidance of conflicts of interest (plus an obligation of notification in such situations), confidentiality, transparency and openness, an obligation of information and sanctions in the case of non-compliance (Annex III).

[284] Decision 2012/235/EU (ECB/2012/6) of the European Central Bank of 29 March 2012 on the establishment of the TARGET2-Securities Board […], OJ 2012 L 117/13, as amended by OJ 2017 L 199/24, Annex III.

[285] Ibid. pt. 5.

[286] See also: Supplementary Code of Ethics Criteria for the members of the Executive Board of the European Central Bank, OJ 2010 C 104/8; Decision (EU) 2016/456 (ECB/2016/3) of the European Central Bank of 4 March 2016 concerning the terms and conditions for European Anti-Fraud Office investigations of the European Central Bank, in relation to the prevention of fraud, corruption and any other illegal activities affecting the financial interests of the Union, OJ 2016 L 79/34, with further information in recital 2.

[287] Decision (EU) 2015/433 (ECB/2014/59) of the European Central Bank of 17 December 2014 concerning the establishment of an Ethics Committee and its Rules of Procedure, OJ 2015 L 70/58, recital 2; emphases added.

[288] Ibid. Art 4(1).

[289] European Data Protection Supervisor Decision of 3 December 2015 establishing an external advisory group on the ethical dimensions of data protection ('the Ethics Advisory Group'), OJ 2016 C 33/1, Art 1(1).

[290] Ibid. recital 5; emphases added.

[291] Regulation participation Horizon 2020, Art 23(9).

[292] Council Decision Research Coal and Steel, Art 29a(6).

It is again Directive GMOs, which states "Member States should be able to consult *any* committee they have established with a view to obtaining advice on the ethical implications of *biotechnology*".[293] This statement stands beside the above-mentioned possibility of the EC, to consult the EGE "on ethical issues of a *general* nature".[294] Evaluation by and consultation with national or local ethics committees is also foreseen for nanosciences and nanotechnologies research,[295] or in the case of ionizing radiation.[296]

In the field of 'clinical trials',[297] 'medical devices'[298] and 'in vitro diagnostic medical devices',[299] the three corresponding regulations all operate based on the same following definition of an ethics committee. "'Ethics committee' means an *independent* body established *in a Member State* in accordance with the law of that Member State and empowered to give *opinions* for the purposes of this Regulation, taking into account the views of *laypersons*, in particular patients or patients' organisations".[300] The ethical review performed by this national ethics committee is a requirement for prior authorisation, where a "clinical trial shall be subject to scientific and ethical review"[301]; similar rules apply for the two other examples mentioned above.[302]

Hence, as we have seen, ethics committees cannot only issue opinions on request or on their own initiative (for example, EGE), but can also play a decisive role in authorization procedures, not only for research grants, but also for manufacturing processes.

One task of ethics committees can also be to issue codes of conduct. Codes of conduct have the clear advantage that they are more detailed than just a general reference to ethical standards. These [5.] codes of conduct can be located both at [a.] EU or at [b.] national level.[303]

---

[293]Directive GMOs, Recital 58; emphases added.

[294]Directive GMOs, Art 29(1); emphasis added.

[295]EC recommendation 2008/345/EC of 7 February 2008 on a code of conduct for responsible nanosciences and nanotechnologies research, OJ 2008 L 116/46 [EC recommendation nanosciences], Annex, pt. 4.1.7.

[296]Council Directive 2013/59/Euratom of 5 December 2013 laying down basic safety standards for protection against the dangers arising from exposure to ionising radiation [...], OJ 2014 L 13/1, as corrected by OJ 2016 L 72/69 [Directive ionising radiation], Art 55(2)(e).

[297]Regulation clinical trials, Art 2(2)(11); see also recital 18. For a comparison of the old and this new regime, see Frischhut (2015, p. 552).

[298]Regulation (EU) 2017/745 of 5 April 2017 on medical devices [...], OJ 2017 L 117/1 [Regulation medical devices], Art 2(56).

[299]Regulation (EU) 2017/746 of 5 April 2017 on in vitro diagnostic medical devices [...], OJ 2017 L 117/176 [Regulation in vitro medical devices], Art 2(59).

[300]Emphases added.

[301]Regulation clinical trials, Art 4 (et passim).

[302]Regulation medical devices, Art 62(3), et passim; Regulation in vitro medical devices, Art 58(3), et passim.

[303]In Council decision Albania, Annex, pt. 3.1., we find reference to a "code of ethics for the prisons system"; see also Directive (EU) 2016/1629 of 14 September 2016 laying down technical requirements for inland waterway vessels [...], OJ 2016 L 252/118, as amended by OJ 2018 L 174/15,

At [5.a.] EU level we find the already mentioned "Code of Conduct for responsible nanosciences and nanotechnologies research".[304] This code is quite detailed, comprising, amongst others, the principles of comprehensibility, respect of fundamental rights, the well-being of individuals and society, sustainability, the precautionary principle, inclusiveness (openness, transparency, and access to information), excellence, innovation, and accountability.[305] Hence, ethics is only part of the general principles mentioned therein.

In the case of 'Directive Services', we find a provision, which encourages "the setting up of codes of conduct, in particular, by professional bodies, organisations and associations at [EU] level". Similar to the case of the example of nanosciences, this code of conduct is also not only about (professional) ethics.[306]

Again at EU level, we find a non-binding recommendation, the already mentioned European Charter for Researchers, which, apart from referring to recognized ethical principles and so forth, also requires researchers to "adhere to [...] ethical standards as documented in the different national, sectoral or institutional codes of ethics".[307] It therefore does not create a code of conduct, but just refers to existing ones, also [5.b.] at national level.

Besides examples of non-binding recommendations, we also find an obligation for the MS regarding the transposition of EU directive against child pornography, according to which MS have to undertake preventive action "such as the drawing up and reinforcement of a code of conduct and self-regulatory mechanisms in the tourism industry, the setting-up of a code of ethics" and so forth.[308] Although the transposition of the directive into national law is binding in itself, thus the MS enjoy some flexibility as regards the form and methods of achieving this goal.

After ethics committees and codes of conduct, the substance of a reference to ethics can also be determined via references to [6.] other (international) documents.

In the context of the already mentioned three related examples of 'clinical trials',[309] 'medical devices'[310] and 'in vitro diagnostic medical devices',[311] reference is made to "the most recent version of the World Medical Association Declaration of

---

Annex VI, pt. 7 ("code of ethics"); Regulation financial rules, Art 136(2)(b) ("ethical standards of the profession").

304 EC recommendation nanosciences, Annex.

305 Ibid. Annex, pt. 3.

306 Directive services, recital 114. Recital 113 is also about ethics, however in this case those codes of conduct (drawn up by "interested parties" at EU level) are only mentioned insofar as they have to be "compatible with legally binding rules governing professional ethics and conduct in the Member States".

307 EC Charter researchers, Annex, Section 1.

308 Directive 2011/93/EU of 13 December 2011 on combating the sexual abuse and sexual exploitation of children and child pornography [...], OJ 2011 L 335/1, as corrected by OJ 2012 L18/7 [Directive combating abuse], recital 33.

309 Regulation clinical trials, recitals 43 and 80. The reference from ethics to the Helsinki declaration is an indirect one, via the notion of "good clinical practice", Art 2(2)(30).

310 Regulation medical devices, recital 64.

311 Regulation in vitro medical devices, recital 66.

Helsinki on Ethical Principles for Medical Research Involving Human Subjects".[312] This Helsinki Declaration[313] has the advantage not only of having been elaborated at a 'worldwide' basis, but also of providing relatively detailed rules as regards ethical behaviour. Of course, it has to be acknowledged that EU law can only refer to such detailed guidelines if they exist and have been elaborated by an acknowledged body in the relevant field.[314]

'Regulation in vitro medical devices' replaces the previous directive in this field, which for ethical requirements in the context of the removal, collection and use of tissues, cells and substances of human origin, has referred to the Council of Europe's Oviedo convention.[315,316]

It is also worth mentioning the example of the directive on statutory audits, which requires adherence to "highest ethical standards".[317] In this context, it is the Commission's task to "adopt implementing measures on professional ethics as minimum standards [and when] doing so, it might consider the principles contained in the International Federation of Accountants (IFAC) Code of Ethics".[318] Thus, the Commission is invited to consider this international code.

Finally, yet importantly, there is also one example, where in the context of biocidal products reference is made to "internationally accepted ethical standards", without further guidance of how these standards are defined.[319]

After ethics committees, codes of conduct, and the determination via references to other (international) documents, we finally come to a category, where some information concerning the content or understanding of ethics can be found [7.] in the relevant legal document itself.

---

[312] Ibid. See also Directive 2001/83/EC of 6 November 2001 on the Community code relating to medicinal products for human use, OJ 2001 L 311/67, as amended by OJ 2017 L 238/44 [Directive medicinal products], Annex I, recital 8: "ethical principles that are reflected, for example, in the Declaration of Helsinki". For further examples, see Frischhut (2015, p. 554).

[313] World Medical Association, WMA Declaration of Helsinki, https://www.wma.net/policies-post/wma-declaration-of-helsinki-ethical-principles-for-medical-research-involving-human-subjects/.

[314] On some criticism concerning the Helsinki Declaration, see: Ehni and Wiesing (2018).

[315] Convention for the protection of Human Rights and Dignity of the Human Being with regard to the Application of Biology and Medicine: Convention on Human Rights and Biomedicine (adopted 4 April 1997, entered into force 1 December 1999), ETS No164.

[316] Directive 98/79/EC of 27 October 1998 on in vitro diagnostic medical devices, OJ 1998 L 331/1, repealed (as of 26.05.2022) by OJ 2017 L 117/176 (= Regulation in vitro medical devices) [Directive in vitro medical devices], Art 1(4).

[317] Directive statutory audits, recital 9.

[318] Ibid.

[319] Regulation (EU) No 528/2012 of 22 May 2012 concerning the making available on the market and use of biocidal products, OJ 2012 L 167/1, as amended by OJ 2017 L 121/45, Annex IV, 1.1.3.

In the field of statutory audit, when mentioning "ethical and independence requirements", etc., the relevant provision on quality assurance of this regulation refers both to other chapters of the same regulation (as well as to another legal document[320]).[321]

Another example of determination of content in the relevant legal document itself can be found in the field of mining. While "ethical mining" is not explicitly defined, a systematic interpretation of the whole directive on supply chain due diligence obligations clearly refers to the affected region ("in particular in the African Great Lakes Region"), to the goods of import in question (gold, etc.), as well as the reasons of concern (conflicts, child labour, sexual violence, the disappearance of people, etc.). All this exhibits why the mining of these goods in these circumstances is deemed wrong.[322]

In the context of placing of proprietary medicinal products on the market, we find an example of a clear statement what is seen as unethical and what should be the consequences. "Since a full placebo comparison will not often be feasible or ethically acceptable in convulsive epilepsy, it is important in the later phases of evaluation to carry out controlled (randomized) clinical trials [...]".[323]

In addition, in the field of medicinal products for human use we find some thoughts on the treatment of control groups against the background of ethical considerations. "[T]hus it may, in some instances, be more pertinent to compare the efficacy of a new medicinal product with that of an established medicinal product of proven therapeutic value rather than with the effect of a placebo".[324] The same directive also exempts applicants from certain documentation if "it would be contrary to generally accepted principles of medical ethics to collect such information".[325]

In Horizon 2020 actions, falling within the scope of 'Regulation participation Horizon 2020' should "be in conformity [...] with ethical principles, which include avoiding any breach of research integrity".[326] In addition, Art 19 (entitled "Ethical principles") of 'Regulation establishing Horizon 2020', after stipulating that "[a]ll the research and innovation activities carried out under Horizon 2020 shall comply with ethical principles [and human rights]", excludes the following fields of research from

---

320 Directive statutory audits.

321 Regulation (EU) No 537/2014 of 16 April 2014 on specific requirements regarding statutory audit of public-interest entities [...], OJ 2014 L 158/77, as corrected by OJ 2014 L 170/66, Art 26(7)(a).

322 Regulation (EU) 2017/821 of 17 May 2017 laying down supply chain due diligence obligations for Union importers of tin, tantalum and tungsten, their ores, and gold originating from conflict-affected and high-risk areas, OJ 2017 L 130/1 [Regulation supply chain], recital 23. On these transparency requirements, see Härkönen (2018).

323 Council Recommendation 87/176/EEC of 9 February 1987 concerning tests relating to the placing on the market of proprietary medicinal products, OJ 1987 L 73/1 [Council Recommendation proprietary medicinal products], Annex IX, pt. 6. To some extent, this example could also be seen as a 'supportive argument'. It should be mentioned that other references in this document to ethics remain undetermined.

324 Directive medicinal products, Annex I, part I, 5.2.5.1.

325 Ibid. Annex I, Part II, 6.

326 Recital 9.

funding: "human cloning for reproductive purposes", "genetic heritage of human beings", as well as "research activities intended to create human embryos solely for the purpose of research or for the purpose of stem cell procurement, including by means of somatic cell nuclear transfer".[327] This can be seen as a European consensus with regard to bioethics, although one could argue that this provision is 'only' about funding and not about the legality of these activities.

Although this book is based on a broad understanding of bioethics, the examples mentioned so far always referred to humans. Nonetheless, there are also examples where the beneficiaries of ethical or moral principles are not humans, but animals, plants or the environment.[328] Especially animals are protected by ethical principles in different fields.

Bearing some resemblance to human dignity, the directive on the protection of animals used for scientific purposes asserts that animals "have an *intrinsic value* which must be respected".[329] As a practical consequence arising from this approach, "animals should always be treated as *sentient* creatures and their use in procedures should be restricted to areas which may ultimately benefit human or animal health, or the environment", and their use "for scientific or educational purposes should therefore only be considered where a non-animal alternative is unavailable".[330] This directive provides even more detailed statements with respect to the practical consequences of the 'intrinsic value' of animals, as there are restrictions for the use of non-human primates.[331] Due to ethical considerations, the directive also sets a maximum threshold of permissible pain and therefore prohibits "the performance of procedures that result in severe pain, suffering or distress, which is likely to be long-lasting and cannot be ameliorated".[332]

Apart from this directive, ethical considerations concerning animals are also the reason why mass slaughtering has been declared as being, amongst other things, "ethically questionable",[333] or, why there can even be "an ethical duty to kill pro-

---

[327] Art 19(3).

[328] EC recommendation nanosciences, Annex, 3.2: "not harm or create a biological, physical or moral threat to people, animals, plants or the environment, at present or in the future".

[329] Directive 2010/63/EU of 22 September 2010 on the protection of animals used for scientific purposes, OJ 2010 L 276/33 [Directive animals], recital 12; emphasis added; and further refers to "the ethical concerns of the general public as regards the use of animals in procedures".

[330] Ibid; emphasis added.

[331] Directive animals, recital 17: "Due to their *genetic proximity* to human beings and to their highly developed *social skills*, the use of non-human primates in scientific procedures raises specific *ethical* and practical problems in terms of meeting their behavioural, environmental and social needs in a laboratory environment"; emphases added.

[332] Directive animals, recital 23. All those ethical considerations have to be taken into account for project evaluation; recital 38; Art 38(2)(d).

[333] Court of Auditors, Special Report No 1/2000 on classical swine fever, together with the Commission's replies, OJ 2000 C 85/1, para 18: "mass slaughtering is expensive, ethically questionable, wasteful of food resources and may destroy genetically valuable animals".

ductive animals which are in severe pain where there is no economically viable way to alleviate such pain".[334]

After a mere declaration annexed to the Maastricht Treaty[335] and a protocol annexed to the Amsterdam Treaty,[336] Art 13 TFEU now entails a horizontal clause according to which both the EU and the MS shall "pay full regard to the welfare requirements of animals", because animals are "sentient beings".[337] In Horizon 2020, this Art 13 TFEU is addressed in the context of respect for "fundamental ethical principles" with the practical consequence that "the use of animals in research and testing should be reduced, with a view ultimately to replacing their use".[338]

Leaving the field of bioethics, the already mentioned directive on statutory audits provides another example pertaining to this category where some understandings of the practical consequences of ethics are provided. After stating that statutory auditors should adhere to "the highest ethical standards", the directive provides that they should be "subject to professional ethics, covering at least their public-interest function, their integrity and objectivity and their professional competence and due care"[339]; further details have to be implemented by the MS.[340]

In the following example, ethics is not determined by the EU, MS and so forth on a collective basis, but by a single business entity. According to the Regulation on European social entrepreneurship funds, so called "[q]ualifying social entrepreneurship funds should invest in a manner consistent with *their* ethical investment strategy, *for instance* they should *not* undertake investments that finance the weapons industry, that risk breaches of human rights or that entail electronic waste-dumping".[341]

334 Council Regulation (EC) No 1099/2009 of 24 September 2009 on the protection of animals at the time of killing, OJ 2009 L 303/1, as amended by OJ 2018 L 122/11, recital 12.

335 OJ 1992 C 191/103.

336 OJ 1997 C 340/110.

337 As protocols also pertain to EU primary law, the transfer from protocol to Treaty provision had more of a symbolic than a legal significance. Neither the declaration nor the protocol had entailed the rationale that animals are sentient beings.

338 Regulation establishing Horizon 2020, recital 29. Similar in Council Regulation (Euratom) No 1314/2013 of 16 December 2013 on the Research and Training Programme of the European Atomic Energy Community (2014–2018) complementing the Horizon 2020 Framework Programme for Research and Innovation, OJ 2013 L 347/948 [Regulation Horizon 2020 Euratom], recital 18 (N.B. This regulation will be repealed by Council Regulation (Euratom) 2018/1563 of 15 October 2018 on the Research and Training Programme of the European Atomic Energy Community (2019–2020) complementing the Horizon 2020 Framework Programme for Research and Innovation, and repealing Regulation (Euratom) No 1314/2013, OJ 2018 L 262/1). Animal welfare "and other ethical issues" are also addressed in Council Decision 2013/743/EU of 3 December 2013 establishing the specific programme implementing Horizon 2020—the Framework Programme for Research and Innovation (2014–2020) [...], OJ 2013 L 347/965, as corrected by OJ 2015 L 102/96, Annex I, Part III, 2.2.3.

339 Directive statutory audits, recital 9.

340 Directive statutory audits, Art 21(1).

341 Regulation 346/2013/EU of 17 April 2013 on European Social Entrepreneurship Funds, OJ 2013 L 115/18, as amended by OJ 2017 L 293/1, recital 21; emphases added.

The combined approach of the ECB, that is to say an Ethics Officer plus principles (such as avoidance of conflicts of interest, confidentiality, transparency and openness, etc.) contained in a code of conduct, has already been mentioned.[342] Likewise, the European Anti-Fraud Office (OLAF) merely follows a substantive approach for their Supervisory Committee. Art 4, entitled 'ethics', requires the members to act independently, neither seeking nor taking instructions from others, not to deal with matters where they have a personal interest, to demonstrate confidentiality, and to adhere to an obligation of notification if any such situation occurs.[343]

In an indirect way, we can also add examples, where reference is made to notions that have a pre-determined meaning from another field, such as public morality,[344] which has been shaped by the CJEU,[345] or moral hazard,[346] as a notion of microeconomics.[347] The example of moral hazard also derives from the financial crisis, where the Commission's banking communication refers several times to 'moral hazard'.[348] In a similar way as for international agreements, moral hazard is addressed in the context of burden sharing.[349] This concept can be explained by referring to a situation caused by the immoral behaviour of a single body that is dangerous for a bigger group (society). Most people would agree to qualify the risky behaviour of certain banks to the detriment of taxpayers (whereas bonuses would still be paid, maybe also with the help of those taxpayers' subsidies) as immoral.[350]

After having seen determination by ethics committees, codes of conduct, references to international documents and further information provided by EU law itself, we finally arrive at the last category, that is, EU law, where ethics [8.] remains undetermined.

The example of patient mobility has already been mentioned in the category of 'non-interference', where patients do not have a right to cross-border healthcare because the directive shall not "undermine the fundamental ethical choices of Member States".[351] This undetermined provision can have a significant impact on patients seeking cross-border healthcare. In fact, some MS feared the application of

---

342 *Supra* at note 283.

343 OLAF Rules of Procedure of the OLAF Supervisory Committee, OJ 2011 L 308/114.

344 Regulation (EU) 2015/478 of 11 March 2015 on common rules for imports, OJ 2015 L 83/16, Art 24(2)(a).

345 See *supra* Sects. 3.1.1 and 3.3.1.1.

346 Directive 2014/59/EU of 15 May 2014 establishing a framework for the recovery and resolution of credit institutions and investment firms […], OJ 2014 L 173/190, as completed by OJ 2018 L 67/8, recital 45.

347 See *supra* at note 89.

348 EC communication on the application, from 1 August 2013, of State aid rules to support measures in favour of banks in the context of the financial crisis ('Banking Communication'), OJ 2013 C 216/1, paras 15, 40, 77 and 84. In this context, see e.g. OJ 2015 L 80, 1 and 49.

349 Ibid. para 15; emphases added.

350 For a good description, see Sandel (2010, pp. 12–13).

351 Directive patient mobility, recital 7. Recital 53 also states that the principle of "recognition of prescriptions from other Member States should not affect any professional or ethical duty that would require pharmacists to refuse to dispense the prescription"; see also Art 11(1)(3).

this directive to sensitive issues "like euthanasia, DNA-testing or IVF".[352] Contrary to what one would expect, it was not the Council of Ministers but the EP that at a very early stage of the legislative procedure, proposed amendments making clear that "[n]o provision of this Directive should be interpreted in such a way as to undermine the fundamental ethical choices of Member States".[353] This was strengthened by emphasizing that "[n]otwithstanding those common values it is accepted that Member States take *different* decisions on *ethical* grounds as regards the availability of certain treatments and the concrete access conditions [and that this] Directive is without prejudice to *ethical diversity*".[354] The question remains, as to whether this provision has to be interpreted in a narrow sense, as it requires 'fundamental' ethical choices. Moreover, only the legal materials help to shed more light on the void of this undetermined concept.

While this example refers to the MS to determine ethics in this regard, the following examples provide no information whatsoever on the understanding behind the term of ethics used in those documents, of both a binding and non-binding nature.

One example of a binding nature is about food law, where it has been acknowledged that scientific risk assessment alone might not provide all necessary information for, but where also "societal, economic, traditional, ethical and environmental factors" have to be considered.[355] The reference to ethics might be very general (one factor amongst others to be taken into account), but does not mitigate the fact that the concept of ethics remains undetermined.

Other examples of non-determined references to ethics are as follows[356]: "*scientific* ethics",[357] "*relevant* ethical principles",[358] "*business* ethics standards",[359] "*professional* ethics",[360] "ethical principles, which *include* avoiding any breach of *research integrity*",[361] or "environmental *and ethical* considerations".[362] In another

[352]Van Hoof and Pennings (2012, p. 194).

[353]EP legislative resolution of 23 April 2009 on the proposal for a directive on the application of patients' rights in cross-border healthcare, OJ 2010 C 184E/368, recital 6.

[354]Ibid. recital 14; emphases added.

[355]Regulation (EC) No 178/2002 of 28 January 2002 laying down the general principles and requirements of food law, establishing the European Food Safety Authority and laying down procedures in matters of food safety, OJ 2002 L 31/1, as amended by OJ 2017 L 117/1, recital 19.

[356]Emphases added.

[357]Regulation data fisheries, Art 20(1)(c).

[358]EC Regulation (EU) 2015/445 of 17 March 2015 amending Regulation (EU) No 1178/2011 as regards technical requirements and administrative procedures related to civil aviation aircrew, OJ 2015 L 74/1, Annex IV.

[359]Directive (EU) 2016/97 of 20 January 2016 on insurance distribution (recast), OJ 2016 L 26/19, as amended by OJ 2018 L 76/28, Annex I.

[360]Directive (EU) 2018/958 of 28 June 2018 on a proportionality test before adoption of new regulation of professions, OJ 2018 L 173/25, recitals 27 and 30, Art 7(3)(c).

[361]Decision (EU) 2017/1324 of 4 July 2017 on the participation of the Union in the Partnership for Research and Innovation in the Mediterranean Area (PRIMA) jointly undertaken by several Member States, OJ 2017 L 185/1, recital 8.

[362]EC decision (EU) 2018/813 of 14 May 2018 on the sectoral reference document on best environmental management practices, sector environmental performance indicators and benchmarks of

reference to "ethical or environmental reasons",[363] this regulation further refers to another document,[364] but without further clarification on the determination of ethics. In addition, the new General Data Protection Regulation (GDPR)[365] refers to "recognised ethical standards for scientific research",[366] as well as "ethics for regulated professions".[367] Besides ethics, in the field of trademark, we find a reference to "accepted principles of morality" in both the corresponding EU directive[368] and regulation.[369,370]

Another example refers to the European Council,[371] which expressed in its Stockholm presidency conclusions from 2001 the need to "strengthen the European biotechnology sector's competitiveness", while ensuring that this is "consistent with common fundamental values and ethical principles".[372] Some could take the view that there is no need for a (purely) political document to provide detailed statements, nonetheless, also in this case we lack further guidance as to the understanding of ethics.

The Council (of Ministers) resolution concerning fundamental health policy choices is another example of a non-binding document, taking 'only' note of some topics, "which warrant joint consideration", such as "revision of medical studies syllabuses in order to incorporate the relevant economic, legal, ethical and social aspects necessary to ensure that practitioners dispense adequate health care".[373] This example is comparable to the one of port State inspectors, where the content of ethics as part of a training programme is not determined.[374] Although there is no

---

excellence for the agriculture sector under Regulation (EC) No 1221/2009 on the voluntary participation by organisations in a Community eco-management and audit scheme (EMAS), OJ 2018 L 145/1, Annex (passim).

[363] EC Regulation (EU) 2016/246 of 3 February 2016 amending Annex I to Regulation (EC) No 794/2004 as regards the forms to be used for the notification of State aid in the agricultural and forestry sectors and in rural areas, OJ 2016 L 51/1, Annex (on p. 78).

[364] European Union Guidelines for State aid in the agricultural and forestry sectors and in rural areas 2014–2020, OJ 2014 C 204/1.

[365] Regulation (EU) 2016/679 of 27 April 2016 on the protection of natural persons with regard to the processing of personal data and on the free movement of such data [...] (General Data Protection Regulation), OJ 2016 L 119/1, as corrected by OJ 2018 L 127/2 [Regulation GDP].

[366] Ibid. recital 33.

[367] Ibid. recital 73, Art 23(1)(g).

[368] Directive (EU) 2015/2436 of 16 December 2015 to approximate the laws of the Member States relating to trade marks, OJ 2015 L 336/1, as corrected by OJ 2016 L 110/5, Art 4(1)(f) and Art 31(1).

[369] Regulation (EU) 2017/1001 of 14 June 2017 on the European Union trade mark, OJ 2017 L 154/1, Art 7(1)(f), Art 76(1) and Art 85(1).

[370] On the diversity argument when applying this concept to the figurative trademark 'La Mafia', see Sect. 3.3.1.2.

[371] Art 15 TEU.

[372] Presidency Conclusions, Stockholm European Council (23./24.3.2001), part I, VI. 44.

[373] Resolution of the Council [etc.] of 11 November 1991 concerning fundamental health-policy choices, OJ 1991 C304/5.

[374] *Supra* at note 61.

further information on what constitutes an ethical syllabus, the MS competence[375] for both education and health might be the legally based reason why this non-legal term should be defined by the MS.

The same idea can hold true for other health related (non-binding) documents in the context of cancer screening[376] and hereditary illnesses[377] on the one hand, and for lifelong learning[378] on the other.

Within the shared competence of the internal market,[379] we find one example of a task in the public interest, which is about "doctors or veterinary bodies ensuring that their members conform to ethical or sanitary rules".[380] This example adds up to our list of undetermined references to ethics, where a possible solution could be to see those bodies in charge of defining those ethical rules.

3.3.3.4 Conclusion

Unethical behaviour can have an impact, both when seeking an authorisation or in the context of research funding. Given the amount of documents that have to be published in the 24 official languages, the inconsistencies identified in this chapter are a minor issue. Nevertheless, it makes a difference whether a document refers to ethics or morality (Directive greenhouse gas emissions), or to ethical or moral principles recognised in one or more MS (Directive Biotech).

Beneficiaries have mainly been humans, however, also animals are protected due to arguments reminding us of 'human dignity'. In order to achieve ethical behaviour, training plays an important role. Therefore, it is no surprise, that also in case of 'EU reference centres for animal welfare' we find the requirement of "suitably qualified staff with adequate training [...] in ethical issues related to animals".[381] In a completely different field, the importance of "[i]ncreased awareness of [...] ethical issues among students and their teachers"[382] is also emphasized.

---

[375] Art 6(a) and (e) TFEU.

[376] Council Recommendation of 2 December 2003 on cancer screening, OJ 2003 L 327/34, recital 10.

[377] Conclusions of the Council [etc.] of 15 May 1992 on hereditary illnesses, OJ 1992 C 148/3, recital 5.

[378] Council Recommendation of 22 May 2018 on key competences for lifelong learning, OJ 2018 C 189/1, Annex (passim).

[379] Art 4(2)(a) TFEU.

[380] EC recommendation of 26 March 2009 on data protection guidelines for the Internal Market Information System (IMI), OJ 2009 L 100/12, Annex, pt. 6 II.

[381] Regulation (EU) 2017/625 of 15 March 2017 on official controls and other official activities performed to ensure the application of food and feed law, rules on animal health and welfare, plant health and plant protection products [...], OJ 2017 L 95/1, as corrected by OJ 2017 L 137/40, Art 95(3)(c).

[382] Council Decision (CFSP) 2016/51 of 18 January 2016 in support of the Biological and Toxin Weapons Convention (BTWC) in the framework of the EU Strategy against Proliferation of Weapons of Mass Destruction, OJ 2016 L 12/50, Annex, pt. 1.6.2.

Concerning humans, special groups that have not been mentioned so far, are incapacitated subjects[383] in respect of clinical trials on medicinal products for human use, as well as children,[384] where specific ethical concerns might arise and should be addressed.

The numerous EU documents referring to ethics and morality can be clustered in the above-mentioned, inductively developed, categories. It has to be emphasized that some examples are overlapping and, hence, could fall in various categories.

The category of ethics serving as a [1.] 'protection shield' clearly is not a very ambitious approach. Using ethics as [2.] a supportive argument is clearly less of a problem, as the legal situation (which it defends) should be able to be self-standing. It is also less of a problem, when ethics is determined by [4.] an ethics committee or via a [5.] code of conduct, in either category either at EU or at national level. Sufficient clarification with regard to the content of references to ethics can also be guaranteed via references to [6.] other (international) documents, such as the Helsinki declaration or the Oviedo convention, or if further information [7.] is provided in the relevant EU document itself.

From the perspective of legal certainty, a [3.] parallel ethical and legal assessment (e.g. Directive Biotech), can be problematic if the criteria for this ethical assessment are not clearly stated, which finally leads us to category [8.], where ethics remains undetermined.

The examples we have seen in the category of ethics committees clearly displays that ethics plays a role in sensitive fields: this is the case for 'science and new technologies' (EGE), in the financial field, in data protection and digitalization, or in the health sector (e.g. clinical trials, medical devices and in vitro diagnostic medical devices). Further recent examples of sensitive fields referring to ethics can be found in the context of 'health in the digital society',[385] 'artificial intelligence',[386] 'robotics',[387] and 'digital ethics'.[388]

---

383 Regulation clinical trials, Art 10(2).

384 Council Recommendation proprietary medicinal products, Annex XIV, pt. 3.2.2(b); Council Resolution of 14 December 2000 on paediatric medicinal products, OJ 2001 C 17/1, recitals 7 and 9; Regulation clinical trials, Art 10(1).

385 Council conclusions on Health in the Digital Society—making progress in data-driven innovation in the field of health, OJ 2017 C 440/3, pt. 23 ("ethical aspects and the differences in digital and health literacy").

386 EC 'EU MS sign up to cooperate on Artificial Intelligence' (10.4.2018), https://ec.europa.eu/digital-single-market/en/news/eu-member-states-sign-cooperate-artificial-intelligence.

387 EP resolution of 16 February 2017 with recommendations to the Commission on Civil Law Rules on Robotics, P8_TA(2017)0051 [EP resolution robotics], passim (50 mentions); the importance of values in the context of robots has also been stressed by Sahlin (2018, p. 85).

388 Ethics Advisory Group (2018). See also: Executive summary of Opinion No 4/2015 of the European Data Protection Supervisor, 'Towards a new digital ethics: Data, dignity and technology', OJ 2015 C 392/9.

3.3.4 The Ethical Spirit in Implementing EU Directives

Some of these documents of EU secondary and tertiary law are EU directives, which need to be implemented into national law.[389] The national provisions implementing these directives in the various MS, are well documented in EUR-Lex, respectively in the relevant national legal databases.[390]

This chapter is related to objective 2, i.e. the question how selected MS have dealt with ethics and morality in the way they have implemented these directives. More precisely: how have these countries implemented the selected EU-Directives regarding ethics and/or morality into national law? In implementing these directives, have they also referred to ethics and/or morality, respectively to similar concepts and related terms, such as EU values and human or fundamental rights? Finally, can we conclude on an 'ethicalization' of national law via EU law?

The countries examined are, in alphabetical order, Austria, the Czech Republic, France, Germany, Ireland, Italy, Slovakia, Spain, and the United Kingdom. While not all 28 Member States could be covered, this chapter covers the biggest Member States, plus taking into account different legal systems (common law, e.g. in the UK and Ireland; civil law system), old and new Member States, from Northern and Southern Europe, as well as from Western and Eastern Europe).

This chapter is based on a research project, which was conducted in two waves, based on a research design developed, as well as the project itself directed by the author, with several students involved. The first round in 2016 covered Austria and Germany,[391] France,[392] Ireland and the United Kingdom,[393] as well as Spain,[394] the second round, in 2017, Italy[395] as well as the Czech Republic and Slovakia.[396] Space precludes a discussion of the numerous findings of these two rounds. Therefore, the most important results are summarized in the following.

The 28 directives identified for this project mainly pertain to the field of health (see Table 3.2), addressing issues of bioethics. Therefore, the majority of references to these concepts can be found in the field of health, mainly referring to 'ethics', less to 'morality'.

As can also be seen from Fig. 3.2, the majority of these 28 directives analysed have been adopted since 2001, which has to be seen against the background of the creation of the EGE in December 1997.[397] While the first directives pertain to the

[389]Art 288(3) TFEU.

[390]That is why in Table 3.2 only those directives are indicated which have been mentioned elsewhere in this book.

[391]Hotarek (2016).

[392]Estermann (2016).

[393]Pacey (2016).

[394]Varona Martín (2016).

[395]Sava (2017).

[396]Kubincová (2017).

[397]See *infra* Sect. 4.2.1.

Table 3.2 EU 'ethics directives', time frame and areas

Time frame	Technology	Health	Employment	Finance & accounting	Children & animals	
1990–1995		1990/385				
		1991/507				
		1993/42				
1996–2000	1998/44[a]	1998/79[b]				
2001–2005		2001/18[c]	2005/36[g]			
		2001/20[d]				
		2001/83[e]				
		2003/63				
		2004/23[f]				
		2004/27				
		2005/28				
2006–2010	2006/87	2007/47	2006/123[i]	2006/43[j]	2010/63[k]	
	2009/30[h]	2009/120	2009/50			
2011–2015		2011/24[l]	2013/55	2014/17	2011/93[n]	
		2013/59[m]		2014/56		
				2014/65		
Number:	3	15	4	4	2	28 (in total)

[a]Directive Biotech
[b]Directive in vitro medical devices
[c]Directive GMOs
[d]Directive clinical trials
[e]Directive medicinal products
[f]Directive 2004/23/EC of 31 March 2004 on setting standards of quality and safety for the donation, procurement, testing, processing, preservation, storage and distribution of human tissues and cells, OJ 2004 L 102/48, as amended by OJ 2009 L 188/14 [Directive tissues and cells]
[g]Directive recognition qualifications
[h]Directive greenhouse gas emissions
[i]Directive services
[j]Directive statutory audits
[k]Directive animals
[l]Directive patient mobility
[m]Directive ionising radiation
[n]Directive combating abuse

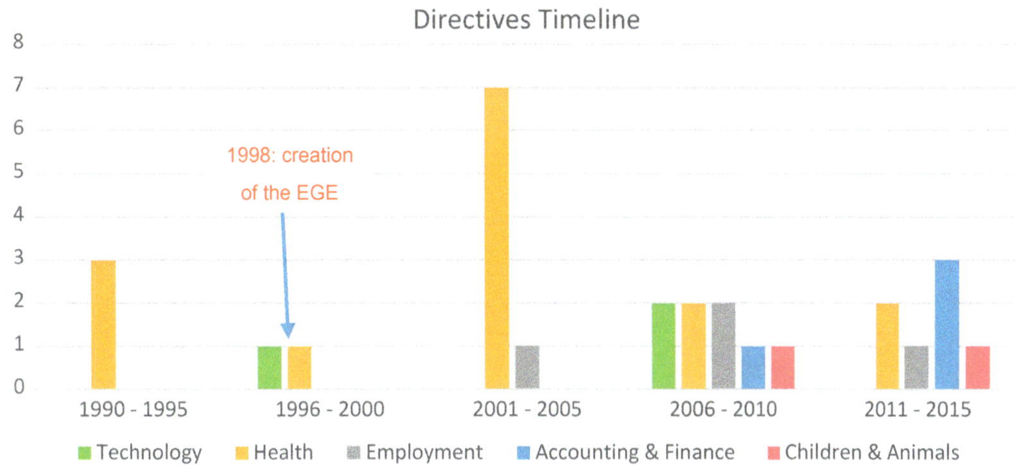

Fig. 3.2 EU 'ethics directives', timeline and areas (total numbers). *Source* Pacey (2016, p. 38)

field of health (which, in total, comprises more than half of these directives), since 2001 we can observe an expansion also to other areas.

These directives have been analysed with regard to the key terms of 'ethics', 'morality' and related terms. These terms plus the different areas, where they occur, can be seen below from Fig. 3.3. 'Ethics' and related terms occur most frequently, especially in the field of 'health', while 'professional ethics' pertains to the field of 'employment', as well as 'accounting & finance'. This is followed by the concept of 'integrity', which primarily occurs in the area of 'accounting & finance'. As mentioned above, the term of morality (primarily only in the field of 'technology') plays a minor role.

When taking a closer look at the term 'ethics' in its various breakdowns, one can see the following picture (see Fig. 3.4), which clearly exhibits, first of all, that the term 'ethics committee' prevails, and, second, that this term clearly pertains to the health field.

When, in a next step, we turn from these EU directives to the national level, the various findings of the national implementation measures (NIM) of the eight MS examined can be summarized as follows[398]:

Although it might sound obvious, keywords in EU directives have only been implemented, when mentioned in those parts of a Directive which have to be implemented, i.e. articles, but not if only mentioned in the recitals of the preamble.[399] For instance, references to fundamental rights or the EU's common values mainly occur in the preamble of directives, thus they play no major role in the NIM.

---

[398]Apart from the limitations specifically mentioned in the respective papers, the following should be mentioned here: firstly, it may be that a MS has not had to transpose all directives [due to an opt-out; see e.g. Pacey (2016, p. 41)] or, in breach of the EU law, at the time of the survey, has in fact not transposed them.

[399]E.g. Hotarek (2016, p. 43).

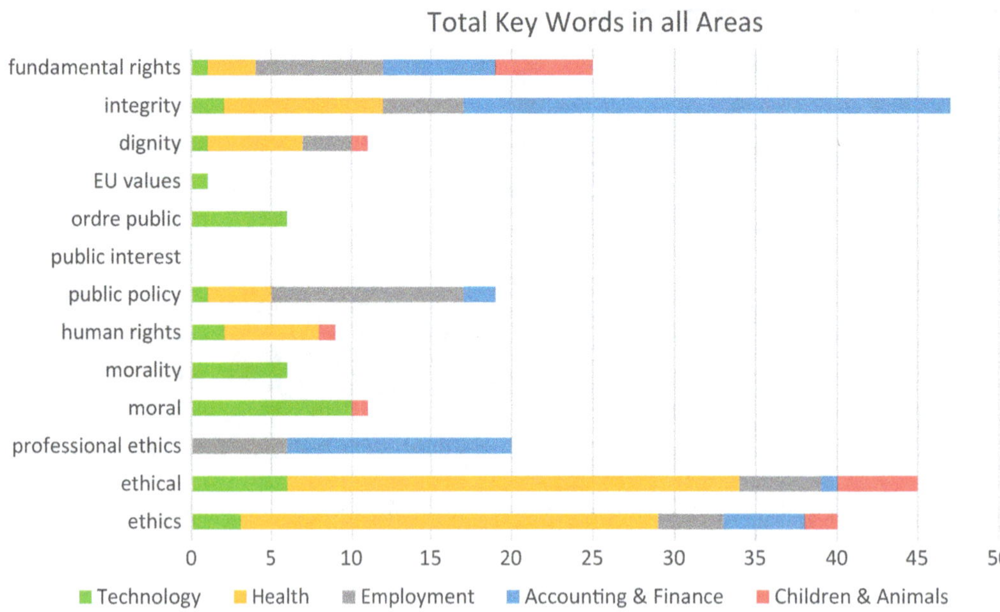

Fig. 3.3 EU 'ethics directives', key terms in different areas (total numbers). *Source* Pacey (2016, A11)

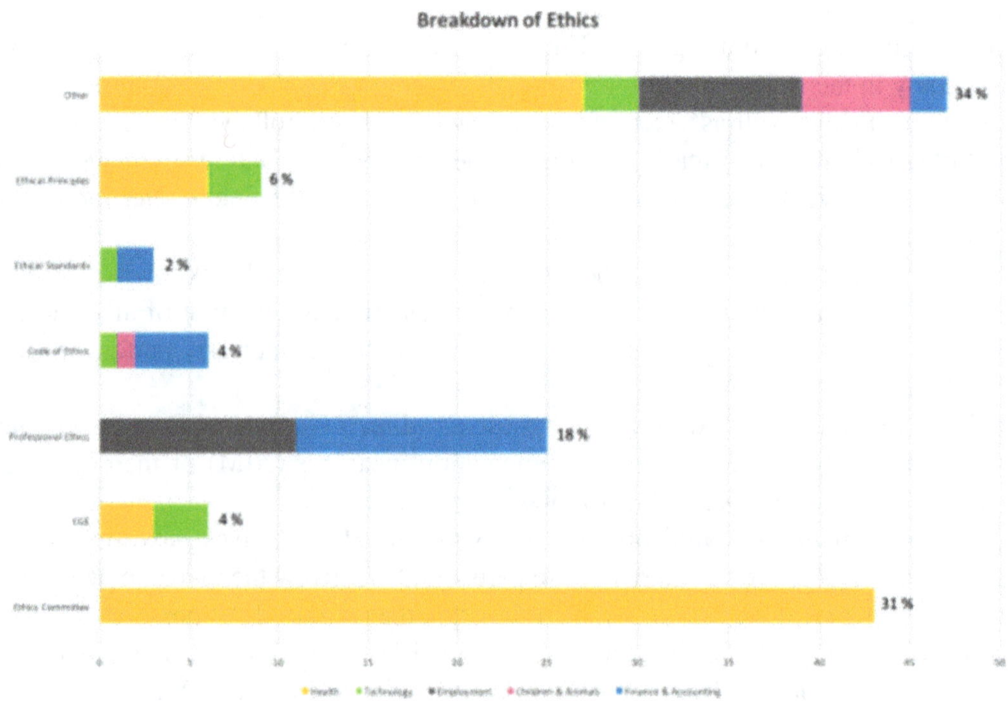

Fig. 3.4 Breakdown of 'ethics' in 'ethics directives' in different areas (percentage). *Source* Sava (2017, 34 and A20)

To make a long story short, there are mainly two reasons why one has to be cautious with over-stressing a quantitative approach.[400] First of all, the degree to which a country (e.g. France) refers to ethics and morality when implementing EU Directives is strongly linked to the pre-existing substantive (e.g. "*les bonnes mœurs françaises*")[401] and procedural (e.g. since 1983: *Comité Consultatif National d'Ethique*, CCNE) approach to ethics and morality in this country. This might also explain the low ratio of NIM referring to keywords (e.g. 15.4%). Second, although a country like Spain has a high number of references to key terms in its NIM, this might be due to the pragmatic 'copy-paste' approach, which, beside the text of the directives, also includes copy-pasting recitals and annexes.[402] Thirdly, a large number of national provisions can implement one single directive, which can distort the validity of quantitative analyses.[403]

Another interesting result could be identified by comparing the results of the different countries. The two waves of this research project revealed, that countries with comparable legal traditions also display similar results. That was true for Austria and Germany,[404] for Ireland and the UK,[405] as well as for the Czech Republic and Slovakia.[406,407] The question of an 'ethicalization' of national law via these EU 'ethics directives' has to be answered in the sense of not playing a major role, as these legal traditions clearly have a higher impact. Again, we can identify an approach, which is not very ambitious, where MS mainly implement these 'ethics elements' of a directive, which are mandatory for them.

In a similar way as for the key terms identified in the directives, also the NIM mainly refer to ethics and especially 'ethics committees', primarily because of Directive clinical trials.[408] This was, for instance, the case in Italy, were 73% of all terms related to ethics, were about 'ethics committees' ('*comitato etico*'),[409] or in France, with the highest number of references to '*comité d'éthique*',[410] and the same for Austria and Germany.[411]

---

[400] A ranking of the amount of NIM in the various MS looks as follows: France: 402; Spain: 125; UK: 104; Austria: 102; Germany: 101; Czech Republic: 73; Slovakia: 61; Ireland: 59; Italy: 36.

[401] Estermann (2016, p. 54).

[402] Varona Martín (2016, 55, 61).

[403] For instance, as in the case of the implementation of Directive patient mobility in Germany; Hotarek (2016, p. 44).

[404] Hotarek (2016, 36, 46, 48).

[405] Pacey (2016, p. 52).

[406] Kubincová (2017, 25, 45).

[407] For instance, it can play a role if MS tend to amend existing laws (e.g. in the case of Austria and Germany; Hotarek (2016, p. 43)), or to create new ones.

[408] Now, Regulation clinical trials; see Sect. 1.2, notes 55 and 56.

[409] Sava (2017, 33 and 43).

[410] Estermann (2016, p. 40).

[411] 220 references to ethics committees (all of them in the field of health), that is to say, by far the highest number, followed by 28 for 'ethical', 27 for 'integrity' and 11 for 'ethics'; and quite the same result for Germany; Hotarek (2016, A15).

Consequently, while some references to ethics, etc. were unavoidable in the sense that it was mandatory for the MS, we cannot observe a uniform 'ethicalization' via EU directives in these nine countries.

References

Arnull, A. (2014). Protocol (30) on the application of the charter of fundamental rights of the European Union to Poland and the United Kingdom. In S. Peers, T. K. Hervey, J. Kenner, & A. Ward (Eds.), *The EU charter of fundamental rights: A commentary* (pp. 1595–1612). Oxford: Hart Publishing.

Bogdandy, A. V., Bogdanowicz, P., Canor, I., Taborowski, M., & Schmidt, M. (2018). Guest Editorial: A potential constitutional moment for the European rule of law: The importance of red lines'. *Common Market Law Review*, *55*, 983–995.

Bogdandy, A. V., & Ioannidis, M. (2014). Systemic deficiency in the rule of law: What it is, what has been done, what can be done. *Common Market Law Review*, *51*, 59–96.

Cohen, I. G. (2012). Circumvention tourism. *Cornell Law Review, 97,* 1309–1398.

Dawson, M., Witte, B. D., & Muir, E. (Eds.). (2013). *Judicial activism at the European Court of Justice*. Cheltenham, Northampton Mass: Edward Elgar Publishing.

de Witte, F. (2013). Sex, drugs & EU law: The recognition of moral and ethical diversity in EU law. *Common Market Law Review, 50,* 1545–1578.

Ehni, H.-J., & Wiesing, U. (2018). Illegitmate authorship and flawed procedures: Fundamental, formal criticisms of the Declaration of Helsinki. *Bioethics.* Advance online publication. https://doi.org/10.1111/bioe.12503.

Estermann, M. (2016). *European law and ethics—implementation of EU directives referring to ethics and/or morality in France*. Master thesis at MCI 'International Business & Law', summer term 2016, Innsbruck.

Ethics Advisory Group. (2018). Towards a digital ethics: Report by the Ethics Advisory Group established by the European Data Protection Supervisor, the EU's independent data protection authority. Retrieved from https://edps.europa.eu/sites/edp/files/publication/18–01-25_eag_report_en.pdf.

European Ombudsman. (2018). *Annual report 2017*. Strasbourg, Brussels: Publications Office of the EU.

Frischhut, M. (2015). "EU": Short for "Ethical" Union?: The role of ethics in European Union Law. *Heidelberg Journal of International Law (HJIL), 75,* 531–577.

Frischhut, M. (2017). Legal and ethical issues of cross-border reproductive care from an EU perspective: Chapter 17. In M. K. Smith & L. Puczkó (Eds.), *The Routledge handbook of health tourism* (pp. 203–218). London, New York: Taylor & Francis.

Grad, J., & Frischhut, M. (2019). Legal and ethical rules in EU decision-making: "Soft law" for targets and actors of lobbying. In D. Dialer & M. Richter (Eds.), *Lobbying in the European Union: Strategies, dynamics and trends* (pp. 305–327). Springer. Retrieved from https://doi.org/10.1007/978-3-319-98800-9_22.

Gruber, N. (2015). *Ethics in the framework of European Union Law with special emphasis on International Agreements*. Master thesis at MCI 'International Business & Law', summer term 2015, Innsbruck.

Hall, C. M. (2013). Medical and health tourism: The development and implications of medical mobility. In C. M. Hall (Ed.), *Medical tourism: The ethics, regulation, and marketing of health mobility* (pp. 3–27). Abingdon, Oxon: Routledge.

Hamm, M. (2018). Transparency in the European crisis: Between ethicization and economicization. In F. Foret & O. Calligaro (Eds.), *European values: Challenges and opportunities for EU Governance* (pp. 119–136). London: Routledge.

Härkönen, E. (2018). Conflict minerals in the corporate supply chain: Is transparency the solution to human rights violations in the tantalum, tin, tungsten and gold supply chains? *European Business Law Review, 29,* 691–727.

Hatzopoulos, V. (2012). *Regulating services in the European Union.* Oxford: Oxford University Press.

Hermerén, G. (2008). European values—and others. Europe's shared values: Towards an ever-closer Union? *European Review, 16,* 373–385. https://doi.org/10.1017/S1062798708000318.

Hermerén, G. (2012). The principle of proportionality revisited: Interpretations and applications. *Medicine, Health Care and Philosophy, 15,* 373–382. https://doi.org/10.1007/s11019-011-9360-x.

Horsley, T. (2013). Reflections on the role of the Court of Justice as the "motor" of European integration: Legal limits to judicial lawmaking. *Common Market Law Review, 50,* 931–964.

Hotarek, T. (2016). *EU law and ethics—implementation of EU directives referring to ethics and/or morality in Austria and Germany.* Master thesis at MCI 'International Business & Law', summer term 2016, Innsbruck.

James, H. S., Jr. (2008). Asymmetric Information. In R. W. Kolb (Ed.), *Encyclopedia of business ethics and society* (pp. 123–125). Los Angeles, London, New Delhi, Singapore: Sage Publications.

Kubincová, M. (2017). *EU law and ethics: Implementation of European Union directives referring to ethics and/or morality in Czechia and Slovakia.* Master thesis at MCI 'Strategic Management & Law', summer term 2017, Innsbruck.

Lienbacher, G. (2013). Die dynamische Rechtsprechung des Gerichtshofes der Europäischen Union und ihre Grenzen: Eine Gedankenskizze. In K. Giese, G. Holzinger, & C. Jabloner (Eds.), *Verwaltung im demokratischen Rechtsstaat: Festschrift für Harald Stolzlechner zum 65. Geburtstag* (pp. 423–450). Wien: Verlag Österreich.

Louden, R. B. (2012). Virtue ethics. In R. F. Chadwick (Ed.), *Encyclopedia of applied ethics* (2nd ed., pp. 503–510). London: Academic Press.

Martinsen, D. S. (2015). *An ever more powerful court?: The political constraints of legal integration in the European Union.* Oxford: Oxford University Press.

Pacey, L. (2016). *EU law and ethics—implementation of EU directives referring to ethics and/or morality in the United Kingdom and Republic of Ireland.* Master thesis at MCI 'International Business & Law', summer term 2016, Innsbruck.

Pechstein, M. (2018). Art. 2 EUV [Werte]. In R. Streinz (Ed.), *EUV/AEUV: Vertrag über die Europäische Union, Vertrag über die Arbeitsweise der Europäischen Union, Charta der Grundrechte der Europäischen Union* (3rd ed.). München: C.H. Beck.

Petrick, J. A. (2008). Integrity. In R. W. Kolb (Ed.), *Encyclopedia of business ethics and society* (pp. 1141-1144). Los Angeles, London, New Delhi, Singapore: Sage Publications.

Pindyck, R. S., & Rubinfeld, D. L. (2018). *Microeconomics* (9th ed.). Harlow, England: Pearson.

Plomer, A. (2018). The duality of human dignity in Europe. In F. Foret & O. Calligaro (Eds.), *European values: Challenges and opportunities for EU governance* (pp. 23–45). London: Routledge.

Prainsack, B., & Buyx, A. (2017). *Solidarity in biomedicine and beyond.* Cambridge, New York: Cambridge University Press.

Rudigier, J. (2015). *Ethics and morality in the European Union—with a special focus on case law of the European Court of Justice.* Master thesis at MCI 'International Business & Law', summer term 2015, Innsbruck.

Sahlin, N.-E. (2018). It's values that matter. In N.-E. Sahlin (Ed.), *Science and proven experience: Johannes* (pp. 77–86). Lund: Media-Tryck.

Sandel, M. J. (2010). *Justice: What's the right thing to do?* New York: Farrar, Straus and Giroux.

Sandel, M. J. (2012). *What money can't buy: The moral limits of markets.* New York: Farrar, Straus and Giroux.

Saurugger, S., & Terpan, F. (2018). The values of the Court of Justice of the European Union. In F. Foret & O. Calligaro (Eds.), *European values: Challenges and opportunities for EU Governance* (pp. 99–115). London: Routledge.

Sava, G. (2017). *EU law and ethics—implementation of EU directives referring to ethics and/or morality in Italy*. Master thesis at MCI 'Strategic Management & Law', summer term 2017, Innsbruck.

Sedmak, C. (Ed.). (2010). *Grundwerte Europas: Band* 1. *Solidarität: Vom Wert der Gemeinschaft*. Darmstadt: WBG Wissen verbindet.

Sedmak, C. (Ed.). (2012). *Grundwerte Europas: Band* 2. *Freiheit: Vom Wert der Autonomie*. Darmstadt: WBG Wissen verbindet.

Sedmak, C. (Ed.). (2013). *Grundwerte Europas: Band* 3. *Gleichheit: Vom Wert der Nichtdiskriminierung*. Darmstadt: WBG Wissen verbindet.

Sedmak, C. (Ed.). (2014). *Grundwerte Europas: Band* 4. *Gerechtigkeit: Vom Wert der Verhältnismässigkeit*. Darmstadt: WBG Wissen verbindet.

Sedmak, C. (Ed.). (2015). *Grundwerte Europas: Band* 5. *Toleranz: Vom Wert der Vielfalt*. Darmstadt: WBG Wissen verbindet.

Sedmak, C. (Ed.). (2016). *Grundwerte Europas: Band* 6. *Frieden: Vom Wert der Koexistenz*. Darmstadt: WBG Wissen verbindet.

Sedmak, C. (Ed.). (2017). *Grundwerte Europas: Band* 7. *Menschenwürde: Vom Selbstwert des Menschen*. Darmstadt: WBG Wissen verbindet.

Tansey, R. (2014). The EU's revolving door problem: How big business gains privileged access. In D. Dialer & M. Richter (Eds.), *Lobbying in der Europäischen Union: Zwischen Professionalisierung und Regulierung* (pp. 257–268). Wiesbaden: Springer.

Van Hoof, W., & Pennings, G. (2012). Extraterritorial laws for cross-border reproductive care: The issue of legal diversity. *European Journal of Health Law, 19,* 187–200. https://doi.org/10.1163/157180912X628226.

Varona Martín, A. (2016). *European law and ethics: Implementation of European Union directives referring to ethics and/or morality in Spain*. Master thesis at MCI 'International Business & Law', summer term 2016, Innsbruck.

Chapter 4
Philosophical Lens (The Normative Theories, etc. Continued)

Ethical conduct must be based on spiritual values that are core to all religions and that are also part of a secular approach to values.

René Smits, The Invisible Core of Values in the European Integration Project (Smits 2018, 224).

4.1 Ethical Approach Identified in EU Legal Documents

While objectives 1–3 have been dealt with in the chapters so far, this chapter is dedicated to objective 4. That is to say, whether we can identify a certain common horizontal (or rather a specific) pattern in referring to these terms of ethics and morality, and whether we can thus identify an ethical spirit based on an analysis of these legal texts; or whether we have to ascertain a gap, which has to be filled by other means?

First, we have to shed some light on the notion of 'spirit', a term that can have manifold meanings. According to the Collins Birmingham dictionary, the spirit of a legal provision "is the way that it was intended to be interpreted or applied",[1] and according to the Oxford dictionary "the real meaning as opposed to lip service or verbal expression (*the spirit of law*)".[2] Often this intention of the authors of a legal provision can be contrasted to the literal meaning, the mere wording. A famous example for this opposition of "wording vs. spirit" can be found in William Shakespeare's "*The Merchant of Venice*",[3] where the promise to give a "pound of flesh" in case a loan cannot be repaid, in the end is solved as follows. As the agreement did not mention blood, hence, there would only be a right to have this "pound of flesh", if no blood would be shed.[4]

[1] Krishnamurthy (1993, p. 948).

[2] Allen et al. (1990, pp. 1173–1174); no emphasis added.

[3] The Hamlyn Publishing Group (1970, pp. 184–208).

[4] Act IV, Scene I. Venice. A Court of Justice; The Hamlyn Publishing Group (1970, p. 204).

M. Frischhut, *The Ethical Spirit of EU Law*,
https://doi.org/10.1007/978-3-030-10582-2_4

However, this book is based on an understanding, where the notion of 'spirit' surpasses the mere 'intention' of a legal provision in various ways. First, this book refers to "the ethical spirit of EU law", hence, a legal system and not only a single legal provision. Second, for the author, 'spirit' is more than just the intention. It is the holistic coming together of different elements, or as Montesquieu called it, the "relations [which] together constitute what I call the Spirit of Laws".[5] When analysing "[h]ow values come to matter at the European Commission", Jim Dratwa has referred to a 'lattice', a "set of bodies and texts, of products and processes".[6] While the author of this book fully acknowledges the difficulty in defining the notion of 'spirit', this book is based on the following understanding:

> the *intention* of the *authors* of a *legal system*, which is reflected in a *lattice* of various different provisions.

In a metaphorical sense, this 'spirit'[7] can be described as a ghost that maybe cannot be seen, but which is nevertheless present in terms of this lattice; or, as mentioned above, the discovery of a common approach which can serve as a basis of understanding of the underlying philosophy of EU law.[8] The reason, why this definition includes "the authors of a legal system" (plural) and not "the legislator" is simply because we have seen several authors in Sects. 3.1–3.3.4. From the MS as "Masters of the Treaties", the EP and the Council (i.e. the ordinary legislative procedure), the CJEU (case-law), and finally to the MS in implementing directives, to name but the most important ones. The spirit of a legal system obviously can change over time. The spirit of EU law in its infancy was different at the beginning (starting with coal and steel, spilling over to the general economic field), compared to what it is today (also comprising the political field and entailing human rights and values). It is also relative to those different provisions and processes. This relativity is reminiscent of the 'relation' aspect, which has also been stressed by Montesquieu. In his famous book, the 'spirit of laws' ('*De L'esprit des Loix*'[9]), he wrote that the spirit of laws "consists in the various *relations* which the laws may have to different objects".[10] In that regard he mentioned the "nature and principle of each government", "the climate of each country", the "relation to the degree of liberty which the constitution will bear, to the religion of the inhabitants, to their inclinations, riches, numbers,

---

[5]This quotation has been retrieved from "The Complete Works of M. de Montesquieu (London: T. Evans, 1777), 4 vols. Vol. 1. 27.8.2018", http://oll.libertyfund.org/titles/837#Montesquieu_0171-01_115; book I, 'chapter III, of positive laws'.

[6]Dratwa (2014, 113 et passim).

[7]See also Brännmark (2017, p. 176), who points out that "a reasonable foundational story does at the same time add something more to a framework than just a philosophical basis; it also adds a spirit in which the rules or principles of the framework can be interpreted and implemented".

[8]*Supra* Sect. 1.4.

[9]Montesquieu, Charles de Secondat, Baron de (1927).

[10]This quotation has been retrieved from "The Complete Works of M. de Montesquieu (London: T. Evans, 1777), 4 vols. Vol. 1. 27.8.2018", http://oll.libertyfund.org/titles/837#Montesquieu_0171-01_115; book I, 'chapter III, of positive laws'; emphasis added.

Table 4.1 Contribution of 'categories of determination' to identification of 'ethical spirit'

Useful	Less useful	Not possible, because determination of content takes place elsewhere
[2.] References only as a supportive argument for a certain legal solution	[1.] References only as an argument against interference from the EU	[4.] Determination via ethics committees, at EU or at national level; exception EGE
[5.] Determination via codes of conduct, at EU or at national level (*in case some principles are mentioned*)	[3.] References in order to create a parallel ethical assessment (beside the legal one)	[5.] Determination via codes of conduct, at EU or at national level (*in case NO principles are mentioned*)
[7.] Determination in document itself (some hints with regard to the content or understanding of ethics)	[8.] No determination at all	[6.] Determination via references to other (international) documents

commerce, manners, and customs".[11] In addition, he continues: "These relations I shall examine, since all these together constitute what I call the Spirit of Laws".[12] These relations[13] add up to this lattice that reflects this spirit, in our case, 'the ethical spirit of EU law'.

To begin with, some introductory remarks. In the context of the above-mentioned determination of the substance of ethics, some categories are more useful to extract this ethical spirit, others less so. The most fruitful categories were those where ethics was used as a supportive argument [2.], or where the determination took place via codes of conduct [5.], especially if these codes of conduct entailed certain principles, as well as if the content of ethics was determined in the relevant legal document itself [7.]. If ethics was only used as an argument against interference from the EU [1.], if 'only' a parallel ethical assessment (besides the legal one) was opened [3.], or if substance wise ethics has not been determined at all [8.], then these categories obviously are less rewarding. Obviously, we cannot harvest any useful 'ethics fruits', if the determination takes place elsewhere, i.e. in case of ethics committees [4.] and in reference to other documents [6.]. The same holds true if in case of codes of conduct [5.], these documents, in the future, will be drafted at a different level (e.g. by MS or companies). The respective contribution of these categories to our quest for the ethical spirit of EU law can be displayed as follows (see Table 4.1).

Hence, in the following, the findings of Chap. 3 will be contrasted with the practical philosophical basics, as covered in Chap. 2. The questions to be answered are the following:

---

[11] Ibid.

[12] Ibid.

[13] In CJEU *Achmea*, C-284/16, paras 33–34, in the context of the autonomy of EU law and the EU's common values, the Court referred to "a structured network of principles, rules and mutually interdependent legal relations".

- Question No 1: In EU law's references to ethics, can we identify any philosophical theory at all?
- Question No 2: If yes, would this comprise one or more philosophical theories?
- Question No 3: If yes, should this be understood as an unconditional reference to one or more philosophical theories, or only as pointing towards a certain idea?

Without wishing to broach fundamental philosophical issues, it should be emphasised that these three normative theories presented in Chapt. 2 can also overlap. As mentioned earlier, deontology rather focuses on an act, consequentialism on its consequences, and the virtue ethics puts an emphasis on the agent itself.[14] Hence, the peculiarity of these three theories is the way in which "good behaviour" is argued. Of course, these three theories arguing in a different way, in the end can come to the same solution. For example, it can be considered good to help children, e.g. to cross a dangerous street. This can be considered intrinsically good (deontology), one can also argue this as in line with consequentialism (the outcome that a child that has not been endangered in this situation), but one can also see it as a positive trait to help children, whereby this inner attitude also manifests itself in the outside (virtue ethics). While a division into these three normative ethical theories is prevailing in literature, one can question if this sharp distinction is the best approach possible. However, as it is not the objective of this book, this question can be left aside.[15]

When now, hereinafter, certain examples will be assigned to the three normative theories, the following has to be emphasized: As far as this can be judged on the basis of the research conducted, the various 'authors' of the EU's legal system have never explicitly referred to one of these normative theories. Hence, question No 1 (identification of any philosophical theory) can only be answered with regard to implicit references. Therefore, the following 'disclaimer' has to be stressed. The following examples can be interpreted as pointing into a certain direction, but it is not the case that sometimes other interpretations would not be possible.

As mentioned above, according to deontology actions are intrinsically right or wrong, irrespective of their consequences.

- In the field of patentability of biotechnological inventions, we seem to have such a deontological approach, when it is stated that "there is a consensus within the [EU] that interventions in the human germ line and the cloning of human beings offends against *ordre public* and morality".[16] This consensus seems to refer to what is intrinsically wrong. As it is against morality, (a) processes for cloning human beings, (b) processes for modifying the germ line genetic identity of human beings, as well as (c) uses of human embryos for industrial or commercial purposes, "shall be considered unpatentable".[17] Especially this stance against commodification of human beings *in statu nascendi* can also be seen as a deontological approach, reminiscent of the concept of human dignity. This is in line with the EP statement

[14]Cf. Louden (2012, p. 504).

[15]On this question, see Parfit (2011).

[16]Directive Biotech, recital 40; no emphasis added.

[17]Directive Biotech, Art 6(2)(a)–(c); (d) refers to animals.

we have seen on surrogacy. According to this statement, surrogacy "undermines the human dignity of the woman since her body and its reproductive functions are used as a commodity".[18]

- A similar deontological and anti-commodification approach can also be found with regard to animals, when the killing of seals "for commercial reasons" is seen as intrinsically wrong due to "public moral concerns", whereas this is not the case for seal hunts traditionally conducted by Inuit and other indigenous communities.[19] Hence, to some extent also a consequentialist approach.
- Another noteworthy example concerns supply chain due diligence obligations and the import of tin, tantalum and tungsten, their ores, and gold, which shall not be imported from conflict-affected or high-risk areas, in particular in the African Great Lakes Region, as this would contravene "ethical mining".[20]
- However, the most important example in this regard is the one that "[a]nimals have an *intrinsic* value which must be respected".[21] This deontological attitude corresponds with what we have seen in the context of animal transports[22] and animal experiments, i.e. the statement that "man has a *moral obligation* to respect all animals and to have due consideration for their capacity for suffering and memory".[23] In addition, we have seen similar approaches with regard to animals in the context of mass slaughtering.[24]
- In addition, the statement on an ethical accountability of researchers "towards society as a whole"[25] can be interpreted as a deontological approach.
- From the CJEU's case-law we have seen so far, we can add the cases on human dignity, where the Court in *Omega* (Oct. 2004) accepted the German notion of human dignity, which has a clear deontological bedrock.[26] In a similar way as Germany has brought forward this national constitutional concept of human dignity, in *Brüstle* (Oct. 2011) the Court had to deal with human dignity as it was mentioned in the 1998 'Directive Biotech'. The Court's approach of opting for a wide interpretation of the notion of 'human embryo' based on human dignity also points into this deontological direction. The entry into force of the Lisbon Treaty (Dec. 2009), enshrining the EU's common values clearly strengthens this approach.

---

[18]EP report human rights, para 115.

[19]Regulation seal products, recitals 1 and 2.

[20]Regulation supply chain, recital 23.

[21]Directive animals, recital 12; emphasis added.

[22]Convention animal transport, recital 2; "every person has a moral obligation to respect all animals and to have due consideration for their capacity for suffering".

[23]Convention animal experiments, recital 2; emphasis added.

[24]*Supra* Sect. 3.3.3.3.

[25]EC Charter researchers, Annex, Section 1.

[26]BVerfG *Shooting down terror plane*, 1 BvR 357/05.

All these examples point towards a deontological understanding and are, as we have seen, closely related to human dignity, or the intrinsic dignity of animals.[27]

As mentioned above, according to consequentialism actions are morally right or wrong depending on the quality of the consequences of action.

- The request "to ensure the ethics of transplantation by adopting measures to eliminate 'transplant tourism'"[28] could be interpreted as a consequentialist approach, as the ethical quality of the action of the addressed states is based on the outcome of their action, i.e. the elimination of transplant tourism.
- In addition, the Korea agreement defines 'ethical business practices' (i.e. the title of this provision) with regard to the pharma industry by its outcome, according to which the contracting parties "shall adopt or maintain appropriate measures to prohibit improper inducements by manufacturers and suppliers of pharmaceutical products or medical devices to health care professionals or institutions".[29]
- The outcome is also the basis for the following example, here to reduce ethical concerns. Moreover, it is an example of the consideration of animal welfare with a consequentialist approach. The outcome in the field of novel food is, where possible, the avoidance of the duplication of animal testing, as "[p]ursuing this goal could reduce possible animal welfare and ethical concerns with regard to novel food applications".[30]

While these examples display a consequentialist approach in order to determine moral correctness and falseness of action, we also have consequentialist examples elsewhere in EU law.

- The effectiveness of EU law, often even in other language versions referred to as "*effet utile*", has become of paramount importance in the case-law of the CJEU. In essence, it states that the provisions of EU law must be interpreted and applied in such a way that they fulfil their practical purpose and have practical effect. On this basis, the requirement of the practical effectiveness of EU law serves the CJEU as an explanatory element with regard to practically all institutes of EU law and in this respect runs like a red thread through the case-law of the Court.[31] In this case-law, the key interpretative approach of the Court is the *outcome*, the assertion of EU law. Although, this '*effet utile*' approach finds its limitations, as there has to be an "appropriate balance between Member State autonomy and the '*effet utile*' of EU law".[32] When analysing the explicitly mentioned "*effet utile*", Advocate General (AG) Kokott referred to "the *spirit* and *purpose* of" the relevant provisions of

[27]For various ethical approaches concerning animals, see the various contributions in Beauchamp and Frey (2014).

[28]Resolution tourism, pt. 33.

[29]Agreement Korea, Annex 2-D, Art 4(1).

[30]Regulation novel foods, recital 32.

[31]See, also for further examples, Ranacher and Frischhut (2009, pp. 68–70).

[32]AG Sharpston opinion of 30 September 2010, *Ruiz Zambrano*, C-34/09, EU:C:2010:560, para 148.

EU law.[33] As mentioned above, this '*effet utile*' case-law is not directly related to ethics and morality. As we have seen above,[34] the Court tackles 'sensitive issues of ethical nature' with a purely legal methodology, which, nevertheless, still renders a decision on this ethical topic. Hence, the '*effet utile*' case-law can also be of indirect relevance for our topic.

- Apart from this supreme 'tool of interpretation', another (non-ethical/moral) consequentialist approach of EU law can be found in case of impact assessments. Impact assessments have already been mentioned as one example indicated in literature in the context of consequentialism.[35] According to Birnbacher, they are not required to assess the outcome of any possible action, but are limited to decisions with far-reaching consequences, as in case of national or supranational legislators.[36] In EU law, impact assessment is one of the "tools for better law-making", in order to "reach well-informed decisions", respecting, amongst others, fundamental rights and "based on accurate, objective and complete information".[37] In essence, an impact shall "cover the existence, scale and *consequences* of a problem".[38] Such an impact assessment can also be required in the context of the precautionary principle, for instance when approving active substances resulting in losses of honeybee colonies.[39]

All these examples point towards a consequentialist approach, both relating to ethics and morality, but also elsewhere in EU law (*effet utile*, impact assessments).

Virtue ethics, sometimes understood rather as a supplement than a basis of normative ethics,[40] puts an emphasis not on the intrinsic quality of the action or its consequences, but on the agent itself. 'Virtues' are character traits, which must also be reflected in corresponding behaviour.[41] As mentioned above, sometimes virtue ethics cannot avoid establishing principles for its part (e.g. the virtue of justice may require principles of justice).[42] 'Integrity' has been described as "an important personal characteristic in ethical systems based on virtue and moral character".[43]

- In the Georgia agreement, we have seen one example for the close link of ethics (precisely, the 'Blueprint on Customs ethics') and "the highest standards of integrity".[44]

---

[33] AG Kokott opinion of 17 July 2014, *UK versus Council*, C-81/13, EU:C:2014:2114, paras 114–117; emphases added.

[34] Section 3.3.1.1.

[35] Section 2.2.

[36] Birnbacher (2013, pp. 194–195).

[37] IIA Better Law-Making, pt. 12–18 (12).

[38] Ibid., emphasis added.

[39] GC judgment of 17 May 2018, *BASF Agro*, T-584/13, EU:T:2018:279, paras 170–171 (because of the principle of proportionality).

[40] Birnbacher (2013, p. 305).

[41] Birnbacher (2013, p. 295).

[42] Birnbacher (2013, p. 304).

[43] Forrest (2002, p. 441).

[44] See at note 52.

- The most important examples referring to integrity can be found in the field of lobbying.[45] Integrity was mentioned for several 'targets' of lobbying, such as the EP, the EC,[46] EU staff, and even for the CJEU, as well as for experts ("ensure the highest level of integrity of experts").[47] However, it has not been addressed for the 'actors' of lobbying.[48]
- Other terms we have seen in the context of lobbying, have been as follows: accountability, dignity, diligence, discretion, disinterest, honesty, impartiality, independence, loyalty, objectivity, openness, responsibility, and transparency. Some of these terms rather fall in the category of legal principles (accountability, diligence, impartiality, independence, objectivity, responsibility, transparency), while (human) dignity is a value[49] and discretion, disinterest, openness, honesty, integrity and loyalty could also qualify as virtues.[50]
- Furthermore, Horizon 2020 addresses "research integrity",[51] as well as Directive statutory audits, which requires statutory auditors to adhere to "the highest ethical standards".[52]
- In the context of the EU 'ethics directives', 'integrity', besides ethics, was the most important key term, mainly occurring in the field of 'accounting & finance', followed by the 'health' field.[53]
- As already mentioned earlier, the three notions of 'values', 'principles' and 'virtues' "can and do overlap".[54] While Art 2 TEU explicitly addresses values, the second sentence of this provision refers to "a society [in the MS,] in which pluralism, non-discrimination, tolerance, justice, solidarity and equality between women and men prevail". For instance, tolerance and solidarity could also be virtues, where justice is even a cardinal virtue.[55]

All these examples can be seen to point towards virtue ethics, if they are also reflected in the corresponding behaviour. Consequently, we have seen examples pointing into the direction of all three normative theories, which answer the above-mentioned three questions. However, as this book follows an inductive approach, likewise, in the following, examples referring to minimal ethics, principlism and communitarianism will be addressed.

Minimal ethics only defines moral norms for a core, while this claim does not exist for the periphery.

---

[45] *Supra* Sect. 3.3.2.

[46] Art 245(2) TFEU.

[47] See Sect. 3.3.2.2 at note 203.

[48] The code of conduct (Sect. 3.3.2.2 note 205) does not mention 'integrity'.

[49] Art 2, 1st sentence TEU.

[50] Keeping in mind the 'moral excellence of behaviour and character', etc., mentioned *supra* in Sect. 2.3.

[51] See Chap. 3 at note 326.

[52] See at note 339.

[53] See Chap. 3 at note 339.

[54] Williams (2010, p. 257).

[55] See at note 105.

- The most prominent example, in this regard, is the field of patentability of biotechnological inventions, a much-contested issue, which we have already seen at various times throughout this book. This has been solved in the following way: Art 6 of this directive defines a core in para 2, where MS and the EP where able to reach a compromise; in the words of AG Cruz Villalón: "a minimum, Union-wide consensus for all Member States".[56] This compromise defined at EU level comprises cloning of humans, modification of the germ line genetic identity of humans, uses of human embryos for commercial purposes, as well as modification of the genetic identity of animals. Obviously, there was no consensus concerning other equally sensitive issues, hence, para 1 of this provision delegates the question of answering the unpatentability to the national level, where the commercial exploitation of inventions has to be assessed against the notions of "*ordre public* or morality". This approach of a minimal ethics at EU level for a core, capable of consensus, and a possible divergent national approach at the periphery, could serve as a role model for other fields.
- This minimum consensus of this 1998 directive has been adopted, in identical terms, in the 2014 agreement with Ukraine.[57] A similar approach is adopted in Horizon 2020, where, under the heading of 'ethical principles', research fields reminiscent of, however not identical to, Art 6(2) Directive Biotech shall not be financed.[58]
- A minimum approach, however of a different kind, can be seen in a resolution, which states that in case sanctions cannot "bring about a change of regime in a particular country, or at least a major change in the policy of that country's government, their imposition may also serve *simply* as an expression of moral condemnation".[59] This is not a true minimum approach which achieves consensus in a core and leaves open questions at the periphery, rather the primary objective (i.e. change of regime) has failed, that is why only moral condemnation remains.

All these examples display a 'minimal ethics' approach. Such an approach might be suitable for areas, where a consensus amongst MS (and the EP) can only be achieved in a (united) core, while the periphery is left to potentially diverse solutions in the MS.

Principlism determines ethics in a substantive way (cf. in the field of medical ethics, Beauchamp and Childress), where ethics is defined based on a certain number of moral principles (e.g. autonomy, beneficence, nonmaleficence, and justice). As mentioned earlier,[60] we can distinguish a legal and a philosophical understanding of 'principles'.

- Against the background of the heated debates on investment protection, Art 8.30 CETA (entitled 'ethics') covers the following principles for the members of the

[56] AG Cruz Villalón opinion of 17 July 2014, *ISC*, C-364/13, EU:C:2014:2104, para 42.

[57] Agreement Ukraine, Art 221(5).

[58] Regulation establishing Horizon 2020, Art 19(3).

[59] Resolution embargoes, pt. 2; emphasis added.

[60] See Chap. 1 at note 92.

multilateral investment tribunal. The independence of its members, as well as the avoidance of both a direct or indirect conflict of interest.[61] The 'Joint Interpretative Instrument' stresses "*independence* and *impartiality*, the *absence of conflict of interest, bias* or *appearance of* bias".[62]

- Likewise, the Korea agreement also refers to the following principles in order to achieve "ethical practices by manufacturers and suppliers of pharmaceutical products and medical devices and by health care providers on a global basis": openness, transparency, accountability and non-discrimination in health care decision-making.[63]
- These principles overlap with those which have been qualified as legal principles above in the context of lobbying: accountability, diligence, impartiality, independence, objectivity, responsibility, transparency. Again, the question of distinguishing virtues from legal as well as philosophical principles remains a challenge.
- One of the most comprehensive examples can be found in the field of nanosciences. The annex of this code of conduct, which is "based on a set of general principles", mentions the following ones.[64] *Meaning* (which comprises comprehensibility for the public, respect for fundamental rights, as well as acting in the interest of the well-being of individuals and society); *sustainability* (referring to the United Nation's Millennium Development Goals, as well as avoidance of harm or creation of "biological, physical or moral threat to people, animals, plants or the environment, at present or in the future"); *precaution* (basically referring to the EU's precautionary principle[65]); *inclusiveness* (principles of openness to all stakeholders, transparency, access to information, as well as stakeholder participation in decision-making); *excellence* (also comprising "integrity of research"); *innovation*; as well as *accountability* (with regard to "social, environmental and human health impacts [...] on present and future generations"). These "general principles" address both the legal as well as the ethical sphere, without providing a clear distinction.
- As we have already seen elsewhere, in the field of biotechnology, reference is made to the national level of MS within the context of "ethical principles",[66] while in the same directive we find an undetermined reference to "basic ethical principles"[67] for the question when the EGE can be consulted.

All these examples can be attributed to principlism. From a theoretical perspective, one could criticize the fact that it is left open whether these principles are purely legal ones, purely philosophical ones, or a combination of both. Yet, from a pragmatic

---

[61] It is worth mentioning that apart from these substantive principles in para 1; paras 2–4 provide procedural safeguards in this respect.

[62] OJ 2017 L11/3 (4); emphases added. See also the Statement by the Commission and the Council on investment protection and the Investment Court System ('ICS'), on p. 20.

[63] Agreement Korea, Annex 2-D, Art 1(e).

[64] EC recommendation nanosciences, Annex, pt. 3.

[65] Recently: GC *BASF Agro*, T-584/13; for further details, see Frischhut and Greer (2017, 331–333).

[66] Directive Biotech, recital 39: "ethical or moral principles recognised in a Member State".

[67] Directive Biotech, recital 44.

perspective, this approach has to be welcomed, as the content of ethics is more clearly determined.

In summary, it can be said that in EU law's references to ethics, we can identify normative theories (question No 1), although only implicit and no explicit ones, covering all three proponents (question No 2). All the examples we have seen cannot be understood as unconditional references, but only as pointing towards these normative theories (question No 3). Can we identify a certain common horizontal (or rather a specific) pattern in referring to these terms of ethics and morality? We have seen different approaches referring to the normative theories of deontology (putting an emphasis on human dignity), consequentialism (with examples in the field of ethics and morality, but also elsewhere in EU law, such as *effet utile* and impact assessments), and virtue ethics (especially, but not only in lobbying), as well as minimal ethics (Directive Biotech, etc.), and principlism (lobbying and nanosciences). There is clearly no horizontal, but a specific approach in addressing different needs in different fields, from independence of members of investment tribunals to research integrity in nanosciences. Hence, we can address both an ethical spirit in the sense of the intention of the various authors of EU law, which is reflected in a lattice of various different provisions, as well as a gap that still needs to be filled. So far, the examples covered those authors authorized to issue binding and non-binding legal provisions, not specifically tasked to deal with ethics. Accordingly, we will now turn to an entity that, while 'only' having an advisory function, is specifically tasked to deal with ethics.

4.2 EGE Opinions

The practical impact of EGE opinions can, amongst others,[68] be seen from the EU's research funding programme Horizon 2020, where the relevant regulation states that "[t]he opinions of the [EGE] should be taken into account".[69,70] In the field of patentability of biotechnological inventions, the already widely covered directive states that the EGE "evaluates all [sic!] ethical aspects of biotechnology".[71] This directive dates from 1998, hence, the year after the EGE's establishment.

---

[68]In addition, several other regulations and directives, as well as courts, e.g. the CJEU and the European Court of Human Rights (ECtHR), as well as AG at the CJEU have referred to EGE opinions; for further details, see Pirs (2017, p. 32). This chapter has been drafted at the same time as the following paper; hence, certain parts can overlap: Pirs and Frischhut (2019, forthcoming).

[69]Regulation establishing Horizon 2020, recital 29.

[70]Similar in Regulation Horizon 2020 Euratom, recital 18.

[71]Recital 44 and Art 7.

4.2.1 EGE History, Institutional Structure and Opinions

Due to rapid scientific developments in biotechnology and genetic engineering in the late 1980s and early 1990s, there was need for an institutionalized framework facilitating debate and addressing public concern as to ethical implications.[72] Hence, in April 1991 the EC stated that there is a need for a "consultative structure on ethics and biotechnology".[73] The Group of Advisers on the Ethical Implications of Biotechnology (GAEIB) was created on 20 November 1991. After the first mandate of two years, the EC addressed the necessity "to clarify further value laden issues in relation to some applications of biotechnology", hence to "reinforce the role of the [GAEIB]".[74] After the mandate had expired on 31 July 1997[75] and the legislative process leading to 'Directive Biotech' was in full swing,[76] the EC on 16 December 1997 decided to replace the GAEIB by the EGE, "extending the Group's mandate to cover all areas of the application of science and technology".[77,78] The EGE was then established in December 1997.[79] As of 2000,[80] the EGE was part of the 'Bureau of European Policy Advisers (BEPA), a Directorate General (DG) of the EC, reporting directly to the EC president.[81] Nowadays, the EGE is docked with DG Research and innovation.[82] While it clearly makes sense to link the EGE to the field of research and innovation, it could also be seen as a downgrading of the EGE, as there is no

---

[72]Plomer (2008, p. 840).

[73]EC 'Promouvoir les conditions de la compétitivité des activités industrielles basées sur la biotechnologie dans la Communauté', SEC(91) 629 final 19.4.1991, p. 18: "*Il est souhaitable que la Communauté dispose d'une structure consultative sur l'éthique et la biotechnologie capable de traiter les questions d'éthique qui se posent dans le cadre des activités communautaires. Cette structure devrait permettre l'ouverture d'un dialogue où seraient débattus ouvertement les problèmes éthiques dont les Etats membres ou d'autres parties intéressées jugeraient la solution nécessaire. Elle permettrait également à des experts délégués par les groupes concernés de contribuer à l'orientation du processus législatif. La Commission estime que cette démarche serait un pas positif en vue d'une meilleure acceptation de la biotechnologie et de la réalisation du marché unique pour les produits Issus de cette technologie.*".

[74]European Commission (1993, p. 103).

[75]EP resolution of 13 June 1997 on the mandate of the Group of Advisers on the Ethical Implications of Biotechnology to the EC (B4-0484/97), OJ 1997 C 200/258 [EP resolution GAEIB], recital A.

[76]On 29 August 1997, the EC had adopted an amended proposal: COM(97)446 final 29.08.1997.

[77]EC decision (EU) 2016/835 of 25 May 2016 on the renewal of the mandate of the European Group on Ethics in Science and New Technologies, OJ 2016 L 140/21 [EGE mandate V 2016], recital 3. This current mandate started on 28.5.2016 and lasts until 27.5.2019.

[78]It seems that the EGE follows a broad understanding of technology.

[79]EC *communication de M. le PRESIDENT, en accord avec M. BANGEMANN, M. FLYNN, Mme CRESSON, Mme BJERREGAARD, M. MONTI, M. FISCHLER et Mme BONINO: Création d'un groupe Européen d'éthique des sciences et des nouvelles technologies*, SEC(97)2404 final 12.12.1997 [EGE mandate I 1997].

[80]That is to say, as of the second mandate (see Table 4.2), Mohr et al. (2012, p. 107).

[81]Plomer (2008, p. 841).

[82]The EGE's website can be accessed via http://ec.europa.eu/research/ege/index.cfm.

direct and regular access to the EC president (Juncker).[83] For an overview of the EGE's development, see Table 4.2.

Moreover due to the increasing role of 'good governance',[84] the already mentioned horizontal rules on the creation and operation of EC expert groups also apply to the EGE; as already mentioned, these rules strive for a balanced composition of expert groups and also comprise rules on conflict of interest, in order to "ensure the highest level of integrity of experts".[85] Likewise, as for all expert groups giving advice to the EC, the core principles of 'quality, openness, and effectiveness' apply to the EGE.[86]

Under the current mandate, the EGE is tasked "to advise the Commission on ethical questions relating to sciences and new technologies and the wider societal implications of advances in these fields".[87] The members are appointed by the EC president, based on a proposal from the Commissioner for research, etc.[88] The EGE, which "shall be independent, pluralist and multidisciplinary", is composed of 15 members serving in personal capacity, and demonstrating "a high level of expertise and pluralism"; furthermore, the mandate strives to establish a geographical balance, as well as a balanced representation of relevant know-how and areas of interest".[89] In its 1997 resolution concerning the GAEIB, the EP had criticized that so far, "too much attention has been paid to the interests of research and not enough to the possible effects on society".[90] Today, besides a balance of qualities, gender and geographical distribution, the current mandate requires "independent advice of the highest quality", "combining wisdom and foresight", as well as "internationally recognised experts, with a track record of excellence and experience at the European

---

[83]Compared to former president Barroso, president Juncker also took a different approach in another field, by "scrapping" the role of the Chief Scientific Adviser (CSA); see Panichi (2015). Nowadays, see the EC's Scientific Advice Mechanism (SAM), also comprising the Group of Chief Scientific Advisors; EC decision on the setting up of the High Level Group of Scientific Advisors, C(2015) 6946 final 16.10.2015, as amended by Decision amending Decision C(2015)6946 on the setting up of the High Level Group of Scientific Advisers, C(2018) 1919 final 5.4.2018.

[84]EC 'European governance—A white paper', COM(2001) 428 final, OJ 2001 C 287/1; addressing principles of openness, participation, accountability, effectiveness, and coherence.

[85]EC decision experts, recital 3, Art 2(4), Art 11.

[86]EC communication on the collection and use of expertise by the Commission: principles and guidelines—"Improving the knowledge base for better policies", COM(2002) 713 final 11.12.2002, p. 1.

[87]EGE mandate V 2016, Art 2.

[88]EGE mandate V 2016, Art 4(3). Since 'EGE mandate III 2005' (see Table 4.2), the EC president has officially appointed the members. However, since the creation of the EGE in 1997, "the President of the Commission has been authorised by the Commission to appoint the EGE members", hence 'EGE mandate III 2005' "has therefore [only] formalised this situation". Source: response of former EC president Barroso on a parliamentary request ('Criteria and methods for the selection of the members of the [EGE]', P6_RE(2006)0430, answer from 17.3.2006); see also EGE mandate I 1997, p. 4. Besides this, the selection process shall be overseen by a new 'Identification Committee'; EGE mandate V 2016, Art 4(3) and (4).

[89]EGE mandate V 2016, Art 4(1), (2) and (4).

[90]EP resolution GAEIB, pt. 3.

Table 4.2 Overview EGE

Term		Time frame	Established by	Number of members ǀ term of years	Opinions (total number)	Chairperson; additional information
GAEIB		1991–1997	EC	6 pers.; 9 pers. as of 1994; ǀ 2 years	1–10 (10)	Marcelino Oreja; followed by Noëlle Lenoir
EGE	1st mandate	1998–2000	(SEC(97) 2404[a]	12 pers. ǀ 3 years	11–15 (5)	Noëlle Lenoir
	2nd mandate	2000–2005	(C(2001) 691[b]	12 pers. ǀ 4 years	16–20 (5)	Göran Hermerén ('president') ǀ New: part of BEPA
	3rd mandate	2005–2010	EC Decision 2005/383/EC[c]	15 pers. ǀ 4 years	21–25 (5)	Göran Hermerén ǀ New: appointed by EC president
	4th mandate	2010–2015	EC Decision 2010/1/EU[d]	15 pers. ǀ 5 years	26–29 (4)	Julian Kinderlerer
	5th mandate	2016–2019	EC Decision (EU) 2016/835[e]	15 pers. ǀ 2.5 years	30 (1)[f]	Christiane Woopen ǀ New: proposal from Commissioner for research, etc., 'Identification Committee'; part of DG Research and Innovation

[a]EGE mandate I 1997

[b]EC *note pour les membres de la Commission 'Groupe européen d'éthique des sciences et des nouvelles technologies (GEE)—modification du mandat'*, C(2001) 691 final 26.3.2001 [EGE mandate II 2001]

[c]EC decision 2005/383/EC of 11 May 2005 on the renewal of the mandate of the European Group on Ethics in Science and New Technologies, OJ 2005 L 127/17 [EGE mandate III 2005]; EC decision 2009/757/EC of 14 October 2009 on the extension of the mandate of the European Group on Ethics in Science and New Technologies and of the period of appointment of its members, OJ 2009 L 270/18 [EGE extension of mandate III 2009]

[d]EC decision 2010/1/EU of 23 December 2009 on the renewal of the mandate of the European Group on Ethics in Science and New Technologies, OJ 2010 L 1/8 [EGE mandate IV 2010]

[e]EGE mandate V 2016

[f]This opinion No 30 was published in December 2018, hence after the manuscript of this book was finished. For further details, see Pirs and Frischhut (2019, forthcoming)

and global level".[91] Furthermore, one of the criteria mentioned is membership in national ethics councils,[92] in order to establish this vertical link between the EGE and national ethics committees.[93] This networking is also related to the international level, in particular the World Health Organisation (WHO), the United Nations Educational, Scientific and Cultural Organisation (UNESCO), and the Council of Europe. This networking is important in terms of exchange of best practice (in either direction). Most important in terms of qualification, the mandate requires the following[94]:

> The Members shall reflect the broad *cross-disciplinary scope* of the group's mandate, embracing *philosophy and ethics*; *natural and social sciences*; and the *law*. However, they shall *not* [!] perceive themselves as *representatives* of a particular discipline, worldview, or line of research; they shall have a *broad vision* which collectively reflects an understanding of important ongoing and emerging *developments*, including inter-, trans-, and multi-disciplinary perspectives, and the need for ethical advice at the European level.

This requirement, more precisely, this rejection of the possibility of sending representatives of a certain political or ideological direction must also be seen in the light of the criticism that in 2005, many members were too closely linked to the Catholic church.[95]

In terms of the inter-institutional role, before the transition from the GAEIB to the EGE, the EP had called for an increasing role on the composition of the new members.[96] These tensions must be seen against the background of fundamental questions about the role of morality in EU law, precisely "the content of any putative European moral norms and the institutional mechanisms through which morally charged EU policy should be decided", as well as the EP's veto against the first draft of 'Directive Biotech'.[97] However, as mentioned above, the EGE's task is to advise one institution, namely the EC.[98] The EP and the Council of the EU only have an 'indirect access' to the EGE, as "the Commission may draw the Group's attention to issues considered by the Parliament and the Council to be of major ethical

---

[91] EGE mandate V 2016, Art 4(6)(a) and (b).

[92] EGE mandate V 2016, Art 4(6)(e).

[93] In 2005, EGE also began formally to network with national ethics committees; Mohr et al. (2012, p. 107). See, for instance, the above-mentioned (preface) 'Meeting of the National Ethics Councils (NEC) Forum and the [EGE]' on 17 & 18 September 2018 in Vienna, organised under the Austrian Presidency of the Council of the EU.

[94] EGE mandate V 2016, Art 4(6)(c); emphases added.

[95] Plomer (2008, p. 844).

[96] EP resolution GAEIB, pt. 4.

[97] Plomer (2008, p. 842).

[98] Quoting former EC president Jacques Santer, in literature (Mohr et al. 2012, p. 107) the EGE was referred to as "the servant of 'European decision-makers', not solely the Commission"; however, in formal terms it is clearly attached to the EC.

importance".[99] Once an opinion has been adopted, besides the general publication, the opinion has to be transmitted to the EP and the Council.[100]

In terms of the intra-institutional role, the current mandate states "the EGE *shall* establish close links with Commission departments concerned by issues the Group is working on",[101] hence, a more prescriptive and less aspirational ('may') language, as this was the case earlier.[102] Links with external representatives have to be agreed with the Commission's representative,[103] while previously this was a prerogative of the EGE itself.[104,105] Finally, as Plomer has emphasized,[106] the EGE does not have a 'president', but a 'chairperson' only; while the first mandate had referred to a chairperson, the second mandate 'upgraded' this job to an EGE 'president', with mandates No 3 to 5 again only referring to a chairperson.[107] While legally speaking this might not change a lot, one should never underestimate the symbolic meaning of such wording.[108]

The EGE develops their opinions and standpoints in a collaborative way, seeking consensus amongst its members, while leaving open the possibility of dissenting opinions,[109] whereas the discussions are confidential.[110] So far, the EGE has deliv-

[99] EGE mandate V 2016, Art 3. However, the EGE has also accepted requests by other institutions (especially in case of a political standstill), followed by an official request of the EC (e.g. in case of EGE opinion No 27, on energy).

[100] EGE mandate V 2016, Art 5(8).

[101] EGE mandate V 2016, Art 5(7); emphasis added. Having access also to other DGs can be important in terms of the impact of the EGE's activities.

[102] Plomer (2008, p. 846).

[103] EGE mandate V 2016, Art 5(7).

[104] See Footnote 102.

[105] However, it seems that the EGE faces no problem in establishing these links, if so desired.

[106] See Footnote 102.

[107] EGE mandate I 1997, pt. 7; EGE mandate II 2001, pt. 7; EGE mandate III 2005, Art 4(1); EGE mandate IV 2010, Art 4(1); EGE mandate V 2016, Art 5(2).

[108] It seems that the EGE has always enjoyed sufficient independence in its work. Göran Hermerén, past president and chairperson of the EGE "[does] not recollect any attempt from BEPA or the Commission to interfere with our work, nor to suggest or put pressure on us to change something in a draft EGE report" (personal communication).

[109] EGE mandate V 2016, Art 5(6) and (8), "as a 'minority opinion'". See for instance the dissenting opinion of Günter Virt on the controversial issue of patenting of human embryonic stem cells, in EGE opinion No 16 (European Group on Ethics in Science and New Technologies (2002, p. 19)).

[110] EGE mandate V 2016, Art 5(10). These internal EGE documents cannot be accessed, "even from within the Commission"; Mohr et al. (2012, p. 109).

ered 30 opinions, as well as statements[111] and reports.[112] EGE opinions[113] have been mentioned in several EU legal documents.[114] They shall include a set of recommendations and shall be based on an overview of the state of the art of sciences and technologies concerned, as well as a thorough analysis of the ethical issues at stake.[115]

The opinions are usually structured in the following three parts[116]: the first part consists of recitals of the reference texts, which form the starting point (e.g. request by EC president, relevant EU law, relevant international law, primary scientific texts, relevant previous EGE opinions, expert reports and roundtable hearings). The second part consists of three sections, which provide the scientific, legal and ethical backgrounds to the opinion, and the third part presents the opinion with recommendations.[117] Since the beginning, EGE opinions have increased in both scope (from bioethics to sciences and new technologies) and size (from six pages to typically around 100 pages).[118] While some argue that theoretically the EGE is not formally bound to the CFR,[119] there are various references in EGE opinions to this key human rights document, as we will also see in the following.

4.2.2 *Key Findings*

As it is the EGE's specific task "to advise [...] on ethical questions", it remains to be seen how many of the gaps concerning the EU's ethical spirit within the lattice identified so far can be filled based on the findings from the EGE's opinions. Thus, in a similar way as Sect. 4.1, this chapter is dedicated to objective 4, which is to say to answer the question whether the EGE substantiates its ethical reasoning on one of the three normative theories.

---

[111]Statements or other forms of analyses can be produced, if operational circumstances require that advice on a particular subject should be given more quickly than in case of the adoption of an opinion (this should be followed, if necessary, by a fuller analysis in the form of an opinion); EGE mandate V 2016, Art 5(9).

[112]According to Busby et al. (2008, p. 840), the EGE was asked to give an opinion on the CFR, however declined to do so and, instead, gave the following report: European Group on Ethics in Science and New Technologies (2000).

[113]For a detailed analysis of their impact on the legislative procedure, see Busby et al. (2008) (concerning opinions 2, 3, 8, 11, 12, 15, 19 and 22) and Mohr et al. (2012) (concerning opinion 19).

[114]E.g. Directive Biotech, recital 19 (GAEIB); EC recommendation nanosciences, recital 6; Regulation advanced therapy, recital 28; Directive tissues and cells, recital 33.

[115]EGE mandate V 2016, Art 5(5).

[116]European Group on Ethics in Science and New Technologies (2005, p. 10).

[117]There are strong indications that, not very surprisingly, lawyers draft the legal parts, philosophers the ethical ones, and scientists the scientific ones.

[118]Cf. Pirs (2017, 27, A7).

[119]Wilms (2013, p. 293).

This chapter is based on a research project, where the research design has been developed by the author, the research itself conducted as well as the research design further specified by Matthias Pirs,[120] and his Master thesis having been supervised within the 'Integrity Research Group' by Lorenzo Pasculli (now: Coventry University) and the author.

With regard to the methodology,[121] this project also took an inductive approach, coding[122] the 1205 pages of the 29 EGE opinions with the aim of deriving 'rules of prediction' in an explorative way.[123] The categories were formed based on a latent analysis, the 'interpretative reading' of the text, so to speak. The opinions where then screened, using the MAXQDA software, which moreover allows to eliminate code redundancies.[124]

As mentioned above, for the first time, the third mandate of the EGE (2005–2010) was based on a formal decision, hence increasing EGE's legitimacy. The research has revealed that starting from the second half of this mandate, the EGE refers to our three normative theories, that is to say mainly since opinion No 23 (issued on 16.01.2008), until opinion No 29 (issued on 13.10.2015).[125] Besides the new (and formally strengthened) mandate, the EGE left its initial turf of biotechnology and bioethics, and moved on to new fields of technological developments in agriculture, energy, information and communication technologies (ICT), security and surveillance, and citizen participation in new health technologies.[126]

In quantitative terms,[127] the total references to deontology prevail (37), followed by virtue ethics (12) and consequentialism (10), with EGE opinions No 25 on 'synthetic biology' and No 28 on 'security and surveillance technologies' exhibiting the largest accumulation of hints to one or more of these three normative theories, 18

---

[120]Pirs (2017).

[121]For further details on the methodology and the limitations, see Pirs (2017, pp. 40–45). Concerning these opinions (in EN), this project applied a qualitative content analysis (QCA) and took a mixed qualitative (assigning code categories in the relevant materials) and quantitative (analysing and interpreting category frequencies) approach. Concerning the footnote references to potential schools of thought, the QCA mainly considered those, "which were primarily referred to in the main line of reasoning (in-text citation or direct references) in the opinions". In other words, the QCA excluded standalone footnote references, if they could not be related to one of the normative theories; Pirs (2017, p. 44).

[122]The coding process contained the following steps: reading opinions, inductive coding, lexical search, refining categories, classification, and finally narrowing down to the results, presented in the following; for further details, see Pirs (2017, pp. 43–44).

[123]The author would like to thank Nils-Eric Sahlin for pointing to the fact that an inductive method cannot lead to a theory.

[124]Pirs (2017, p. 42). As mentioned above (Table 4.2), for opinion No 30 see Pirs and Frischhut (2019, forthcoming).

[125]Opinion No 30 is on the 'future of work'.

[126]Pirs (2017, p. 49).

[127]It has to be emphasized that sometimes it could be the case that, for instance, three hits occur on the same page of the same opinion, while in other cases three hits occur in different parts of the same opinion, or in total three hits in three different opinions. That is why these numbers shall not be overestimated.

and 16 respectively (see Table 4.3). In terms of philosophers, John Rawls accounts for most hits (10[128]), followed by Hugo Grotius (7), Thomas Hobbes and Hans Jonas with 5 each, Hannah Arendt (4), Jeremy Waldron, Jeremy Bentham, John Stuart Mill, Peter Singer, Michel Foucault and Aristotle with 3 each, John Locke with 2, as well as Immanuel Kant and Jean-Jacques Rousseau with one each, to name but a few.[129]

Overall,[130] the qualitative content analysis (QCA) revealed that thinkers in a deontological tradition of thought dominate the reasoning in the EGE (see Table 4.3).[131]

In its opinion (No 24) on 'ethics of modern developments in agriculture technologies', the EGE referred to justice, as the "institutional dimension of ethics".[132] When broaching issues of global as well as intergenerational justice, the EGE referred to Harvard philosopher John Rawls (1921–2002)[133] and his 'original position', where everyone decides questions of justice from behind a 'veil of ignorance; hence, one would adopt "a 'maximin' strategy which would maximise the position of the least well-off".[134] For the global justice discourse, the EGE refers to this question of distributive justice, which deals with the question of which goods a society or a collective group shall distribute among its individual members. This geographical dimension addresses similar questions as along the timeline (i.e. 'justice between generations'), where "*future* or *past* generations can be viewed as holding legitimate claims or *rights* against present generations, who in turn bear correlative *duties* to future or past generations".[135] It is worth mentioning that this involves not only the perspective of rights, but also of duties, similar to the discussion on human rights and human rights obligations.[136]

As we have seen earlier, conflict of interest is a key issue in ethics. Likewise, in this context, by again referring to Rawls, the EGE emphasizes that "if there is an intergenerational *conflict of interests*, considerations of *justice* could place an *obligation* on *present* generations not to pursue policies that create benefits for themselves but at the expense of those who will live in the future".[137] One year later (in 2009), the EGE picked up the same ideas of Rawls on justice in its opinion on 'synthetic biology'.[138]

---

[128]Five in EGE opinion No 24 ('agricultural technologies') and five in EGE opinion No 25 ('synthetic biology').

[129]For a detailed overview, see Pirs (2017, p. 50).

[130]In the following, some key findings will be presented; for further details see Pirs (2017, pp. 52–64), respectively the above-mentioned opinions, and Pirs and Frischhut (2019, forthcoming).

[131]As far as possible, the different philosophers have been categorized according to the three normative theories.

[132]EGE opinion No 24, p. 48.

[133]Rawls (1971).

[134]EGE opinion No 24, pp. 51–52.

[135]EGE opinion No 24, p. 52; emphases added.

[136]See Weß (2010, pp. 258–259); Assmann (2018).

[137]EGE opinion No 24, p. 52; emphases added.

[138]EGE opinion No 25, p. 45.

Table 4.3 EGE opinions normative theories (quantitative analysis)[a]

EGE opinions/normative theories	No 23 animal cloning 1/2008[b]	No 24 agriculture 12/2008[c]	No 25 synthetic biology 11/2009[d]	No 26 ICT 2/2012[e]	No 27 energy 1/2013[f]	No 28 security and surveillance technologies 5/2014[g]	No 29 health technologies and citizen participation 10/2015[h]	In total
Deontology	0	5	17	0	3	12	0	37
Consequentialism	7	1	0	0	0	2	0	10
Virtue ethics, and related[i]	0	0	1	4	0	2	5	12
In total	7	6	18	4	3	16	5	59

[a]This table does not mention references that cannot be assigned to one of the three normative theories. In the following, opinions will be cited as follows: EGE opinion [No], [page]. Source and further details: Pirs (2017, p. 48); for opinion No 30, see Pirs and Frischhut (2019, forthcoming)
[b]European Group on Ethics in Science and New Technologies (2008a)
[c]European Group on Ethics in Science and New Technologies (2008b)
[d]European Group on Ethics in Science and New Technologies (2009)
[e]European Group on Ethics in Science and New Technologies (2012)
[f]European Group on Ethics in Science and New Technologies (2013)
[g]European Group on Ethics in Science and New Technologies (2014)
[h]European Group on Ethics in Science and New Technologies (2015)
[i]While their classification to a normative theory is debated in literature and clearly challenging, Foucault and Arendt are covered here in 'virtue ethics, and related'. The author would like to thank Johan Brännmark for addressing the fact that Foucault is more about social theory than normative theory; the reason why he was addressed by the EGE in the field of surveillance might be that he is a relevant source because of his work on disciplining and governmentality

Hans Jonas (1903–1993), a philosopher focussing on relationship of man to nature and his handling of technology, has also highlighted this responsibility towards future generations. Based on Kant's 'categorical imperative',[139] in his 1979 book "*Das Prinzip Verantwortung*", he developed an 'ecological imperative', which states as follows: "Act so that the effects of your action are compatible with the permanence of real human life on earth".[140] The development of this deontological concept has to be seen against the historical background, where he saw the need to develop a new concept of ethics, since in the past technology did not have such ranges of action in space and time. In opinion No 27 on energy, the EGE has referred to Jonas, stating that his approach "is echoed in part in the implementation of the 'precautionary principle' in the legal EU framework, which reverses the burden of proof—the argument for the greater overall benefit of an action—in cases of expected harms or risk of envisioned technologies".[141] Likewise, the EGE links Jonas' ideas of obligations towards future generations to the 'principle of sustainability' with respect to the impact of present actions on future generations.[142] In this regard, the EGE refers to the values of human dignity (and human rights), justice (including distributive, social, political, and intergenerational justice), as well as solidarity (the shared responsibility and concern for EU and global welfare). These overarching rights and values shall "guide the development of an ethics framework oriented at a responsible design of the EU energy policy".[143]

The aforementioned value of human dignity is another deontological concept, which the EGE in its opinion on 'synthetic biology' sees as "the *core* of the ethics framework for synthetic biology".[144] Although the EGE only refers to it as "[o]ne such attempt" to define human dignity, it quotes the following definition of medical expert William P. Cheshire[145]:

> The exalted *moral status* which *every* being of human origin uniquely possesses. Human dignity is a given reality, *intrinsic* to human substance, and *not contingent upon* any functional capacities which vary in degree. […] The possession of human dignity carries certain *immutable moral obligations*. These include, concerning the treatment of all other human beings, the duty to preserve life, liberty, and the security of persons, and concerning animals and nature, responsibilities of stewardship.

This deontological concept of the 'intrinsic value' comprises, according to the "Kantian understanding of human dignity [which] emphasises moral responsibility", a prohibition of "treating human beings as mere 'objects' of the interests of others".[146] According to the EGE, this is especially important in case of vulnera-

---

[139]See *supra*, Sect. 2.1.

[140]Jonas (1979, p. 36); translated with DeepL. This book is also quoted in EGE opinion No 25, p. 16.

[141]EGE opinion No 27, p. 49.

[142]See Footnote 141.

[143]EGE opinion No 27, p. 50.

[144]EGE opinion No 25, p. 39; emphasis added.

[145]Cheshire (2002, p. 10); emphases added.

[146]EGE opinion No 25, p. 39.

ble human beings,[147] referring to an idea addressed by Beyleveld & Brownsword in their seminal work 'Human Dignity in Bioethics and Biolaw'. Based on "the notion of dignity as a virtue", the idea of responsible behaviour, according to them, should be taken seriously; in that regard, the responsibility that underlies the notion of dignity, is a "responsibility that goes to questions of character as much as to the appearance".[148] Then they continue with the part that was (partially) quoted by the EGE[149]: "Specifically, it is the idea of dignity as a particular practical attitude to be cultivated in the face of human finitude and vulnerability (and, concomitantly, the natural and social adversity that characterizes the human condition)".[150] Hence, for the EGE, dignity "is the *basis* for more specific principles, *rights and obligations*, and is closely connected to the principle of *justice* and *solidarity*".[151] This corresponds to human dignity enshrined in Art 1 CFR and Art 2 TEU (EU's common values), as well as the above-mentioned emphasis not only on rights, but also on obligations.

With regard to patentability of biotechnological inventions, the EGE addresses the danger of commercial exploitation ('commodification'), which can offend human dignity, thus proposing three types of categories of inventions. First, that "which is common to all *humankind*, and should not be patentable or directly exploited for commercial gain", second, that "which, for a variety of reasons, should be placed in the *public domain* for all to use and exploit (the 'commons')", and finally, inventions that can be protected "at the inventor's discretion".[152] In summary, it can be said that based on the EGE's emphasis on human dignity, deontology plays an important role in bioethics.[153]

Also in the field of 'security and surveillance technologies', the EGE emphasized that human dignity "is at the heart of ethics and is also of crucial importance regarding the debate" in this field.[154] Against the background of debates of increasing security by limiting freedom, the EGE makes a clear statement: "Human dignity is the *core* principle of the European moral framework, and as such it cannot be 'traded off'".[155] However, according to the EGE, "dignity is intimately associated with freedom and responsibility", and here a balance needs to be struck between those two.[156] In this context, the EGE draws on Jeremy Waldron (1953–), a New Zealand professor of law and philosophy, who uses the respect for the dignity of citizens as an argument

---

[147] See Footnote 146.

[148] Beyleveld and Brownsword (2001, p. 2).

[149] See Footnote 146.

[150] See Footnote 148.

[151] EGE opinion No 25, p. 39; emphases added.

[152] EGE opinion No 25, pp. 45–46; emphases added. For further details on the notion of 'common heritage' and Grotius, see Pirs (2017, pp. 57–59).

[153] Cf. also Pirs (2017, p. 56) with further details.

[154] EGE opinion No 28, p. 71.

[155] EGE opinion No 28, p. 77; emphasis added.

[156] EGE opinion No 28, p. 77.

for a moral entitlement to "transparency or the reasons why [the citizens] should apply certain laws".[157]

This relationship of citizens and the state (rulers and the ruled) is also broadly addressed in terms of 'social contract theories'.[158,159] Starting from famous philosophers such as Thomas Hobbes (1588–1679) and the like,[160] the EGE reflects on security and "the moral justification of the absolute power of the state and of the citizens' limitation of freedom",[161] based on Hobbes' 1651 book 'Leviathan'.[162] While theoretically the elected representatives are bound by the 'people's will' (and can be held accountable), "this has turned out to be a challenge under the new security policies".[163] Pirs argues that in this field of security and surveillance technologies, the EGE applies "a more subtle approach towards a deontological understanding of human dignity", where rights are balanced based on the principles of proportionality and effectiveness.[164]

According to the above-mentioned qualitative content analysis, there were clearly fewer references in EGE opinions to consequentialism (see Table 4.3).[165]

This normative theory plays a role when assessing the consequences that arise from developments in the field of science and new technologies, i.e. the EGE's turf. In the context of risk assessment, these consequences relate to possible benefits versus possible risks. Anthropocentric approaches, placing humans in the centre of the universe, focus "on *consequential* considerations and issues related to potential consequences from the use of *synthetic biology* for human beings (risk assessment and management and hazard considerations [...])".[166] The analysis of risk comprises the three elements of risk assessment, risk management and risk communication, where the already mentioned precautionary principle[167] is particularly relevant for risk management.[168] Such risk assessment is emphasized by the EGE "in order to protect

---

157 EGE opinion No 28, p. 78.

158 The EGE provides the following definition: "social (or political) contract arguments classically posit that individuals have consented, either explicitly or tacitly, to surrender some of their freedoms and submit to the authority of the sovereign (or to the decision of a majority) in exchange for protection of their remaining rights". These theories can be distinguished between some that are concerned with the origin of the state, while others focus on "the contract—the modus vivendi—between the ruler(s) and the ruled"; EGE opinion No 28, p. 62.

159 EGE opinion No 28, pp. 61–68.

160 John Locke (1632–1704), mentioned twice, and Jean-Jacques Rousseau (1712–1778) mentioned once (in EGE opinion No 28, pp. 61, 64).

161 EGE opinion No 28, p. 61.

162 Cf. Hobbes (2008).

163 EGE opinion No 28, p. 66.

164 Pirs (2017, p. 60).

165 The author would like to thank Göran Hermerén for addressing the fact that, where a consequentialist approach was (also) called for, the EGE often discussed proportionality; on the latter, see Hermerén (2012).

166 EGE opinion No 25, p. 42; emphases added.

167 See *supra* at note 141.

168 EC 'On the precautionary principle', COM(2000) 1 final 2.2.2000, p. 2.

human dignity and the autonomy of persons", in a similar way as the importance of the precautionary principle.[169] Hence, linking this consequentialist approach to human dignity, as mentioned above in the context of deontology.

Moreover, a consequentialist approach is applied by the EGE in the context of 'animal cloning for food supply'. Here, the EGE takes a more bio-centric attitude,[170] comprising ethical concerns for the cloned animals, for humans, for the environment, as well as for society.[171] Jeremy Bentham (1748–1832) is considered as the founder of modern utilitarianism, the most prominent form of consequentialism. As already mentioned, utilitarianism is egalitarian (as the well-being of each person is of equal value), and even the feelings of animals can be taken into account.[172] That is why Bentham is often regarded as one of the earliest proponents of animal rights. The EGE refers to Bentham, John Stuart Mill (1806–1876) and Peter Singer (1946–), etc., in order to argue 'the moral status of animals', as "actions causing *pain* in *sentient* animals are morally unacceptable, since animals are considered *moral subjects*".[173] At the same time, the EGE also refers to a deontological line of argumentation, based on the 'intrinsic value argument', referring especially to literature focusing on animals' intrinsic value[174] and integrity.[175] In summary, the EGE concludes that it "has doubts as to whether cloning for food is justified", and "does not see convincing arguments to justify the production of food from clones and their offspring".[176]

Accounting for slightly more hints than consequentialism (i.e. 10), the research of Pirs identified 12 references in EGE opinions to [3.] virtue ethics (see Table 4.3), which has been defined as "[a]n approach to both understanding and living the *good life* that is *based on virtue*".[177] What does this concept of 'human flourishing' imply for today's potential dangers arising from the corroding of privacy due to the introduction of new ICT tools? This 'good life' is addressed in the opinion on ethics of ICT in the sense that "giving up privacy would determine the flourishing of a personal and social virtue [...] based on people's freedom to introduce and share whatever data on their own lives they desire".[178] In the end, the EGE calls for building "a stronger and more coherent data protection framework".[179] In this context, the EGE also refers to Hannah Arendt (1906–1975), one of the most important philosophers

[169]EGE opinion No 25, p. 42.

[170]It is worth mentioning that from the perspective of Art 37 CFR ('environmental protection'), we shall apply a broad understanding, as according to Rudolf (2014, 558–559, 562), the notion of 'environment' comprises air, soil, water, flora and fauna, humans and the environment created and shaped by humans and animals (but no pets).

[171]EGE opinion No 23, p. 32.

[172]*Supra* Sect. 2.2.

[173]EGE opinion No 23, p. 33; emphases added.

[174]Dol et al. (1999).

[175]Dol et al. (1997).

[176]EGE opinion No 23, p. 45.

[177]Chara (2002, p. 915); emphases added.

[178]EGE opinion No 26, p. 45; similar in EGE opinion No 28, p. 73.

[179]Ibid. This opinion was delivered four years before the adoption of Regulation GDP.

of the 20th century, as "one of the first scholars to observe the political importance of privacy". The EGE states that "Arendt's defence of the importance of the private sphere warns about dangers arising from the erosion of the private, a situation which some consider as deriving from the use of ICT as communication tools".[180] Also in the context of new health technologies and citizen participation, the EGE refers to Arendt[181] when addressing the danger of "downgrading of individual rights in pursuit of the collective good".[182]

A famous representative of virtue ethics, Aristotle (384–322 B.C.), is mentioned in the context of ethics in ICT, where the EGE reflects on his "friendship as mutual care between equals" against the background of the "ethically important change" in the way in which social networks shape the concept of friendship and community.[183] Hence, we can see various examples of old concepts being applied to current as well as future challenges. However, despite these examples, it is important to emphasize that the EGE "does not clearly stipulate any normative ethical guidance on the basis of virtue ethics in this regar[d]".[184] One exception can be found in 'security and surveillance technologies'. There, the EGE refers to 'virtuous behaviour' in the context of the tension between privacy and new technologies, which has been addressed with regard to four instruments: technology, education, self-regulation and the law; in terms of the third one, according to the EGE, "[s]elf-regulatory governance works to promote (virtuous) behaviour by involving stakeholders and establishing bottom-up soft regulations".[185]

As mentioned above, based on the first formal mandate (in 2005), since 2008 (i.e. Opinion No 23) the EGE has started to refer to normative theories, especially via their proponents. In this regard, it is fascinating to see a similar development in the legal sphere. As of Opinion No 16 (patenting of human stem cells inventions, May 2002), which falls in the 2nd mandate,[186] the EGE has also increasingly (9 hits) started to refer to EU and international documents, mainly in the field of human rights (see Fig. 4.1).

The number became double-digit (14 hits) with Opinion No 17 (clinical research in developing countries, February 2003), 54 hits in Opinion No 25 (synthetic biology, November 2009), with a maximum of 80 hits in Opinion No 28 (security and surveillance technologies, May 2014). From these documents, the CFR ranks first with 142 hits, followed by the European Convention for the Protection of Human Rights and Fundamental Freedoms (ECHR) with 79 hits, the Oviedo convention (61

[180]The EGE refers to the first edition in 1958; see nowadays: Arendt et al. (2018).

[181]Arendt (1951).

[182]EGE opinion No 29, p. 41. In this context, the EGE also refers to Michel Foucault (1926–1984); p. 40.

[183]EGE opinion No 26, p. 42; Aristotle was also mentioned in EGE opinion No 25, p. 11, and EGE opinion No 28, p. 64.

[184]Pirs (2017, p. 63).

[185]EGE opinion No 28, p. 59.

[186]2000–2005; here, the EGE became part of BEPA.

International Ethical Framework - main references	Charter of Fundamental Rights (CFR)	European Convention on Human Rights (ECHR)	Convention on Human Rights and Biomedicine (Oviedo)	Universal Declaration on the Human Genome and Human Rights	International Covenant on Economic, Social and Cultural Rights (ICESC)	WMA Declaration of Helsinki	Universal Declaration on Bioethics and Human Rights	Convention for the Protection of Automatic Processing	Universal Declaration of Human Rights 1948	International Declaration on Human Genetic Data	International Covenant on Civil and Political Rights (ICCPR)	SUM
ss	0	0	0	0	0	0	0	0	0	0	0	0
Opinion no. 02 human blood or human plasma products	0	0	0	0	0	0	0	0	0	0	0	0
Opinion no. 03 biotechnology directive	0	1	0	0	0	0	0	0	0	0	0	1
Opinion no. 04 gene therapy	0	0	0	0	0	0	0	0	0	0	0	0
Opinion no. 05 food labelling modern biotechnology	0	0	0	0	0	0	0	0	0	0	0	0
Opinion no. 06 prenatal diagnosis	0	0	0	0	0	0	0	0	0	0	0	0
Opinion no. 07 genetic modification of animals	0	0	0	0	0	0	0	0	0	0	0	0
Opinion no. 08 patenting human origin inventions	0	0	0	0	0	0	0	0	0	0	0	0
Opinion no. 09 cloning techniques	0	0	0	1	0	0	0	0	0	0	0	1
Opinion no. 10 5th research framework programme	0	0	1	1	0	1	0	0	0	0	0	3
Opinion no. 11 human tissue banking	0	0	1	1	0	0	0	0	0	0	0	2
Opinion no. 12 human embryo FP5 research	0	0	3	1	0	0	0	0	0	0	0	4
Opinion no. 13 healthcare in the information society	0	2	1	1	0	0	0	3	0	0	0	7
Opinion no. 14 doping in sport	0	0	0	1	0	0	0	0	0	0	0	1
Opinion no. 15 human stem cell research and use	3	0	2	1	0	0	0	0	0	0	0	6
Opinion no. 16 patenting human stem cells inventions	5	1	1	2	0	0	0	0	0	0	0	9
Opinion no. 17 clinical research in developing countries	2	1	2	0	0	9	0	0	0	0	0	14
Opinion no. 18 genetic testing in the workplace	1	0	1	0	0	0	0	0	0	0	0	2
Opinion no. 19 umbilical cord blood banking	1	0	3	1	0	0	0	0	0	0	0	5
Opinion no. 20 ICT implants in the human body	15	0	5	4	0	1	1	1	1	0	0	28
Opinion no. 21 nanomedicine 2007	12	3	9	8	0	2	4	1	0	1	0	40
Opinion no. 22 hESC FP7 research projects	2	0	13	2	0	1	2	2	0	2	0	24
Opinion no. 23 animal cloning for food supply	2	0	0	0	0	0	0	0	0	0	0	2
Opinion no. 24 modern agricultural technologies	7	0	0	0	3	0	0	0	2	0	0	12
Opinion no. 25 synthetic biology	16	2	11	16	0	5	3	0	0	1	0	54
Opinion no. 26 information and communication technologies	19	0	1	1	0	0	1	1	0	1	0	24
Opinion no. 27 research, production and use of energy	24	2	0	0	6	0	0	0	0	0	0	32
Opinion no. 28 security and surveillance technologies	28	44	1	0	2	0	0	0	3	0	2	80
Opinion no. 29 NHT and citizen participation	5	23	6	0	17	2	1	0	1	0	1	56
SUM	*142*	*79*	*61*	*41*	*28*	*21*	*12*	*8*	*7*	*5*	*3*	*407*

Fig. 4.1 EGE references to key documents. *Source* Pirs (2017, A37); N.B: this overview of Pirs continues with seven other documents on page A38; for opinion No 30, see Pirs and Frischhut (2019, forthcoming)

hits), the Universal Declaration on the Human Genome and Human Rights[187] with 41 hits, the International Covenant on Economic Social and Cultural Rights (ICESC) with 28 hits, and the Helsinki declaration with 21 hits.[188] This tendency goes hand in hand with the increase in number of pages, around 20 pages until Opinion No 19 (March 2004), to around 100 starting with Opinion No 21 (January 2007).[189]

Overall, we can observe an extension not only in pages, in references to normative theories as well as to these EU and international documents, but also in scope, as the group has moved from purely bioethics also to broader principles of human rights, as well as an increase in group members. There has also been an increase of the duration of the mandates, except for the last one.[190] As we know from the job of the president of the European Council, newly created by the Lisbon Treaty,[191] an appointment for two times 2.5 years allows for more control, compared to an appointment for five years. Apart from the normative theories covered in this chapter and based on the terminological delimitation,[192] the EGE has referred to values (human dignity, justice, freedom, solidarity, etc.), to human rights, as well as to principles (privacy, informed consent, non-discrimination, equity, precaution, sustainability, etc.).

4.3 Conclusion

It is evident, that both in EU legal documents (Sect. 4.1) as well as in case of the EGE (Sect. 4.2), ethics enters the scene in sensitive areas. This was the case with CETA (investment protection and the fear that big companies can 'buy justice'), as well as the Korea agreement (inappropriate influence of the pharma industry). In addition we can name the saving of Islandic banks in the context of EFTA (taxpayers' money and moral hazard), scepticism with regard to (regulation of) the financial world in general (cf. ethics committees in the field of ECB and EIB), and lobbying (the fear that big companies can 'buy law'), to name but a few. In case of the EGE, one reason for its establishment was also to address public concern on the new challenges raised by new (bio-)technologies.[193]

In the following, the questions mentioned at the beginning[194] will be answered in more detail, as the results of Sect. 4.2 on the EGE will supplement those of Sect. 4.1.

With regard to the possible identification of normative theories (i.e. question No 1), we have seen implicit references in EU legal documents, implicit as well as explicit ones in EGE opinions. The latter have mainly referred to several proponents of

187 Dating from 11.11.1997.

188 Source: Pirs (2017, A37); mentioning twelve other documents in descending order.

189 Pirs (2017, A7).

190 See *supra* Table 4.2.

191 Art 15(5) TEU.

192 See *supra* Sect. 1.5.

193 Cf. Plomer (2008, p. 840).

194 See *supra* Sect. 1.2 (objectives).

these normative theories, but have also explicitly addressed these normative theories. Implicit references in EGE opinions especially addressed deontological ideas via the EU value of human dignity.

Question No 2 can clearly be answered in terms of addressing several normative theories, although these three theories are not equally represented. In EGE opinions, deontology clearly prevails, and we find less examples of virtue ethics.[195] However, it is important to emphasize that often the EGE refers to one normative theory, by emphasizing the consequences if the decision-makers opt for this theory, besides pointing to another normative theory, also emphasizing the consequences for this other theory. Hence, while there are most references to deontology, this disclaimer has to be kept in mind.

It was also remarkable to see justice as the "institutional dimension of ethics".[196] Justice occurred both in terms of distributive justice (Rawls), as well as with regard to future generations (Jonas). Human dignity, in Waldron's interpretation, also has an institutional component, in terms of citizens' entitlement to transparency in the decision-making process.

In both EU legal documents, as well as in EGE opinions, human dignity plays a paramount role. It was addressed to be at the 'core' of synthetic biology, at the 'heart' of ethics in the field of security and surveillance technologies, and was even addressed as the "core principle of the European moral framework".[197] This EU value clearly has a deontological connotation, when referring to the *intrinsic* value of humans, with similar ideas expressed with regard to animals. Throughout EU law, human dignity has been an argument against 'commodification' of the human body, based on the Kantian idea of not treating humans as mere objects. For the same reason, it has been emphasized that there can be no trade-offs.[198] Human dignity has been emphasized especially in case of vulnerable groups, which also links it to solidarity. This 'core principle', in more correct terms one would have to speak of 'core value', is the basis for further rights, principles and obligations, as we can also observe it in the CFR.[199]

Consequentialism has been addressed by the EGE in the context of risk assessment. Apart from ethics, in EU law in general we have seen that impact assessment plays an important role in EU decision-making, as well as the '*effet utile*' principle in CJEU case-law, both of which also have a consequentialist connotation. Utilitarian philosophers have been addressed when taking a more bio-centric approach, in particular with regard to animals. It is worth mentioning that the EGE both in case of risk assessment and with regard to animals has also taken a deontological approach,

[195]Given the information available, it remains unfortunately a challenge to address the question "why and when" a certain approach has been applied.

[196]EGE opinion No 24, p. 48.

[197]EGE opinion No 28, p. 77.

[198]However, this was possible in case of freedom and responsibility.

[199]The 'Explanations relating to the Charter of Fundamental Rights', OJ 2007 C 303/17, state as follows: "The dignity of the human person is not only a fundamental right in itself but constitutes the real basis of fundamental rights."

as it has emphasized the importance to protect human dignity and the autonomy of persons (in case of risk assessment), and has also referred to the intrinsic value of animals, as mentioned above.

Social contract theories have been addressed in terms of security and surveillance technologies. Although drafted during the age of enlightenment to legitimate the authority of the state, this concept is still of relevance and was applied to these new challenges.

Both for EU legal documents, as well as for the EGE opinions, all the examples we have seen cannot be understood as unconditional references to one or more normative theory(ies), but only as pointing towards them (question No 3). The EGE often refers to several views, for instance to deontology and to consequentialism,[200] without explicitly favouring the one, or rejecting the other view. In other words, in case of explicit references to normative theories, the EGE contrasts different philosophical views; hence, it is not possible to assign the EGE exclusively to one of these three normative theories.

Another question was, whether we can identify a certain common horizontal (or rather a specific) pattern, when referring to these terms of ethics and morality in EU legal documents (Sect. 4.1), respectively when addressing these normative theories (Sect. 4.2). As we have seen above with regard to EU legal documents, there is clearly no horizontal, but a specific approach in addressing different normative theories in different fields. Deontology plays a role in order to refer to general principles of morality, consequentialism to address effects of the ethical challenge at hand, and virtue ethics is addressed in the context of 'pursuing a good life'.[201] Against the background of the diverse topics of the 30 opinions so far, the EU's values with their corner stone of human dignity, a deontological concept, can be seen as the most horizontal approach in this regard.

Having now analysed the different 'layers' (in the sense of the hierarchy) and the different 'areas' (in the sense of the 'separation of powers') of EU law, the final question (i.e. objective 4), as to whether we can identify an ethical spirit of EU law, can be answered as follows. As stated above, in this book, the notion of spirit is understood as "the intention of the authors of a legal system, which is reflected in a lattice of various different provisions". In Sect. 4.1 with regard to EU legal documents, we have already identified both an ethical spirit, as well as a gap that still needs to be filled. The findings of Sect. 4.2 point in a similar direction, further emphasizing the predominant role of the EU's common values and the corner stone of human dignity. Apart from explicitly referring to these concepts from a legal angle as the values enshrined in Art 2 TEU, the deontological normative arguments addressed in the EGE's opinions also point in the same direction, hence further closing the gap addressed earlier. Having identified this 'lattice' of ethics in the different layers and areas, both binding legal provisions and soft-law, including the EGE's opinion, this does not mean that we have reached a final position. This analysis is valid as of 2018, might however be different in the future, and was clearly less elaborated in the past.

---

[200] EGE opinion No 12, p. 8.

[201] Lucivero (2016, p. 15).

One example in this regard is Opinion No 12, on ethical aspects of research involving the use of human embryo in the context of the fifth framework programme, from November 1998. The EGE appropriately states that the EU has no proper competence in medicine, hence such protection falls within national competence. Nonetheless (i.e. first limitation), EU authorities "should be concerned with ethical questions resulting from medical practice or research dealing with early human development".[202] However, (limitation to the first limitation), in doing so, EU authorities have to take into account "the *moral and philosophical* differences, reflected by the extreme *diversity* of legal rules applicable to human embryo research", as "because of lack of consensus, it would be inappropriate to impose one exclusive *moral* code".[203] The question remains, if this diversity stipulated in 1998 with regard to embryo-related questions is still valid today, having in mind the growing importance of EU values, especially since 2009. To sum up, this ethical spirit is *in statu nascendi*, as we can also see from the 'united in diversity' approach we have seen in case of EU primary law.

Addressing these elements of constant development on a time line, it is worth mentioning that also the status quo, as viewed from today, has addressed retrospective elements (the historical responsibility for climate change and the moral obligation to assist ACP countries),[204] as well as the obligations with regard to future generations (nanosciences, Hans Jonas, etc.).

The ethical spirit of EU law identified in this book is subject to the following limitation. It only applies to EU law. Hence, this does not cover all the examples where reference is made to the national or local level (e.g. "compliance with local codes of ethics"[205]). In those situations, the ethical spirit of EU law can only have an indirect influence, especially via the EU's common values. This is similar to 'morality' being determined by the different MS, but constrained by the EU's proportionality principle (especially the requirement of 'coherence'), as well as the prohibition of double morality, etc., as stated in the CJEU's case-law.

One final word about the just addressed difference in terminology, i.e. ethics versus morality. The reason why this book has not coined the term of the 'moral spirit of EU law' is primarily due to the reason that the notion of 'public morality' has essentially been used as a protection shield, in EU primary law (called 'reason of justification'), in international agreements (called 'exception clause'), as well as in EU secondary law.[206] Besides this, 'public morality' is a legal term while ethics is a term of practical philosophy. In terms of morality, 'public morality' is a collective term, while we have also seen a lot of variations of morality: 'moral

---

[202] EGE opinion No 12, p. 10.

[203] Ibid.; emphases added.

[204] *Supra* Sect. 3.2.1 (at note 74).

[205] *Supra* Sect. 3.2.1 (at note 56).

[206] One exception to this statement is the "competence of Member States as regards ethical issues", we have seen in the context of GMOs; *supra* Sect. 3.3.3.3.

support',[207] 'moral condemnation',[208] 'moral development',[209] a 'high moral standing',[210] 'moral safety',[211] 'moral responsibility',[212] as well as the economic term of 'moral hazard'.[213] The notion of 'ethics',[214] on the other hand, has not been used in such a collective way.[215] It has the advantages of not being a legal term (although used in legal texts) and it has not been used as a 'protection shield'.[216] Now that we have examined the 'ethical spirit of EU law' from a philosophical point of view, we turn to the legal perspective.

References

Allen, R. E., Fowler, H. W., & Fowler, F. G. (1990). *The concise Oxford dictionary of current English* (8th ed.). Oxford: Clarendon Press.

Arendt, H. (1951). *The origins of totalitarianism*. New York: Schocken Books.

Arendt, H., Allen, D. S., & Canovan, M. (2018). *The human condition: With an introduction by Margaret Canovan and a New Foreword by Danielle Allen (Sixtieth anniversary edition)*. Chicago, London: University of Chicago Press.

Assmann, A. (2018). *Menschenrechte und Menschenpflichten: Schlüsselbegriffe für eine humane Gesellschaft*. Wien: Picus Verlag.

Beauchamp, T. L., & Frey, R. G. (Eds.). (2014). *Oxford handbooks. The Oxford handbook of animal ethics*. Oxford, New York: Oxford University Press.

Beyleveld, D., & Brownsword, R. (2001). *Human dignity in bioethics and biolaw*. Oxford: Oxford University Press.

Birnbacher, D. (2013). *Analytische Einführung in die Ethik*. Berlin: De Gruyter.

Brännmark, J. (2017). Respect for persons in bioethics: Towards a human rights-based account. *Human Rights Review, 18*, 171–187. https://doi.org/10.1007/s12142-017-0450-x.

Busby, H., Hervey, T. K., & Mohr, A. (2008). Ethical EU law? The influence of the European Group on Ethics in science and new technologies. *European Law Review (E.L.Rev.), 33*, 803–842.

Chara, P. J. (2002). Virtue. In J. K. Roth (Ed.), *International encyclopedia of ethics* (pp. 912–915). London, Chicago, Illinois: Fitzroy Dearborn.

Cheshire, W. D. (2002). Toward a common language of human dignity. *Ethics & Medicine, 18*, 7–10.

Dol, M., Kasanmoentalib, S., Lijmbach, S., Rivas, E., & van den Bos, R. (Eds.). (1997). *Animal consciousness and animal ethics: Perspectives from the Netherlands*. Assen: Van Gorcum.

[207] *Supra* Sect. 3.2.1, at note 78 (to the Burundian people), and at note 93 (EFTA States' obligation to provide moral support in the context of EU enlargement).

[208] *Supra* Sect. 3.2.1, at note 79.

[209] *Supra* Sect. 3.2.1, at note 80.

[210] *Supra* Sect. 3.2.1, at note 81.

[211] *Supra* Sect. 3.2.1, at note 82.

[212] *Supra* Sect. 3.3.3.3, at note 264.

[213] *Supra* Sect. 3.2.1, at note 89.

[214] As mentioned above, ethics has not been mentioned in EU primary law. Apart from this, ethics also remains untouched by the CJEU (judicial self-restraint).

[215] On communitarianism, see *infra* Chap. 6.

[216] Apart from the Polish GMO case, where, by the way, the Polish line of argumentation was not successful.

Dol, M., van Fentener Vlissingen, M., Kasanmoentalib, S., Visser, T., & Zwart, H. (Eds.). (1999). *Recognizing the intrinsic value of animals: Beyond animal welfare*. Assen: Van Gorcum.

Dratwa, J. (2014). How values come to matter at the European Commission: Ethical experimentations of Europe. *Politique Européenne*, 86–121.

European Commission. (1993). Growth, competitiveness, employment. The challenges and ways forward into the 21st century: Bulletin of the European Communities. Supplement 6/93. White paper. COM(93)700 final 5 December 1993.

European Group on Ethics in Science and New Technologies. (2000). *Citizens rights and new technologies: A European challenge*. Report of the European Group on Ethics in Science and New Technologies on the Charter on Fundamental Rights related to technological innovation as requested by President Prodi on February 3, 2000: CHARTE 4370/00 CONTRIB 233.

European Group on Ethics in Science and New Technologies. (2002). Ethical aspects of patenting inventions involving human stem cells: Opinion No 16.

European Group on Ethics in Science and New Technologies. (2005). *General report on the activities of the European Group on Ethics in Science and New Technologies to the European Commission 2000–2005*. Luxembourg: Office for Official Publications of the European Communities.

European Group on Ethics in Science and New Technologies. (2008a). Ethical aspects of animal cloning for food supply: Opinion No 23.

European Group on Ethics in Science and New Technologies. (2008b). *Ethics of modern developments in agriculture technologies: Opinion No 24*. Luxembourg: Publications Office of the EU.

European Group on Ethics in Science and New Technologies. (2009). *Ethics of synthetic biology: Opinion No 25*. Luxembourg: Publications Office of the EU.

European Group on Ethics in Science and New Technologies. (2012). *Ethics of information and communication technologies: Opinion No 26*. Luxembourg: Publications Office of the EU.

European Group on Ethics in Science and New Technologies. (2013). *An ethical framework for assessing research, production and use of energy: Opinion No 27*. Luxembourg: Publications Office of the EU.

European Group on Ethics in Science and New Technologies. (2014). *Ethics of security and surveillance technologies: Opinion No 28*. Luxembourg: Publications Office of the EU.

European Group on Ethics in Science and New Technologies. (2015). *The ethical implications of new health technologies and citizen participation: Opinion No 29*. Luxembourg: Publications Office of the EU.

Forrest, B. (2002). Integrity. In J. K. Roth (Ed.), *International encyclopedia of ethics* (pp. 441–442). London, Chicago, Illinois: Fitzroy Dearborn.

Frischhut, M., & Greer, S. L. (2017). EU public health law and policy—Communicable diseases. In T. K. Hervey, C. Young, & L. E. Bishop (Eds.), *Research handbook on EU Health Law and Policy* (pp. 315–346). Cheltenham: Edward Elgar Publishing.

Hermerén, G. (2012). The principle of proportionality revisited: Interpretations and applications. *Medicine, Health Care and Philosophy, 15*, 373–382. https://doi.org/10.1007/s11019-011-9360-x.

Hobbes, T. (2008). *Leviathan: Edited with an introduction by J. C. A. Gaskin. Oxford world's classics*. Oxford: Oxford University Press.

Jonas, H. (1979). *Das Prinzip Verantwortung: Versuch einer Ethik für die technologische Zivilisation* (1st ed.). Frankfurt am Main: Insel Verlag.

Krishnamurthy, R. (Ed.). (1993). *English learner's dictionary (Reprint)*. London, Glasgow: Harper Collins Publishers.

Louden, R. B. (2012). Virtue ethics. In R. F. Chadwick (Ed.), *Encyclopedia of applied ethics* (2nd ed., pp. 503–510). London: Academic Press.

Lucivero, F. (2016). *Ethical assessments of emerging technologies: Appraising the moral plausibility of technological visions*. Cham, Heidelberg, New York, Dordrecht, London: Springer International Publishing.

Mohr, A., Busby, H., Hervey, T. K., & Dingwall, R. (2012). Mapping the role of official bioethics advice in the governance of biotechnologies in the EU: The European Group on Ethics' opinion on commercial cord blood banking. *Science and Public Policy, 39,* 105–117. https://doi.org/10.1093/scipol/scs003.

Montesquieu, Charles de Secondat, Baron de. (1927). *De L'esprit des Loix: Avec des notes de Voltaire, de Crevier, de Mably, de la Harpe, etc.* Nouvelle édition entièrement refondue. Tome premier. Paris: Librairie Garnier Frères.

Panichi, J. (2015, February 3). Former science adviser goes public on British television. *EuropeanVoice*. Retrieved from http://www.europeanvoice.com/article/former-science-adviser-goes-public-on-british-television/.

Parfit, D. (2011). *On what matters. The Berkeley Tanner Lectures*. Oxford: Oxford University Press.

Pirs, M. (2017). *Ethical Integration in EU Law by The European Group on Ethics in Science and New Technologies: A qualitative content analysis of the prevailing philosophical schools of thought*. Master thesis at MCI 'Strategic Management & Law', summer term 2017, Innsbruck.

Pirs, M., & Frischhut, M. (2019. forthcoming). Ethical Integration in EU Law: The prevailing normative theories in EGE opinions. In N. Ryder & L. Pasculli (Eds.), *Corruption, integrity and the law: Global regulatory challenges*. Milton Park, Abingdon, Oxon, New York, NY: Routledge.

Plomer, A. (2008). The European group on ethics: Law, politics and the limits of moral integration in Europe. *European Law Journal, 14,* 839–859. https://doi.org/10.1111/j.1468-0386.2008.00447.x.

Ranacher, C., & Frischhut, M. (2009). *Handbuch Anwendung des EU-Rechts: Mit Judikatur (EuGH, VfGH, VwGH, OGH)*. Wien: facultas wuv.

Rawls, J. (1971). *A theory of justice*. Cambridge: Belknap Press of Harvard University Press.

Rudolf, B. (2014). Artikel 37. In J. Meyer (Ed.), *Charta der Grundrechte der Europäischen Union* (4th ed., pp. 558–564). Baden-Baden: Nomos.

Smits, R. (2018). The invisible core of values in the European Integration Project. *Legal Issues of Economic Integration, 45,* 221–227.

The Hamlyn Publishing Group. (1970). *The complete works of William Shakespeare: Comprising his plays and poems with a preface by the late Sir Donald Wolfit, CBE. Introduction and glossary by Dr Bretislav Hodek* (12th impression). London, New York, Sydney, Toronto: Spring Books.

Weß, P. (2010). *Glaube aus Erfahrung und Deutung: Christliche Praxis statt Fundamentalismus*. Salzburg: Otto Müller Verlag.

Williams, A. T. (2010). *The ethos of Europe: Values, law and justice in the EU. Cambridge studies in European law and policy*. Cambridge: Cambridge University Press.

Wilms, H. C. (2013). Ethisierung des Europarechts – Grundrechtliche Grenzen und politische Praktiken. In S. Vöneky, B. Beylage-Haarmann, A. Höfelmeier, & A.-K. Hübler (Eds.), *Ethik und Recht - Ethics and Law: Die Ethisierung des Rechts - The Ethicalization of Law* (pp. 285–298). Heidelberg: Springer.

Chapter 5
Legal Lens

The question whether references to ethics should be understood as an unconditional reference (to one or more philosophical theories), or only as pointing towards a certain idea (question No. 3), has already been answered in the previous chapter (in terms of the second option). This question (concerning the philosophical lens) is separate from another question (now, concerning the legal lens), whether these notions shall be imported in an unaltered way (i.e. absolute approach), or whether they shall be imported by placing them in the legal context (i.e. relative approach? As mentioned above,[1] for the relation of law and science, a relative approach has been preferred.[2] I have argued elsewhere[3] that references in legal texts to ethics and morality have to be seen within the limitation that those philosophical concepts necessarily have to be reflected within the legal order itself.[4] In other words, concepts that cannot, in one way or another be traced in the legal order itself (and which therefore are alien to this legal order), consequently cannot come into consideration. The same argumentation is also upheld in this book; hence, these normative theories and other philosophical concepts have to be imported in a relative way and need to be reflected in the EU legal order. While this legal order can be seen as autonomous, it shall nevertheless respect principles of justice (relative autonomy). Thus, in the following, this legal lens will add some pieces to further enrich the lattice developed so far, and, as we will see, will confirm some of the findings of the previous chapter.

---

[1] *Supra* Sect. 1.4.

[2] Wahlberg (2010, 208, 213, 2017, p. 63), Wahlberg and Persson (2017).

[3] Frischhut (2015).

[4] This approach has previously also been adopted by the Austrian Supreme Court judgment of 18 April 2012, *Prostitution not against public morals*, 3 Ob 45/12g, para 4.6.1: "When it comes to the understanding of 'public morals', generally accepted moral concepts can be taken into account. This applies, however, with the limitation that moral concepts are only relevant to the extent that they have been reflected in the legal system itself" (own translation).

M. Frischhut, *The Ethical Spirit of EU Law*,
https://doi.org/10.1007/978-3-030-10582-2_5

5.1 From the *Schuman* Plan to Today's Vertical Distribution of Competences

On 9 March 1950, the then French foreign minister and founding father of the EU, Robert Schuman highlighted, amongst others, the following idea in his groundbreaking declaration[5]: "Europe will not be made all at once, or according to a single plan. It will be built through concrete achievements which first create a de facto solidarity".[6] The same applies to the 'ethical spirit of EU law', which has developed since then, and which will continue to do so in the future. The background of this declaration was World War II and its atrocities. Hence, the atmosphere of this time might have been inspired by deontology, while neo-functionalism can rather be seen as consequentialist.

This integration process, started with the "pooling of coal and steel production" and has further developed according to the spill-over phenomenon, resulting in the vertical distribution of competences,[7] as we know it today. This distribution of competences to pass legal documents can also have an impact on the ethical spirit. For instance, 'public health' falls within the MS competence. As we have seen above,[8] in order to alleviate the fear of MS that, based on economic single market rights, patients could seek unethical treatment abroad, the relevant EU directive states as follows: "[n]o provision of this Directive should be interpreted in such a way as to undermine the fundamental ethical choices of Member States".[9] This is quite remarkable as the directive, besides a clear statement in EU primary law,[10] emphasizes several times the competences of MS in this regard, that is to say from a legal perspective. From a strictly legal angle, this reference to ethics would not have been necessary; nevertheless, it clearly demonstrates the increasing role of ethics in EU law. Although this example, like others classified in this 'protection shield' category, is not very ambitious, it can be taken as a role model where the vertical distribution of legal competences can also play a role for the question at which vertical level ethical questions would be decided. These considerations can be summarised as follows: based on this vertical distribution of competences, one can, in case of doubt assume that the

[5]This plan was initiated by Jean Monnet and Paul Reuter; Simon (1998, p. 16). On Monnet, see Schwabe (2016).

[6]Source: https://europa.eu/european-union/about-eu/symbols/europe-day/schuman-declaration_en.

[7]Art 2-6 TEU.

[8]*Supra* Sect. 3.3.3.3, at note 351.

[9]Directive patient mobility, recital 7.

[10]Art 168(7) TFEU: "Union action shall respect the responsibilities of the Member States for the definition of their health policy and for the organisation and delivery of health services and medical care. The responsibilities of the Member States shall include the management of health services and medical care and the allocation of the resources assigned to them [...]".

legal competence also includes the competence for ethical questions.[11] On the other hand, if EU secondary law explicitly refers to the MS for deciding issues of ethical nature, this goes in the same direction as this presumption. Likewise, as in similar cases, the EU's common values can be a limitation to this 'national competence'.

5.2 Preambles TEU and CFR

Based on what we have already seen in Sect. 3.1.1, the preambles of the TEU and the CFR provide important guidance with regard to the ethical spirit of EU law.

Searching for the groundwork of ethics in EU law, one comes across the preamble of the CFR, which refers to the "spiritual and moral heritage" of the Union.[12] It is worth mentioning that the preamble only uses the wording "conscious of", as opposed to the wording used for the common values[13]: "based on",[14] respectively "is *founded on* the indivisible, universal values of human dignity, freedom, equality and solidarity".[15] In terms of the already covered terminology, presumably the term of 'morality' has been chosen, in order to refer to a factual (historically developed) situation, and not to the one of 'ethics', which would be the philosophical approach to define morality. As one might already suspect, these terms ('spiritual' and 'moral' heritage) are not defined regarding their content. In terms of geography, they can be seen as to refer to Europe, presumably as composed at the time of the drafting of the Charter.[16] We are faced with the same challenge that we have already seen many times in this book, that is to say the reference of law to another discipline, which in this case requires primarily a historical approach.[17] Hence, this moral heritage does not define the 'ethical spirit', it just adds up to the lattice identified so far.

This goes hand in hand with the reference to the "cultural, religious and humanist inheritance of Europe", from which the TEU draws 'inspiration'.[18] While the previous reference of the CFR (i.e. the 'spiritual and moral heritage') opened the legal field for this 'ethical spirt',[19] this second reference can fill it regarding its content. Let us start with the reference to humanism.[20] Although covering a broad range, humanism

---

[11] I already argued this way in Frischhut (2015, p. 570).

[12] CFR, recital 2.

[13] *Infra* Sect. 5.4.

[14] CFR, recital 1.

[15] CFR, recital 2, which continues, "*based o*n the principles of democracy and the rule of law"; emphases added.

[16] However, this cannot be taken as a reason against including future MS, given the dynamic interpretation of EU law by the CJEU.

[17] For a brief overview, albeit primarily from a Christian perspective, see Rauscher (2005).

[18] TEU, recital 2. Similar to what was mentioned before (notes 14 and 15), this is also a 'softer wording'.

[19] N.B. Besides all the other examples identified so far in this book.

[20] 'Culture' can also have in impact on the ethical spirit. However, since this influence is of a rather indirect nature, it will not be pursued further.

can be understood as "any philosophical perspective that assigns preeminent value to human beings, their experiences, their interests, and their rights",[21] "based on the freedom, responsibility, and rationality of human beings".[22] This goes hand in hand with the recitals of the preambles of the CFR, which "places the individual at the heart of [the Union's] activities",[23] as well as of the TEU, according to which "decisions are taken as closely as possible to the citizen".[24] Recently in the context of ethical challenges of robotics, the EP referred to the "intrinsically European and universal humanistic values that characterise Europe's contribution to society".[25]

The two references in the CFR ("spiritual and moral heritage") and in the TEU ("cultural, *religious* and humanist *inheritance*")[26] require a few words on the relationship between EU law and religion. When the European Convention drafted the CFR, there were 'highly emotional disputes'[27] concerning a possible reference to God (*invocatio dei*), respectively a reference to (one or more) religion(s).[28] These have finally been solved by deviating language versions referring to the already mentioned 'spiritual and moral heritage', whereas only the German version refers to religion and none of them to 'God'.[29] Therefore, on the one hand, the reference to the 'spiritual and moral heritage' can neither be seen as a commitment to a single religion (for example, Christianity), nor to several religions (such as, Christianity, Judaism, while excluding Islam); on the other hand, also atheists and agnostics should be seen as bearers of this heritage.[30]

'Time is a great healer', and this heated dispute was finally 'resolved' years later with the amendments brought by the Lisbon Treaty, as the second recital of the TEU refers to the inspiration, drawn "from the cultural, religious and humanist inheritance of Europe". A similar analysis applies with regard to humanism. As mentioned above,[31] a reference to humanism in an earlier draft[32] in the end has not made it into the preamble of the CFR, and now figures in this (second) recital of the TEU.

We have already seen another similarity between religion and humanism in the Polish GMO case mentioned above, where Poland had argued with "Christian and Humanist ethical principles", opening the door for intriguing questions of the rela-

---

21 Steelwater (2012, p. 674); see also *supra* Sect. 1.5, at note 108.

22 Radest (2002, p. 411).

23 CFR, recital 2.

24 TEU, recital 13.

25 EP resolution robotics, recital U.

26 Emphases added.

27 Meyer (2014, p. 70).

28 Schmitz (2005, 86), refers to the influence of French laicism and to the distance of many European citizens from church and religion.

29 For further details, see Meyer (2014, pp. 70–73).

30 Meyer (2014, p. 71).

31 *Supra* Sect. 1.5, at note 109.

32 CONV 722/03 of 28 May 2003, p. 2.

tionship of EU law and religion, as well as humanism.[33] However, since Poland did not fulfil its burden of proof, there was no room for the CFEU to make any statement in this regard; however, against the background of the principle of judicial restraint, one had not much to hope for in terms of content anyway.

The reserved relationship of EU law and religion is somehow also confirmed by some Eurobarometer surveys. During the last years, peace, respect for human life and human rights have constantly been ranked top in terms of personal values of Europeans, and peace, human rights and democracy in terms of values representing the EU (see Fig. 5.1), while religion has been constantly ranked very low in both categories.[34]

Nonetheless, it would be wrong to state that there is no influence of religion for our quest for the 'ethical spirit of EU law'. Moyn has convincingly argued that "religious constitutionalism" had some influence and inspired the concept of dignity.[35] To make a long story short, religion has had an influence on the understanding of 'human dignity', which plays a key role for the 'ethical spirit of EU law'.[36] In summary, one can speak of an indirect influence of religion on the ethics of the EU.

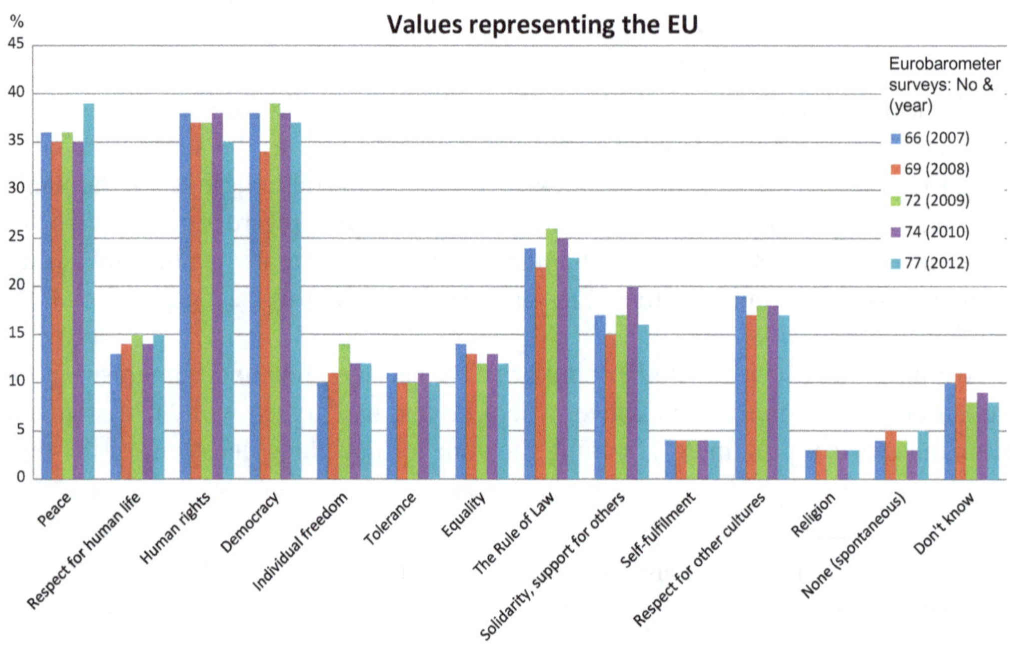

Fig. 5.1 Eurobarometer surveys on EU values [*Source* Eurobarometer 77 (2012), pp. 9 and 12; Eurobarometer 74 (2010), pp. 32 and 33; Eurobarometer 72 (2009), Vol. 2, pp. 148 and 152; Eurobarometer 69 (2008), 1. Values of Europeans, pp. 15 and 22; Eurobarometer 66 (2007), p. 28]

---

[33] *Supra* Sect. 3.3.1.1, at note 149.

[34] On the ranking of values, see Hermerén (2006).

[35] Moyn (2012, 2014).

[36] As stated already several times, and as further outlined in Sect. 5.3.

Referring to the EU integration process in its entirety, the four references to the "ever closer union"[37] can also be applied to the 'ethical spirit of EU law' in the sense of a steadily developing concept, a 'spirit *in statu nascendi*', so to speak.[38] According to Meyer, the ideal picture of a draft for the future is also associated with an 'ethical claim'.[39] This evolutionary aspect goes hand in hand with the above comments on the *Schuman* declaration.

Several times throughout this book, we have seen examples of ethics comprising not only rights, but also duties.[40] According to Meyer, although there were concerns about 'basic obligations' in totalitarian regimes, the Convention did not want to completely ignore the idea of an 'asymmetric guarantee of connection' to fundamental rights, not least because of classical philosophical guidelines.[41] This finally resulted in the following recital of the CFR preamble: "Enjoyment of these rights entails *responsibilities* and duties with regard to other *persons*, to the *human community* and to *future generations*."[42] The distinction between ethical and legal obligations is likely to echo in the pair of concepts of responsibilities and duties, where ethical obligations may arise both in relation to fellow human beings and to human society, and in relation to future generations.[43]

Values and human dignity have already been addressed several times. To finish with the guidance provided by the preambles of the TEU and the CFR with regard to the ethical spirit of EU law, the CFR addresses the "peaceful future *based on* common values" as well as "the indivisible, universal values of human dignity, freedom, equality and solidarity", on which "the Union is *founded*".[44] The TEU preamble refers to the inspiration, drawn "from the cultural, religious and humanist inheritance of Europe, from which have developed the *universal values* of the inviolable and inalienable rights of the human person, freedom, democracy, equality and the rule of law".[45] This leads us to human dignity in the next chapter, as well as to the other values in the subsequent one.

---

[37] TEU, recital 13; Art 1(2) TEU; TFEU, recital 1; CFR, recital 1. The counterpart to this is the respect of the national identities of MS; Art 4(2) TEU.

[38] Similar to the debates in the CFR Convention on religion, this concept of 'ever closer union' is also a partly controversial issue, as the EU offer (of 18 and 19 February 2016) to the UK before the Brexit referendum (of 23 June 2016) shows; 'A New Settlement for the United Kingdom within the European Union', OJ 2016 CI 69/1. On the concept of respect for national identities, see *infra* note 100.

[39] Meyer (2014, p. 49).

[40] *Supra* Sect. 3.2.1, note 74, (moral obligation to assist ACP countries), Sect. 4.2.2, notes 136 (with regard to EGE opinion No 24, p. 52) and 145 (for the definition of human dignity by William P. Cheshire).

[41] Meyer (2014, p. 88).

[42] CFR, recital 6; emphases added.

[43] Meyer (2014, p. 89).

[44] CFR, recitals 1 and 2; emphases added.

[45] TEU, recital 2.

5.3 Human Dignity

> Regardless of whether one sees the origin of human dignity in the Christian emphasis on the image of man as God or in a mixture of ancient and humanistic traditions and the Enlightenment, it is a central theme in the European philosophy and history of law.[46]
>
> All in all, human dignity has its roots deep in the origins of a conception of mankind in European culture that regards man as an entity capable of spontaneity and self-determination. Because of his ability to forge his own free will, he is a person (subject) and must not be downgraded to a thing or object.[47]

Despite its paramount role today, it is remarkable that human dignity[48] was not initially part of the ECHR, signed on 4 November 1950.[49] Human dignity entered the Council of Europe sphere with the Oviedo convention, and it was only in 2002 that the ECtHR held that "[t]he very essence of the Convention is respect for human dignity and human freedom".[50,51] Also in France, the *Conseil Constitutionnel* first dealt with human dignity in the field of bioethics.[52] Likewise elsewhere in Europe, human dignity has also only slowly emerged as the supreme constitutional principle in the constitutions of the MS.[53] Besides the above-mentioned influence of religion,[54] also the German constitution as well as Roman Herzog, who chaired the European Convention elaborating the CFR (1999–2000), had some influence on our understanding of human dignity.[55]

Human dignity is not only the first value mentioned in Art 2 TEU, it is both the first title, as well as the first article of the CFR. According to Meyer, the CFR Convention refused to address human dignity as a value only in the preamble, thereby depriving it of the character of a fundamental right.[56] Consequently, human dignity can be seen as a value, as a human right,[57] as well as according to both the CFR explanations and the EGE,[58] as the basis for principles that are more specific, rights[59] and obligations.

---

[46]Meyer (2014, p. 73); translated with DeepL.

[47]AG Stix-Hackl *Omega*, C-36/02, para 78.

[48]See the various contributions in McCrudden (2014), as well as in Feuillet-Liger and Orfali (2018).

[49]For the UN-perspective, see e.g. AG Stix-Hackl *Omega*, C-36/02, para 82.

[50]ECtHR judgment of 29 April 2002, *Pretty vs. the United Kingdom*, 2346/02, para 65.

[51]Rensmann (2005, 58, 60).

[52]Rensmann (2005, 60).

[53]Rensmann (2005, 58).

[54]*Supra* note 35.

[55]Rensmann (2005, 58); for further details on the other MS see pp. 59–60.

[56]Meyer (2014, p. 53).

[57]As a human right, human dignity is both a 'defensive right' ("must be respected") and also entails a 'duty to protect' ("must be [...] protected"); Streinz (2018, no. 4).

[58]*Supra* Sect. 4.3.

[59]"Human dignity, as a fundamental expression of an element of mankind founded simply on humanity, forms the underlying basis and starting point for all human rights distinguishable from it [...]"; AG Stix-Hackl *Omega*, C-36/02, para 76.

This is why human dignity has been referred to as the corner stone[60] of both the CFR and the values.

However, as accentuated by Di Fabio, in law, human dignity must also be respected in its non-legal meaning.[61] This is in line with the statement of the EGE, according to which "[t]he respect of the dignity of the human person is at the *root* of the *ethics* of science and new technologies *as well as of human rights*".[62] In a resolution 1.5 years before the mandate of the GAEIB expired, the EP emphasized, "that it is essential to establish ethical standards, based on respect for human dignity".[63] Human dignity as the bridge between the two disciplines of law and practical philosophy, so to speak.[64]

As we have already seen especially with regard to EGE opinions, human dignity predominantly has this notion of treating human beings as subjects, not merely as objects.[65] Also in literature, human dignity is usually explained with reference to Immanuel Kant.[66] As Dickson and Eleftheriadis highlighted, "in a way, Kant's theory is a predecessor to that of Rawls and a predecessor to some relevant contemporary views of the European Union".[67] This Kantian notion of human dignity can be exemplified by the following current[68] example. In a recent resolution on integrity in sports, the EP pointed out that "athletes, in particular minors, face increasing economic pressures, and are treated as *commodities*, and have therefore to be protected against any form of abuse, violence or discrimination that may occur in the course of their participation in sport".[69] Although the Union, with its commitment to human dignity, which places the human person at the centre of its action, clearly sees itself as an anthropocentric order of values,[70] animals can also enjoy protection and respect due to their intrinsic value.

In summary, the legal lens confirms the importance of the corner stone of human dignity for the 'ethical spirit of EU law', just as we have already seen it from the philosophical lens.

---

[60]Frischhut (2015, p. 532).

[61]Di Fabio (2004, p. 5).

[62]European Group on Ethics in Science and New Technologies (2000, p. 11).

[63]EP resolution GAEIB, pt. 1.

[64]See also Frischhut (2015, p. 565).

[65]See also AG Stix-Hackl *Omega*, C-36/02, paras 77–78 and 94 on 'dwarf-tossing'.

[66]Cf. for instance: Borowsky (2014, p. 96), Müller-Graff (2017, 47).

[67]Dickson and Eleftheriadis (2012, pp. 12–13).

[68]For an older example see: EP resolution on compulsory gynaecological examinations at the Dutch-German border, OJ 1991 C 106/113; N.B: on suspicion of having had an abortion in the Netherlands. On Kant, see *supra* Sect. 2.1.

[69]EP resolution sport and integrity; emphasis added.

[70]Rensmann (2005, 61).

5.4 EU Values (Continued) and Human Rights

Does this also hold true for the other common values of the EU and for human rights,[71] do they also contribute to the lattice forming the 'ethical spirit'? The increasing role of human rights, culminating in the now legally binding CFR, corresponds to the before mentioned anthropocentric view and humanism.

As also reflected in the CJEU's case-law, values can entail not only rights, but also obligations: They can also result in negative consequences, as in the following example. This was about a Dutch decision declaring a foreigner to be an "undesirable immigrant", where "a disposition hostile to the fundamental values enshrined in Articles 2 and 3 TEU, such as human dignity and human rights", can be qualified as being against 'public policy'.[72,73]

If we turn to this concept of 'values', it is necessary to differentiate, as values can have an ethical, political, legal, artistic and economic connotation, though the latter two are not discussed any further.

From a social science point of view, according to Di Fabio "values are the basic attitudes of people who stand out due to their special firmness, conviction of correctness and emotional foundation". He continues as follows: "values appear like relics from a past epoch, they have not yet taken part in the disenchantment and rationalization of the modern world, they stand between 'is' and 'ought', they act normatively, but are subject to change through social factuality".[74] The latter statement corresponds with the evolutionary aspect of the 'ethical spirit'.

Values in the sense of political science ('*Staatswissenschaften*') are "guiding ideas for the activities of political institutions based on political-philosophical value judgements. Every political community needs a bundle of guiding ideas, to which its basic order is oriented. Two types of guiding ideas can be distinguished, namely values (value-based guiding ideas) and other (in themselves value-neutral) guiding ideas."[75]

Finally, from the legal point of view, "values describe goods that a legal system recognises as given or abandoned".[76] In this context, values may serve as interpretive guidelines as well as standards of norm control, and unfold a legitimatory meaning.[77] The challenge is the determination of the content, as values are indeterminate, multi-layered, subjective, contextual, and culturally shaped.[78] As mentioned earlier,[79] values are more abstract than principles, as the former lack specific lim-

---

[71] Although officially coined 'fundamental rights', most of the CFR rights apply to all 'humans', 'persons', 'everyone', etc.

[72] For this notion, see *supra* Sect. 3.3.1.1, at note 146.

[73] CJEU judgment of 2 May 2018, *K*, joined cases C-331/16 and C-366/16, EU:C:2018:296, para 60.

[74] Di Fabio (2004, p. 3); translated with DeepL.

[75] Schmitz (2005, 80); translated with DeepL; emphases in the original.

[76] Reimer (2003, p. 209); translated with DeepL.

[77] Calliess (2004, p. 1034).

[78] See Footnote 77.

[79] *Supra* Sect. 1.5, at note 99.

itations, in particular with regard to specific legal consequences and addressees.[80] The lack of these limitations contrasts values from state objectives (principles) or fundamental rights (subjective rights).[81] With regard to the German Basic Law, the Federal Constitutional Court has stated that the Basic Law is not a value-neutral order and that its value order expresses a fundamental strengthening of the validity of fundamental rights.[82]

According to Walter Hallstein, certain values have been part of the integration process, even before the Lisbon Treaty has officially enshrined them in Art 2 TEU.[83] The EU has transformed itself from, an 'association of functional integration' ('*Zweckverband funktioneller Integration*'[84]), as Hans Peter Ipsen coined it, into a political union (Maastricht Treaty), that also respects human rights (CFR, etc.), and finally into a 'community of values'.[85,86] The key word for this metamorphosis is 'homogeneity'. Homogeneity demands, "a supranational Union and its Member States must have the same basic political and philosophical orientation", where this "requirement of homogeneity of value systems is already known from another federal organizational form, namely the federal state".[87] However, homogeneity of value orders does not mean uniformity of value orders, "homogeneity means affinity of essence, not equality of essence, congruence in essential points, not total congruence".[88] Applying this concept of homogeneity to EU integration means that the Union must also implement the common fundamental values; however, it can do so "in its own specific way".[89] "This is part of the development of the Union's own identity, which must be more than a mere mirror of the identity of the Member States", where an important step was the development of a separate catalogue of fundamental rights.[90]

---

[80]Reimer (2003, p. 209).

[81]See Footnote 77.

[82]BVerfG judgment of 15 January 1958, *Lüth*, 1 BvR 400/51, BVerfGE 7, 198, para 25; see also Di Fabio (2004, pp. 1–2).

[83]Hallstein (1979, pp. 66–71): peace, uniformity, equality, freedom, solidarity, prosperity, progress and security (own translation).

[84]Ipsen (1972, pp. 196–200).

[85]On this notion, see *infra*.

[86]On the 'constitutional debate' see, for instance, Weiler (1999).

[87]Schmitz (2005, 81); translated with DeepL.

[88]Schmitz (2005, 82); and he continues: "Only the basic values that characterise the system must agree, but not the many simple values—be it in the laws or in the constitution—that go beyond them; these must only be compatible with the common basic values", translated with DeepL.

[89]Schmitz (2005, 82); translated with DeepL.

[90]See Footnote 89.

Nowadays, the EU's values have mainly been shaped and further enriched in its practical application by the CJEU.[91] For the EU's common[92] values, we have also seen a sector-specific approach also comprising distinct values, when looking at health, non-financial reporting, sports and digitalization.[93] There is a resemblance to ethics, where the CJEU clearly took a sector-specific approach, if we only compare the *Brüstle* and the *Mayr* case (fertilization vs. transfer into uterus).[94]

As part of the Court's 'judicial self-restraint', when dealing with the notion of 'public morality', the Court referred to national values.[95] However, the Court's statement in *Omega*[96] that there is no need for a consensus amongst all MS could be answered differently today, now having legally binding *common* values.[97] In other words, a more uniform rather than diverse approach from a vertical (EU vs. MS) perspective.

However, the Court will always be willing to recognise certain circumstances, which have a specific importance for a country, for example because of the historical context. This was the case in the following examples. For instance, the national value of human dignity in Germany,[98] due to the atrocities of the Nazi regime, falling under 'public policy'. The fight against the mafia as a specifically important principle of morality in Italy, which corresponds with the EU's values (see *infra*).[99] Finally, the 'Law on the abolition of the nobility', an element of national identity in the context of Austrian constitutional history, falling under 'public policy' as well as under Art 4(2) TEU (respect for the national identities of MS).[100] In the Italian case on EU trademark law, the GC has referred to EU values in the following way:

> The Court takes the view that such criminal activities breach the *very values* on which the European Union is *founded*, in particular the values of respect for *human dignity and freedom* as laid down in Article 2 TEU and Articles 2, 3 and 6 of the Charter of Fundamental Rights

---

[91] As the Court stated, "EU law is based on the fundamental premiss that each [MS] *shares* with all the other [MS], and *recognises* that they share with it, a set of common values on which the [EU] is *founded*, as stated in Article 2 TEU. That premiss implies and justifies the existence of *mutual trust* between the [MS] that those values will be recognised, and therefore that the EU law that implements them will be respected"; CJEU *LM*, C-216/18 PPU, para 35; emphases added.

[92] Recently it has been argued that "differentiation [in integration] should not be permissible when it comes to the respect of existing fundamental rights and values"; EP draft report of 2 August 2018 on differentiated integration (2018/2093(INI)), PE626.719v01-00, pt. 9.

[93] *Supra* Sect. 3.1.3.

[94] *Supra* Sect. 3.3.1.1, at note 128. Also Herrmann and Rowlandson have observed that "[a]t first glance it seems as if the role of ethics and morality in EU law does not hold any uniform legal significance"; Herrmann and Rowlandson (2008, p. 241).

[95] *Supra* Sect. 3.3.1.1, at note 101.

[96] *Supra* Sect. 3.3.1.1, at note 143.

[97] N.B. However, this would not change much for the *Omega* case as such, as we have seen that the German notion of human dignity very much corresponds with the EU counterpart.

[98] In Germany, human dignity is referred to as the 'fundamental constitutional principle' of human rights; AG Stix-Hackl *Omega*, C-36/02, para 76.

[99] GC *La Mafia Franchises*, T-1/17, para 36; see *supra* Sect. 3.3.1.2, at note 155.

[100] CJEU judgment of 22 December 2010, *Sayn-Wittgenstein*, C-208/09, EU:C:2010:806, paras 83, 84, 92.

> of the European Union. Those values are *indivisible* and make up the *spiritual and moral heritage* of the European Union.[101]

We have already seen various links between the EU's values (including human dignity), the legal lens so to speak, and the philosophical[102] one. According to Larenz, to 'judge' ('*werten*') is an inner invitation to comment with regard to a moral value, whereby not according to one's own highly personal values, but according to the general consciousness of values of a legal community.[103] These values have to be *objective*, correspond with a *general* mode of action and judgement and must be an *adequate* expression of this value requirement; in other terms, bad habits cannot be such a yardstick.[104] While in previous times, values have also been considered as non-legal concepts, which need to be imported into the legal sphere,[105] nowadays we have to accept that values do not only have a legal meaning, but also a philosophical one.[106] In other words, values stand between law and morality,[107] and in this way, they fulfil a bridge function.

As mentioned above, starting with a market for coal and steel, the EU finally also turned into a 'community of values'. According to Mandry, this notion, "on the one hand, describes the supranational European collectivity founded on common value convictions and a sense of belonging together, and on the other hand, the political-ethical quality of the political organization, namely the institutions and attitudes of the European Union."[108] As mentioned earlier, the notion of 'ethos' refers to the attitude, convictions, customs and behaviours of a person,[109] or even of an institution.[110] From an ethical perspective, the self-image as a 'community of values' can help to describe the 'ethos' of the EU.[111] From a social perspective, the 'community of values' is obviously an idea that is intended to express the 'identity' of the EU.[112] As Calliess rightly points out, the totality of values forms the value system of a society, which, according to social science, constructs identity over it.[113] Besides the more institutional angle of the 'community of values', what is most important are the expectations of citizens with regard to legitimate and 'good' political action.[114]

---

[101]GC *La Mafia Franchises*, T-1/17, para 36.

[102]On the notion of 'philosophy of values', see Berthold and Hügli (2004, pp. 611–614).

[103]Larenz (1960, p. 216).

[104]Larenz (1960, p. 219).

[105]Di Fabio (2004, p. 4), referring to older German case-law.

[106]Cf. e.g. Scheler (1916).

[107]Calliess (2004, p. 1034), with reference also to Di Fabio (2004, p. 3).

[108]Mandry (2009, p. 17); translated with DeepL.

[109]*Supra* Sect. 1.5, at note 89.

[110]*Supra* Sect. 1.5, at note 90.

[111]Mandry (2009, p. 99).

[112]See Footnote 111.

[113]Calliess (2004, p. 1034).

[114]See Footnote 111.

As we know, the 'community of values' has a threefold impact: on the EU, on the Member States and on citizens.[115] Focussing on the citizens, as the EP has recently emphasized, "European democracy needs a European identity, a genuinely European demos".[116] The question of whether and how a 'European identity' is further developed and strengthened, has to be differentiated from the question of how the 'community of values' affects the citizens, keeping in mind that they are closely connected. As mentioned earlier,[117] the first sentence of Art 2 TEU mentions the values the EU is founded on. This sentence affects all three 'stakeholders', the EU, the MS and the citizens. The second sentence mentions values that "are common to the Member States in a society", which is then further described by means of these values. These values are societal values, which also concern the relationship of private persons.[118] Already thirteen years ago, Rensmann argued that the metamorphosis of the EU into a 'community of values', which has been legally implemented for a long time, must still be understood by the citizens in order to become the basis for the development of a European consciousness, respectively EU identity.[119] To close the circle with the homogeneity mentioned above, "despite their feedback to national values, European values have their own independent content, which must be worked out."[120] Citizen participation will be of utmost importance for both the 'community of values', as well as for the 'ethical spirit'.

References

Berthold, J., & Hügli, A. (2004). Wertphilosophie. In J. Ritter, K. Gründer, & G. Gabriel (Eds.), *Historisches Wörterbuch der Philosophie: Band 12: W-Z* (pp. 611–614). Basel: Schwabe AG.

Borowsky, M. (2014). Titel I Würde des Menschen. In J. Meyer (Ed.), *Charta der Grundrechte der Europäischen Union* (4th ed., pp. 94–106). Baden-Baden: Nomos.

Calliess, C. (2004). Europa als Wertegemeinschaft: Integration und Identität durch europäisches Verfassungsrecht? *Juristenzeitung (JZ), 59,* 1033–1084.

Di Fabio, U. (2004). *Grundrechte als Werteordnung. Juristenzeitung (JZ), 59,* 1–8.

Dickson, J., & Eleftheriadis, P. (2012). Introduction: The puzzles of European Union law. In J. Dickson & P. Eleftheriadis (Eds.), *Philosophical foundations of law. Philosophical foundations of EU law* (pp. 1–22). Oxford: Oxford University Press.

European Commission. (2007). Public Opinion in the European Union. Eurobarometer 66.

European Commission. (2008). Values of Europeans. Eurobarometer 69.

European Commission. (2009). Public Opinion in the European Union. Vol. 2. Eurobarometer 72.

European Commission. (2010). Public Opinion in the European Union. Eurobarometer 74.

European Commission. (2012). The Values of Europeans. Eurobarometer 77.

---

[115] Calliess (2004, p. 1038).

[116] EP draft report of 19 July 2018 on State of the debate on the Future of Europe (2018/2094(INI)), PE625.528v01-00, pt. 21.

[117] *Supra* Sect. 3.1.3.

[118] Streinz et al. (2010, pp. 79–80).

[119] Rensmann (2005, 54).

[120] Calliess (2004, p. 1042).

European Group on Ethics in Science and New Technologies. (2000). Citizens rights and new technologies: A European challenge. Report of the European Group on Ethics in Science and New Technologies on the Charter on Fundamental Rights related to technological innovation as requested by President Prodi on February 3, 2000: CHARTE 4370/00 CONTRIB 233.

Feuillet-Liger, B., & Orfali, K. (Eds.). (2018). *The reality of human dignity in law and bioethics*. Cham: Springer.

Frischhut, M. (2015). "EU": Short for "Ethical" Union?: The role of ethics in European Union law. *Heidelberg Journal of International Law (HJIL), 75,* 531–577.

Hallstein, W. (1979). *Die Europäische Gemeinschaft* (5th ed.). Düsseldorf, Wien: Econ.

Hermerén, G. (2006). European values, ethics and law: Present policies and future challenges. *Jahrbuch Für Wissenschaft Und Ethik, 11,* 5–40.

Herrmann, J. R., & Rowlandson, M. (2008). The role of ethics and morality in EU law. *Journal of International Biotechnology Law, 5,* 241–251. https://doi.org/10.1515/JIBL.2008.39.

Ipsen, H. P. (1972). *Europäisches Gemeinschaftsrecht*. Tübingen: Mohr.

Larenz, K. (1960). *Methodenlehre der Rechtswissenschaft*. Berlin, Göttingen, Heidelberg: Springer.

Mandry, C. (2009). *Europa als Wertegemeinschaft: Eine theologisch-ethische Studie zum politischen Selbstverständnis der Europäischen Union. Denkart Europa: Vol. 9*. Baden-Baden: Nomos.

McCrudden, C. (Ed.). (2014). *Understanding human dignity*. Oxford: Oxford University Press.

Meyer, J. (2014). Präambel. In J. Meyer (Ed.), *Charta der Grundrechte der Europäischen Union* (4th ed., pp. 43–93). Baden-Baden: Nomos.

Moyn, S. (2012). The secret history of constitutional dignity. Retrieved from http://papers.ssrn.com/sol3/papers.cfm?abstract_id=2159248.

Moyn, S. (2014). The secret history of constitutional dignity. In C. McCrudden (Ed.), *Understanding Human Dignity* (pp. 95–111). Oxford: Oxford University Press.

Müller-Graff, P.-C. (2017). A. Verfassungsordnung der Europäischen Union: I. Verfassungsziele der Europäischen Union. In M. A. Dauses & M. Ludwigs (Eds.), *Handbuch des EU-Wirtschaftsrechts: Band 1* (pp. 1–76). München: C.H. Beck.

Radest, H. B. (2002). Humanism. In J. K. Roth (Ed.), *International encyclopedia of ethics* (pp. 411–412). London, Chicago, Illinois: Fitzroy Dearborn.

Rauscher, A. (2005). Die christlichen Wurzeln der Europäischen Einigung. In D. Blumenwitz, G.-H. Gornig, & D. Murswiek (Eds.), *Die Europäische Union als Wertegemeinschaft* (pp. 19–27). Berlin: Duncker & Humblot.

Reimer, F. (2003). Wertegemeinschaft durch Wertenormierung?: Die Grundwerteklausel im europäischen Verfassungsvertrag. *Zeitschrift Für Gesetzgebung*, 208–217.

Rensmann, T. (2005). Grundwerte im Prozeß der europäischen Konstitutionalisierung: Anmerkung zur Europäischen Union als Wertegemeinschaft aus juristischer Perspektive. In D. Blumenwitz, G.-H. Gornig, & D. Murswiek (Eds.), *Die Europäische Union als Wertegemeinschaft* (pp. 49–72). Berlin: Duncker & Humblot.

Scheler, M. (1916). *Der Formalismus in der Ethik und die materiale Wertethik: Neuer Versuch der Grundlegung eines ethischen Personalismus*. Sonderdruck aus: „Jahrbuch für Philosophie und phänomenologische Forschung", Bd. I und II, herausgegeben von EDMUND HUSSERL, Freiburg i. Br. Halle a. d. Saale: Verlag von Max Niemeyer.

Schmitz, T. (2005). Die Charta der Grundrechte der Europäischen Union als Konkretisierung der gemeinsamen europäischen Werte. In D. Blumenwitz, G.-H. Gornig, & D. Murswiek (Eds.), *Die Europäische Union als Wertegemeinschaft* (pp. 73–97). Berlin: Duncker & Humblot.

Schwabe, K. (2016). *Jean Monnet: Frankreich, die Deutschen und die Einigung Europas*. Baden-Baden: Nomos.

Simon, D. (1998). *Le système juridique communautaire* (2e édition mise à jour). *Droit politique et théorique*. Paris: Presses universitaires de France.

Steelwater, E. (2012). Humanism. In R. F. Chadwick (Ed.), *Encyclopedia of applied ethics* (2nd ed., pp. 674–682). London: Academic Press.

Streinz, R. (2018). Art. 1 EU-Grundrechte-Charta Würde des Menschen. In *EUV/AEUV: Vertrag über die Europäische Union, Vertrag über die Arbeitsweise der Europäischen Union, Charta der Grundrechte der Europäischen Union* (3rd ed.). München: C.H. Beck.

Streinz, R., Ohler, C., & Herrmann, C. (2010). *Der Vertrag von Lissabon zur Reform der EU: Einführung mit Synopse; [mit Lissabon-Entscheidung und Begleitgesetz]* (3. aktualisierte und erw. Aufl.). *Aktuelles Recht für die Praxis*. München: Beck.

Wahlberg, L. (2010). *Legal questions and scientific answers: Ontological differences and epistemic gaps in the assessment of causal relations*. Lund: Media-Tryck.

Wahlberg, L. (2017). Legal ontology, scientific expertise and the factual world. *Journal of Social Ontology, 3,* 49–65. https://doi.org/10.1515/jso-2015-0022.

Wahlberg, L., & Persson, J. (2017). Importing notions in health law: Science and proven experience. *European Journal of Health Law, 24,* 565–590. https://doi.org/10.1163/15718093-12453308.

Weiler, J. H. H. (1999). *The constitution of Europe: "Do the new clothes have an emperor?" and other essays on European integration*. Cambridge: University Press.

Chapter 6
Conclusion and Suggestions for Improvement

For decades, the Union's techno- and bureaucrats have successfully worked on a process of economic integration between countries, but in their paper mills they have overlooked the fact that unions between countries must also have a soul, an idea or an ideal that is above individual interests and in which everyone feels united.

Leon de Winter, *Wo steckt Europas Seele*? (de Winter 2004, p. 158; translated with DeepL.).

While so far, this book was clearly about the legal situation as it stands, I now want to conclude with some own suggestions for improvement. Much has already been written about the multiple crisis of the EU. However, even if these crises did not exist, it would be high time to further develop a new Union, which is 'inspired by an ethical spirit'. Without going into details, such a development has the advantage that it does not necessarily require an amendment of primary law,[1] which was the 'mission impossible' in all the crises the EU had to deal with recently.[2] There are good philosophical and legal arguments supporting this idea, but the pragmatic reasons might even prevail. Why should the European Union (EU) act and be perceived as an 'Ethical Union'?[3]

We can observe various gaps between the EU and the citizens, a geographic one (Brussels is further away than your municipality or your capital city), an emotional one (to some extent also due to the first point), and a content-related one (EU law often is very sophisticated, especially for citizens). That is why trust is of utmost importance

---

[1]Art 48 TEU.

[2]One idea which would not be a 'mission impossible' from a formal perspective (as there would be no necessity to change EU primary law), but in terms of the likelihood of its implementation, would be an 'ethical impact assessment'. Without going into details, combining the current role of the EGE and the impact assessment, as we know it today, this could be an EGE 2.0.

[3]This was the title of my paper (Frischhut 2015), which can be seen as the starting point of this bigger research project, which is part of this Jean Monnet Chair, entitled 'European integration & ethics'.

M. Frischhut, *The Ethical Spirit of EU Law*,
https://doi.org/10.1007/978-3-030-10582-2_6

even more important than at a nation state level. As the Court has recently held in a case on access to EU documents, "by increasing the legitimacy of the Commission's decision-making process, transparency ensures the credibility of that institution's action in the minds of citizens",[4] a statement, which holds true for to the EU as a whole. This quotation also corresponds with the moral entitlement of citizens as argued by Waldron.[5] However, this procedural component has to be accompanied by a substantive one, where the 'ethical spirit' of EU law plays a role for either perspective. While the author strongly rejects populism, the EU has to focus more on citizens and their concerns.[6] Otherwise, it risks failing, if it is perceived as the supporter of big companies, which can 'buy justice' or 'buy legislation'. Without going into details and, in a very simplified way, if we add the two perspectives of content and the way how it was perceived by the general public, the EU has clearly done a better job on 'roaming' and 'passenger's rights', than providing transparency in case of CETA,[7] or handling the issue of glyphosate. In the already mentioned report on the CFR,[8] the EGE has referred to the 'precautionary principle' as "the expression of prudence as a genuine ethical virtue".[9] To make a long story short, a true application of this principle[10] could also lead to a different outcome. Acting in the citizens' interest and not being open to unethical lobbying is one element of this 'ethical spirit', where the EU can demonstrate the added value of acting at EU level, for a single state realistically has no chance of overcoming these challenges. However, these statements should be seen as encouragement, knowing that much improvement has already happened and also having in mind the important work of the European Ombuds(wo)man.

Hence, the question is, what should this 'ethical spirit' look like? Well, for a big part, it already exists; in terms of all the opening clauses we have seen in EU law, through the EU's values, including human dignity, the EU's human rights, as well as the 'spiritual and moral heritage'. Tallacchini has argued that from the beginning, "ethics never embodied or related to any existing specific morality or moral philosophy".[11] This statement has been confirmed in the various analyses throughout this book. Although we have seen that from the three normative theories deontology

---

[4]CJEU judgment of 4 September 2018, *ClientEarth vs. Commission*, C-57/16 P, EU:C:2018:660, para 104.

[5]*Supra* Sect. 4.2.2, at note 157.

[6]In an open letter in the '*Frankfurter Allgemeine Zeitung*', Supiot et al. (2018) argue that "the EU can still be resuscitated by giving clear priority and safeguarding the ideals it proclaims over the economic and financial postulates that lead to its loss"; translated with DeepL. They refer to the three options (exit, voice or loyalty) available in times of a crises, as developed by Hirschman (1970).

[7]It seems that the Commission has clearly learned its lessons, if we nowadays look at the Brexit negotiations.

[8]*Supra* Sect. 4.2.1, note 112.

[9]European Group on Ethics in Science and New Technologies (2000, p. 10).

[10]Apart from the above-mentioned disclaimer (Sect. 1.5 note 92), one has to acknowledge the difficulties in establishing a common understanding in this regard; see e.g. Dratwa (2002).

[11]Tallacchini (2015, p. 157).

prevails, it would be wrong to attribute the EU's 'ethical spirit' exclusively to this one. Rather should we see this 'ethical spirit' as a lattice, not only linking various provisions of EU law that address ethics and morality in different ways, but also as a lattice of different input.[12]

In *Van Gend en Loos*, the Court has not only referred to the 'spirit' of (EU) law, it has also coined the term of the 'new legal order'.[13] In line with this ground-breaking statement, the 'ethical spirit' of EU law cannot be attributed to a certain pre-existing and worldwide uniform philosophical approach. Some might argue that it would be desirable if one could define the 'stone of the philosophers' (*lapis philosophorum*) in the sense of such a uniform normative theory.[14] However, one has to be so realistic that a theory of ethics is always relative to the current challenges of the time and the community we are living in.[15] This corresponds to the step-by-step approach inherent to the *Schuman* declaration.[16]

As mentioned above,[17] according to a particularistic moral understanding, the claim of morality can also be limited to the members of a certain group. This 'communitarianism' has been developed against the background of multiple crises,[18] emphasizing rights and responsibilities,[19] stressing the importance of shared common values and the 'common good', which requires that "we have to reason together about the meaning of the good life".[20] This idea goes hand in hand with the analysis of human dignity in the CFR, which according to Rensmann "does not only embrace man as a being isolated in his freedom, but also in his social integration".[21] Therefore, I argue that the 'ethical spirit of EU law' should also be seen from such a communitarian perspective. The limitation to the EU should not be understood in a way excluding others. Rather should it be seen as a rejection of a 'colonialist approach' and a rejection of the wish to develop a universally applicable system,

---

[12]On Montesquieu see *supra* Sect. 4.1 at note 5, and on CJEU *Achmea*, C-284/16, paras 33–34 (same chapter) at note 13.

[13]CJEU *Van Gend en Loos*, 26/62, p. 12; see also *supra* Sect. 1.2, notes 37–39 and 45.

[14]On Parfit (2011) see *supra* Chap. 2, note 1.

[15]As Sangiovanni (2008, p. 164) points out, "principles of justice therefore vary, at a fundamental level, with respect to the institutional context they are meant to regulate".

[16]Without the atrocities of World War II, human dignity would most likely not play the same role as it does today.

[17]Section 2.4.3.

[18]Hence, it seems perfectly suitable for the EU.

[19]Briefly to mention, that also CJEU *Van Gend en Loos*, 26/62, p. 12, addressed rights and obligations, the citizens as key stakeholders, as well as the 'legal heritage'.

[20]Sandel (2010, p. 261).

[21]Rensmann (2005, 61); translated with DeepL.

which would fit every community and culture,[22] worldwide and at any time.[23] This communitarian perspective entails the idea that we reason together about the 'good life', hence involving citizens. This comprises not only rights, but also obligations,[24] not only freedom, but also engaging in and for society.

Also the analysis of the preambles of the EU treaties point to a specific EU approach, as they do not refer to one of these three normative theories, but to the EU's 'spiritual and moral heritage'. Within this Jean Monnet chair, not only was the research on this book conducted, but it also included a course,[25] in which an exchange student from Asia provided the following valuable external perspective. This statement may sound banal, but it shows exactly what it is all about. Asked to write down what *should be* a value of the EU, he wrote, 'community'. While since the entry into force of the Lisbon Treaty, for reasons of linguistic accuracy EU lawyers tend only to refer to the Union, not to the Community any more,[26] this notion of 'community' better reflects how the EU, its members and its citizens should see themselves in it.

The 'ethical spirit' of EU law should not only be seen from and benefit from the idea of 'communitarianism'. In addition, 'principlism' ought to be embraced as well. Making this 'ethical spirit' more easily applicable to different challenges in different sectors,[27] we might need an approach as we have seen it in the context of lobbying. These principles (sometimes also virtues[28]) can translate abstract values into principles that are able to guide the individual to the 'right solution'. In a similar way as we have seen the general common values of the EU (Art 2 TEU) also specified to different fields,[29] we could think about both specific values for other fields, as well as developing further principles, linked to these general or specific values. Hence, values could be general (Art 2 TEU) or specific (e.g. sports), while these principles would mainly be specific. This does of course not mean that a principle like 'integrity'

---

[22]This does not mean that the author is not of the opinion that also other cultures could benefit from (parts of) this 'ethical spirit' and adopt it, as for instance other elements of the EU integration process have been adopted in other parts of the world. On the example of the CJEU and the Andean Community, see Frischhut (2003, pp. 209–301).

[23]Although it might be still relevant today, also the social contract theory was developed against the background of the emerging role of the state, and although it was highly developed, ancient Greek philosophy had no problem with slavery.

[24]In CJEU judgment of 7 February 1973, *Commission vs. Italy*, EU:C:1973:13, paras 24–25, the Court has emphasized "the equilibrium between advantages and obligations", which is an essential part of solidarity (now: one of the common values), where a failure in the duty of solidarity "strikes at the fundamental basis of the [EU] legal order".

[25]Available at: https://jeanmonnet.mci.edu/jean_monnet_mooc.

[26]See also the disclaimer in this book, *supra* Sect. 1.1, note 15.

[27]Besides this differentiation in different (horizontal) sectors, principles can also be differentiated from a vertical perspective in those mainly governing the relationship between the EU and the MS, and those mainly concerning the individuals (in relation to the EU, respectively the MS when applying, etc. EU law); for a similar approach, see Dickson and Eleftheriadis (2012, p. 14).

[28]As mentioned above (Sect. 1.5 note 107), principles and virtues can sometimes be difficult to define and overlap.

[29]*Supra* Sect. 3.1.3.

would not make sense in various sectors. This approach goes into a similar direction as a position called 'moral disunitarianism', "according to which moral generalities, to the extent that they exist, are at best domain-specific".[30]

While sometimes terminology might differ, this approach can go into a similar direction as primary and secondary principles, or in other terms: more abstract primary principles, and below that, more detailed secondary principles.[31] We have also seen that virtues might require principles,[32] and that the 2006 Council conclusions might serve as a role model, where "[b]eneath these overarching values, there is also a set of operating principles".[33]

Finally, the 'ethical spirit of EU law', which, as we have seen, is constantly developing, can also embrace some ideas of 'minimal ethics'. We have seen this approach in Art 6 Directive Biotech. Although it can be desirable to have a uniform approach, the step-by-step shift from diversity to more uniformity can simply require a pragmatic minimal approach (i.e. only to define the core, but not the periphery), which, in the future, might become more 'united'.

These ideas for an 'ethical spirit of EU law' can contribute to the statement that "unions between countries must also have a soul", as mentioned in the quote at the beginning of this chapter. It is important to emphasize that other approaches, for instance Williams arguing for a "new philosophy of EU law based on a theory of justice that is constitutionally enshrined" and "an institutional ethos that prioritizes fundamental values" can be complementary to this book.[34] Not only is justice a value of the EU, also citizens would highly value a more just EU.

As this book has summarized the research conducted with this Jean Monnet Chair 'European integration & ethics', kindly supported by the European Commission under Erasmus+, one funding requirement was to publish this book 'open access'. The author is thankful for this stimulus, as this 'ethical spirit' cannot be covered by one single book. In addition, every day, new documents can add up to this 'lattice'. That is why this open access book and hopefully other research will contribute to this "research agenda where I hope that others will contribute to this process".[35]

Finally, and for the sake of this debate, the book is summarized in the following 28[36] theses. This will include both the summary of the status quo identified so far, as well as the author's suggestions for improvement (high lightened by "I argue").

---

[30]Brännmark (2016, p. 481); see also Brännmark and Sahlin (2010), and the following quotation on medical ethics, which can be applied analogously to our topic: "what disunitarianism points to is a conception of medical ethics where morality, politics, and law are more strongly integrated"; Brännmark (2018, p. 10).

[31]*Supra* Sect. 2.2, at note 34.

[32]*Supra* Sect. 2.3, at note 57.

[33]*Supra* Sect. 3.1.3, at note 28.

[34]Williams (2009, p. 577).

[35]Taken from my paper "'EU': Short for 'Ethical Union'", Frischhut (2015, p. 577).

[36]28, because the author believes in #StrongerTogether.

1. Striving to identify the 'ethical spirit' of EU law, the notion of spirit, I argue, shall be understood as "the intention of the authors of a legal system, which is reflected in a lattice of various different provisions".
2. We can observe an increasing role of ethics in EU law since the 1990s.
3. Not surprisingly, ethics in EU law plays a role above all, but not only, in sensitive areas.
4. In EU law, we can find both implicit (e.g. in case of rules on lobbying) as well as explicit references to ethics (and morality).
5. There are various categories for the question, how the content of ethics (in case EU law refers to this non-legal concept) is determined. [1.] Ethics serving as a mere 'protection shield' (not a very ambitious approach, indeed), [2.] ethics as a supportive argument, or a [3.] parallel ethical and legal assessment. Often ethics is determined by [4.] an ethics committee or via [5.] a code of conduct, in either category either at EU and/or at national level, via [6.] references to other (international) documents (e.g. Helsinki declaration or Oviedo convention), or [7.] further information provided in the relevant EU document itself. Finally, there is also one category [8.], where ethics remains undetermined.[37]
6. In case of implementation of EU directives, which refer to ethics and morality, in the MS, we cannot observe a uniform 'ethicalization' in the nine countries covered, rather can we observe countries with comparable legal traditions displaying similar results.
7. The CJEU applies a judicial self-restraint when being confronted with cases involving ethical implications, thus leaving more discretion to the MS.[38]
8. The limitations to this national discretion are the prohibition of double morality and the requirements of coherence and legislative transparency, or in others terms, a reduced (or 'procedural') proportionality review.
9. Based on the vertical distribution of competences in the EU, one can assume in case of doubt that the legal competence also includes the competence for ethical questions. The just mentioned limitations also apply here.
10. The corner stone of human dignity and the other values, I argue, can be seen as a bridge between the legal and the philosophical 'world'.
11. For various reasons, it cannot be argued that religion should play a direct role in determining the content especially of ethics and human dignity, but it clearly has had an indirect impact in shaping our understanding of human dignity.
12. References to all three normative theories, I argue, also support the claim for a distinct 'ethical spirit of EU law'.
13. These references to ethics and morality cannot only be attributed to one, but to all three normative theories (deontology, consequentialism, virtue ethics),

[37]The author agrees to the feedback of Karl Harald Søvig (University of Bergen | Faculty of Law) that law should be more concrete (the argument of legal certainty), when referring to ethics.

[38]While harmonisation in some areas might be desirable, it can be difficult to achieve, especially because of different historical, political, religious traditions, different economical and/or technical development. The author would like to thank Göran Hermerén for valuable feedback in this regard.

where deontology clearly prevailed. However, this does not mean that the other two do (and shall) not play an important role.

14. The references to these normative theories do not follow a common horizontal, but rather a sector-specific approach.
15. These references from the legal sphere to non-legal concepts, I argue, should only be understood as pointing towards certain philosophical theories, not as unconditional reference.
16. A distinct question addresses the way, how these normative theories and other philosophical concepts (as non-legal concepts) shall be imported in the legal sphere. Here I argue that they have to be imported in a relative way, as they need to be reflected in EU law itself (i.e. a relative approach), and not be imported in an unaltered way (i.e. absolute approach); hence, the same approach as it has been argued for references of law to natural science.
17. The references to the "cultural, religious and humanist inheritance of Europe", human dignity and human rights clearly point to an anthropocentric view, while we can also find examples for a bio-centric attitude, emphasizing the intrinsic value of animals.
18. The 'ethical spirit' of EU law identified in this book is '*in statu nascendi*', following a step-by-step approach comparable to the *Schuman* declaration, where future developments will also contribute to the lattice of this spirit, hopefully rendering it more uniform than diverse.
19. This 'ethical spirit', which hopefully contributes to adding a 'soul' to the EU, is important for various reasons, nowadays, however, most important to increase citizens' trust in the EU.[39] In the external field, the EU could thus serve as a 'shining torch' for other countries or organisations.[40]
20. In this context, I argue, it is also important to involve citizens and other stakeholders. However, if citizens are engaged (i.e. citizen participation) and 'have a talk', then this input should be taken into account as far as possible ('walk the talk').[41]
21. This 'ethical spirit' as well as the 'community of values' hopefully contribute to the emergence of an EU identity.
22. The gap that still exists in between this lattice, but equally other references to ethics and morality, I argue, have to be filled by the EU's common values and the corner stone of human dignity, which play a predominant role.
23. The 'ethical spirit of EU law', I argue, should also be seen from a communitarian perspective, where communitarianism has been developed against the background of multiple crises, emphasizing rights and responsibilities, stressing the importance of shared common values and the 'common good', which requires to reason together about the meaning of the good life.
24. Likewise, being a community could also be seen as a value, as long as it is not used simply to exclude others.

---

[39] It is a different question, but such an ethical spirit will hopefully also lead to ethical laws.

[40] The author would like to thank Dean Harris for valuable feedback in this regard.

[41] See Frischhut (2015, p. 574).

25. The 'ethical spirit of EU law', I argue, should also embrace principlism, as different principles might render abstract values more easily applicable to different challenges in different sectors.[42]
26. The 'ethical spirit of EU law', I argue, should also encompass ideas of minimal ethics, especially if this is the only possible way of moving step-by-step from a temporarily diverse, to a more uniform approach in the future.
27. Other approaches, for instance arguing for a "new philosophy of EU law based on a theory of justice that is constitutionally enshrined" and "an institutional ethos that prioritizes fundamental values" (Williams), can be seen to be complementary to this book.
28. Finally, I argue that this 'ethical spirit' should equally apply if there are no references in EU law to ethics or morality.

References

Brännmark, J. (2016). Moral disunitarianism. *The Philosophical Quarterly, 66,* 481–499. https://doi.org/10.1093/pq/pqv114.

Brännmark, J. (2018). The independence of medical ethics. *Medicine, Health Care, and Philosophy.* Advance online publication. https://doi.org/10.1007/s11019-018-9842-1.

Brännmark, J., & Sahlin, N.-E. (2010). Ethical theory and the philosophy of risk: First thoughts. *Journal of Risk Research, 13,* 149–161. https://doi.org/10.1080/13669870903126192.

de Winter, L. (2004). Wo steckt Europas Seele? *Der Spiegel*, pp. 152–158.

Dickson, J., & Eleftheriadis, P. (2012). Introduction: The Puzzles of European Union Law. In J. Dickson & P. Eleftheriadis (Eds.), *Philosophical foundations of law. Philosophical foundations of EU law* (pp. 1–22). Oxford: Oxford University Press.

Dratwa, J. (2002). Taking risks with the precautionary principle: Food (and the environment) for thought at the European Commission. *Journal of Environmental Policy & Planning, 4,* 197–213. https://doi.org/10.1002/jepp.110.

European Group on Ethics in Science and New Technologies. (2000). *Citizens rights and new technologies: A European challenge*. Report of the European Group on Ethics in Science and New Technologies on the Charter on Fundamental Rights related to technological innovation as requested by President Prodi on February 3, 2000: CHARTE 4370/00 CONTRIB 233.

Frischhut, M. (2003). *Die Rolle der Judikative in der Ausformung der Verbandsgewalt supranationaler Organisationen: EuGH, Andengerichtshof, Supreme Court und Conseil Constitutionnel im Vergleich*. Frankfurt am Main: Peter Lang.

Frischhut, M. (2015). "EU": Short for "Ethical" Union?: The role of ethics in European Union Law. *Heidelberg Journal of International Law (HJIL), 75,* 531–577.

Hirschman, A. O. (1970). *Exit, voice and loyalty: Responses to decline in firms, organizations, and states* (6. printing). Cambridge, Massachusetts, London, England: Harvard University Press.

Parfit, D. (2011). *On what matters. The Berkeley Tanner lectures*. Oxford: Oxford University Press.

[42]The author would like to thank Winfried Löffler (University of Innsbruck | Department of Christian Philosophy) for pointing out the following. While the three normative theories mentioned so far are intended to answer the general question of the nature of good actions, principlism and minimal ethics are attempts to offer an ethical tool that can also be applied to 'mere practitioners' beyond difficult fundamental debates. In addition, for various reasons, it can be challenging to apply the concept of principlism beyond medical ethics. There will clearly be a need for further debate here.

Rensmann, T. (2005). Grundwerte im Prozeß der europäischen Konstitutionalisierung: Anmerkung zur Europäischen Union als Wertegemeinschaft aus juristischer Perspektive. In D. Blumenwitz, G.-H. Gornig, & D. Murswiek (Eds.), *Die Europäische Union als Wertegemeinschaft* (pp. 49–72). Berlin: Duncker & Humblot.

Sandel, M. J. (2010). *Justice: What's the right thing to do?*. New York: Farrar, Straus and Giroux.

Sangiovanni, A. (2008). Justice and the priority of politics to morality. *Journal of Political Philosophy, 16,* 137–164. https://doi.org/10.1111/j.1467-9760.2007.00291.x.

Supiot, A., Mückenberger, U., Allamprese, A., Boruta, I., Casas Baamonde, M. E., Deliyanni Dimitrakou, C., … Triomphe, C.-E. (2018, September 23). Gastbeitrag: Die EU muss neu gegründet werden. *Frankfurter Allgemeine Zeitung*.

Tallacchini, M. (2015). To bind or not bind?: European ethics as soft law. In S. Hilgartner, C. A. Miller, & R. Hagendijk (Eds.), *Genetics and society. Science and Democracy: Making knowledge and making power in the biosciences and beyond* (pp. 156–175). New York: Routledge, Taylor & Francis Group.

Williams, A. T. (2009). Taking values seriously: Towards a philosophy of EU law. *Oxford Journal of Legal Studies, 29,* 549–577. https://doi.org/10.1093/ojls/gqp017.

Appendix

Case-Law (Clustered According to Relevant Court etc., then in Chronological Order)

CJEU judgment of 5 February 1963, *Van Gend en Loos*, 26/62, EU:C:1963:1
CJEU judgment of 7 February 1973, *Commission vs. Italy*, EU:C:1973:13
CJEU judgment of 14 December 1979, *Henn and Darby*, C-34/79, EU:C:1979:295
CJEU judgment of 12 November 1981, *Meridionale Industria Salumi*, 212 to 217/80, EU:C:1981:270
CJEU judgment of 11 March 1986, *Conegate*, 121/85, EU:C:1986:114
CJEU judgment of 4 October 1991, *Society for the Protection of Unborn Children [SPUC]*, C-159/90, EU:C:1991:378
CJEU judgment of 24 March 1994, *Schindler*, C-275/92, EU:C:1994:119
CJEU judgment of 5 December 1996, *Merck*, C-267/95, EU:C:1996:468
CJEU judgment of 12 July 2001, *Smits and Peerbooms*, C-157/99, EU:C:2001:404
CJEU judgment of 9 October 2001, *Netherlands vs. EP and Council*, C-377/98, EU:C:2001:523
CJEU judgment of 20 November 2001, *Jany*, C-268/99, EU:C:2001:616
CJEU judgment of 14 October 2004, *Omega*, C-36/02, EU:C:2004:614
CJEU judgment of 18 July 2006, *Meca-Medina*, C-519/04 P, EU:C:2006:492
CJEU judgment of 6 March 2007, *Placanica*, joined cases C-338/04, C-359/04 and C-360/04, EU:C:2007:133
CJEU judgment of 14 February 2008, *Dynamic Medien*, C-244/06, EU:C:2008:85
CJEU judgment of 26 February 2008, *Mayr*, C-506/06, EU:C:2008:119
CJEU judgment of 16 July 2009, *Commission vs. Poland (GMOs)*, C-165/08, EU:C:2009:473
CJEU judgment of 8 September 2009, *Liga Portuguesa*, C-42/07, EU:C:2009:519
CJEU judgment of 9 November 2010, *Schecke*, C-92/09, EU:C:2010:662
CJEU judgment of 22 December 2010, *Sayn-Wittgenstein*, C-208/09, EU:C:2010:806
CJEU judgment of 18 October 2011, *Brüstle*, C-34/10, EU:C:2011:669
CJEU judgment of 21 December 2011, *N. S.*, C-411/10 and C-493/10, EU:C:2011:865
CJEU judgment of 18 March 2014, *D*, C-167/12, EU:C:2014:169
CJEU judgment of 18 March 2014, *Z*, C-363/12, EU:C:2014:159
CJEU judgment of 18 December 2014, *International Stem Cell [ISC]*, C-364/13, EU:C:2014:2451
CJEU judgment of 27 February 2018, *Associação Sindical dos Juízes Portugueses*, C-64/16, EU:C:2018:117

M. Frischhut, *The Ethical Spirit of EU Law*,
https://doi.org/10.1007/978-3-030-10582-2

CJEU judgment of 6 March 2018, *Achmea*, C-284/16, EU:C:2018:158
CJEU judgment of 17 April 2018, *Egenberger*, C-414/16, EU:C:2018:257
CJEU judgment of 2 May 2018, *K*, joined cases C-331/16 and C-366/16, EU:C:2018:296
CJEU judgment of 5 June 2018, *Coman*, C-673/16, EU:C:2018:385
CJEU judgment of 25 July 2018, *LM*, C-216/18 PPU, EU:C:2018:586
CJEU judgment of 4 September 2018, *ClientEarth vs. Commission*, C-57/16 P, EU:C:2018:660
CJEU judgment of 11 September 2018, *IR*, C-68/17, EU:C:2018:696

AG Stix-Hackl opinion of 18 March 2004, *Omega*, C-36/02, EU:C:2004:162
AG Sharpston opinion of 30 September 2010, *Ruiz Zambrano*, C-34/09, EU:C:2010:560
AG Cruz Villalón opinion of 17 July 2014, *ISC*, C-364/13, EU:C:2014:2104
AG Kokott opinion of 17 July 2014, *UK vs. Council*, C-81/13, EU:C:2014:2114
GC judgment of 15 March 2018, *La Mafia Franchises*, T-1/17, EU:T:2018:146
GC judgment of 17 May 2018, *BASF Agro*, T-584/13, EU:T:2018:279
ECtHR judgment of 29 April 2002, *Pretty vs. the United Kingdom*, 2346/02
ECtHR judgment of 1 June 2010, *Gäfgen vs. Germany*, 22978/05
ECtHR judgment of 29 April 2014, *L.H. vs. Latvia*, 52019/07
Austrian Supreme Court judgment of 18 April 2012, *Prostitution not against public morals*, 3 Ob 45/12g
BVerfG judgment of 15 January 1958, *Lüth*, 1 BvR 400/51, BVerfGE 7, 198
BVerfG judgment from 15 February 2006, *Shooting down terror plane*, 1 BvR 357/05

EU Primary Law, etc. (in Chronological Order)

Treaty of Maastricht, signed 7 February 1992, OJ 1992 C 191/1
Treaty of Amsterdam, signed 2 October 1997, OJ 1997 C 340/1
Accession Treaty, signed 16 April 2003, OJ 2003 L 236/1
Treaty of Lisbon, signed 13 December 2007, OJ 2007 C 306/1
Treaty on European Union (TEU), OJ 2016 C 202/13 (consolidated version)
Treaty on the Functioning of the European Union (TFEU), OJ 2016 C 202/47 (consolidated version)
Charter of Fundamental Rights of the European Union (CFR), OJ 2000 C 364/1 (Nice, 7 December 2000), OJ 2007 C 303/1 (Strasbourg, 12 December 2007), OJ 2016 C 202/389 (consolidated version)

Directives and Regulation (in Alphabetical Order)

N.B. The following are acts of the European Parliament and of the Council of the EU, unless specifically stated otherwise.

Council Directive 2013/59/Euratom of 5 December 2013 laying down basic safety standards for protection against the dangers arising from exposure to ionising radiation […], OJ 2014 L 13/1, as corrected by OJ 2016 L 72/69 [Directive ionising radiation]
Council Directive (EU) 2017/159 of 19 December 2016 implementing the Agreement concerning the implementation of the Work in Fishing Convention, 2007 of the International Labour Organisation […], OJ 2017 L 25/12
Council Regulation No. 1 Determining the Languages to be Used by the European Economic Community, OJ 1958 P 17/385, as amended by OJ 2013 L 158/1

Council Regulation (EC) No. 440/2008 of 30 May 2008 laying down test methods pursuant to Regulation (EC) No. 1907/2006 on the Registration, Evaluation, Authorisation and Restriction of Chemicals (REACH), OJ 2008 L 142/1, as amended by OJ 2017 L 112/1

Council Regulation (EC) No. 1099/2009 of 24 September 2009 on the protection of animals at the time of killing, OJ 2009 L 303/1, as amended by OJ 2018 L 122/11

Council Regulation (Euratom) No. 1314/2013 of 16 December 2013 on the Research and Training Programme of the European Atomic Energy Community (2014–2018) complementing the Horizon 2020 Framework Programme for Research and Innovation, OJ 2013 L 347/948 [Regulation Horizon 2020 Euratom]

Council Regulation (EU) 2016/369 of 15 March 2016 on the provision of emergency support within the Union, OJ 2016 L 70/1

Directive 98/44/EC of 6 July 1998 on the legal protection of biotechnological inventions, OJ 1998 L 213/13 [Directive Biotech]

Directive 98/79/EC of 27 October 1998 on in vitro diagnostic medical devices, OJ 1998 L 331/1, repealed (as of 26.05.2022) by OJ 2017 L 117/176 (= Regulation in vitro medical devices) [Directive in vitro medical devices]

Directive 2001/18/EC of 12 March 2001 on the deliberate release into the environment of genetically modified organisms [...], OJ 2001 L 106/1, as amended by OJ 2018 L 67/30 [Directive GMOs]

Directive 2001/20/EC of 4 April 2001 on the approximation of the laws, regulations and administrative provisions of the MS relating to the implementation of good clinical practice in the conduct of clinical trials on medicinal products for human use, OJ 2001 L 121/34, as repealed by OJ 2014 L 158/1 (= Regulation clinical trials) [Directive clinical trials]

Directive 2001/83/EC of 6 November 2001 on the Community code relating to medicinal products for human use, OJ 2001 L 311/67, as amended by OJ 2017 L 238/44 [Directive medicinal products]

Directive 2004/23/EC of 31 March 2004 on setting standards of quality and safety for the donation, procurement, testing, processing, preservation, storage and distribution of human tissues and cells, OJ 2004 L 102/48, as amended by OJ 2009 L 188/14 [Directive tissues and cells]

Directive 2005/36/EC of 7 September 2005 on the recognition of professional qualifications, OJ 2005 L 255/22, as amended by OJ 2017 L 317/119 [Directive recognition qualifications]

Directive 2006/43/EC of 17 May 2006 on statutory audits of annual accounts and consolidated accounts [...], OJ 2006 L 157/87, as amended by OJ 2014 L 158/196 [Directive statutory audits]

Directive 2006/123/EC of 12 December 2006 on services in the internal market, OJ 2006 L 376/36 [Directive services]

Directive 2009/30/EC of 23 April 2009 [amending certain other directives], OJ 2009 L 140/88 [Directive greenhouse gas emissions]

Directive 2010/63/EU of 22 September 2010 on the protection of animals used for scientific purposes, OJ 2010 L 276/33 [Directive animals]

Directive 2011/24/EU of 9 March 2011 on the application of patients' rights in cross-border healthcare, OJ 2011 L 88/45, as amended by OJ 2013 L 353/8 [Directive patient mobility]

Directive 2011/93/EU of 13 December 2011 on combating the sexual abuse and sexual exploitation of children and child pornography [...], OJ 2011 L 335/1, as corrected by OJ 2012 L 18/7 [Directive combating abuse]

Directive 2012/29/EU of 25 October 2012 establishing minimum standards on the rights, support and protection of victims of crime, and replacing Council Framework Decision 2001/220/JHA, OJ 2012 L 315/57

Directive 2013/33/EU of 26 June 2013 laying down standards for the reception of applicants for international protection, OJ 2013 L 180/96

Directive 2014/59/EU of 15 May 2014 establishing a framework for the recovery and resolution of credit institutions and investment firms […], OJ 2014 L 173/190, as completed by OJ 2018 L 67/8

Directive 2014/95/EU amending Directive 2013/34/EU as regards disclosure of non-financial and diversity information by certain large undertakings and groups, OJ 2014 L 330/1

Directive (EU) 2015/2436 of 16 December 2015 to approximate the laws of the Member States relating to trade marks, OJ 2015 L 336/1, as corrected by OJ 2016 L 110/5

Directive (EU) 2016/97 of 20 January 2016 on insurance distribution (recast), OJ 2016 L 26/19, as amended by OJ 2018 L 76/28

Directive (EU) 2016/1629 of 14 September 2016 laying down technical requirements for inland waterway vessels […], OJ 2016 L 252/118, as amended by OJ 2018 L 174/15

Directive (EU) 2018/958 of 28 June 2018 on a proportionality test before adoption of new regulation of professions, OJ 2018 L 173/25

Regulation No. 31 (EEC), 11 (EAEC), laying down the Staff Regulations of Officials and the Conditions of Employment of Other Servants of the European Economic Community and the European Atomic Energy Community, OJ 1962 45/1385, as amended by OJ 2017 C 429/9 [Regulation staff]

Regulation (EC) No. 178/2002 of 28 January 2002 laying down the general principles and requirements of food law, establishing the European Food Safety Authority and laying down procedures in matters of food safety, OJ 2002 L 31/1, as amended by OJ 2017 L 117/1

Regulation (EC) No. 1829/2003 of 22 September 2003 on genetically modified food and feed, OJ 2003 L 268/1, as amended by OJ 2015 L 327/1 [Regulation GM food]

Regulation (EC) No. 1394/2007 of 13 November 2007 on advanced therapy medicinal products […], OJ 2007 L 324/121, as amended by OJ 2010 L 348/1 [Regulation advanced therapy]

Regulation (EU) No. 1169/2011 of 25 October 2011 on the provision of food information to consumers, OJ 2011 L 304/18, as amended by OJ 2015 L 327/1

Regulation (EU) No. 528/2012 of 22 May 2012 concerning the making available on the market and use of biocidal products, OJ 2012 L 167/1, as amended by OJ 2017 L 121/45

Regulation 346/2013/EU of 17 April 2013 on European Social Entrepreneurship Funds, OJ 2013 L 115/18, as amended by OJ 2017 L 293/1

Regulation (EU) No. 1290/2013 of 11 December 2013 laying down the rules for participation and dissemination in "Horizon 2020 - the Framework Programme for Research and Innovation (2014–2020)" […], OJ 2013 L 347/81, as amended by OJ 2014 L 174/14 [Regulation participation Horizon 2020]

Regulation (EU) No. 1291/2013 of 11 December 2013 establishing Horizon 2020—the Framework Programme for Research and Innovation (2014–2020) […], OJ 2013 L 347/104, as amended by OJ 2015 L 169/1 [Regulation establishing Horizon 2020]

Regulation (EU) No. 536/2014 of 16 April 2014 on clinical trials on medicinal products for human use […], OJ 2014 L 158/1, as complemented by OJ 2017 L 238/12 [Regulation clinical trials]

Regulation (EU) No. 537/2014 of 16 April 2014 on specific requirements regarding statutory audit of public-interest entities […], OJ 2014 L 158/77, as corrected by OJ 2014 L 170/66

Regulation (EU) 2015/478 of 11 March 2015 on common rules for imports, OJ 2015 L 83/16

Regulation (EU) 2015/1775 of 6 October 2015 amending Regulation (EC) No. 1007/2009 on trade in seal products […], OJ 2015 L 262/1 [Regulation seal products]

Regulation (EU) 2015/2283 of 25 November 2015 on novel foods […], OJ 2015 L 327/1 [Regulation novel foods]

Regulation (EU) 2016/679 of 27 April 2016 on the protection of natural persons with regard to the processing of personal data and on the free movement of such data […] (General Data Protection Regulation), OJ 2016 L 119/1, as corrected by OJ 2018 L 127/2 [Regulation GDP]

Regulation (EU) 2017/625 of 15 March 2017 on official controls and other official activities performed to ensure the application of food and feed law, rules on animal health and welfare, plant health and plant protection products […], OJ 2017 L 95/1, as corrected by OJ 2017 L 137/40

Regulation (EU) 2017/745 of 5 April 2017 on medical devices [...], OJ 2017 L 117/1 [Regulation medical devices]

Regulation (EU) 2017/746 of 5 April 2017 on in vitro diagnostic medical devices [...], OJ 2017 L 117/176 [Regulation in vitro medical devices]

Regulation (EU) 2017/1004 of 17 May 2017 on the establishment of a Union framework for the collection, management and use of data in the fisheries sector and support for scientific advice regarding the common fisheries policy [...], OJ 2017 L 157/1 [Regulation data fisheries]

Regulation (EU) 2017/821 of 17 May 2017 laying down supply chain due diligence obligations for Union importers of tin, tantalum and tungsten, their ores, and gold originating from conflict-affected and high-risk areas, OJ 2017 L 130/1 [Regulation supply chain]

Regulation (EU) 2017/1001 of 14 June 2017 on the European Union trade mark, OJ 2017 L 154/1

Regulation (EU, Euratom) 2018/1046 of 18 July 2018 on the financial rules applicable to the general budget of the Union, OJ 2018 L 193/1 [Regulation financial rules]

EC Regulation (EU) 2015/445 of 17 March 2015 amending Regulation (EU) No. 1178/2011 as regards technical requirements and administrative procedures related to civil aviation aircrew, OJ 2015 L 74/1

EC Regulation (EU) 2016/246 of 3 February 2016 amending Annex I to Regulation (EC) No. 794/2004 as regards the forms to be used for the notification of State aid in the agricultural and forestry sectors and in rural areas, OJ 2016 L 51/1

EC Regulation (EU) 2017/735 of 14 February 2017 amending, for the purpose of its adaptation to technical progress, the Annex to Regulation (EC) No. 440/2008 laying down test methods pursuant to Regulation (EC) No. 1907/2006 on the Registration, Evaluation, Authorisation and Restriction of Chemicals (REACH), OJ 2017 L 112/1

Other Legal Documents (in Alphabetical Order)

Agreement between the EP and the EC on the transparency register for organisations and self-employed individuals engaged in EU policy-making and policy implementation, OJ 2014 L 277/11 [Agreement transparency register]

Agreement establishing an Association between the EU and its MS, and Central America, OJ 2012 L 346/3, as amended by OJ 2015 L 196/59

Agreement on Port State Measures to Prevent, Deter and Eliminate Illegal, Unreported and Unregulated Fishing, OJ 2011 L 191/3

Agreement on the European Economic Area, OJ 1994 L1/3, as amended by OJ 2016 L 141/3

Association Agreement between the EU and the EAEC and their MS, and Georgia, OJ 2014 L 261/4, as amended by OJ 2018 L 140/107 [Agreement Georgia]

Association Agreement between the EU and the EAEC and their MS, and Moldova, OJ 2014 L 260/4, as amended by OJ 2018 L 176/21

Association Agreement between the EU and the European Atomic Energy Community [EAEC] and their MS, and Ukraine, OJ 2014 L 161/3, as amended by OJ 2018 L 188/17 [Agreement Ukraine]

CJEU Code of Conduct for Members and former Members of the Court of Justice of the European Union, OJ 2016 C 483/1

Comprehensive Economic and Trade Agreement (CETA) between Canada, and the EU and its MS, OJ 2017 L11/1 [CETA]

Conclusions of the Council [etc.] of 15 May 1992 on hereditary illnesses, OJ 1992 C 148/3

Conclusions of the Council [etc.] on promoting the common values of the EU through sport, OJ 2018 C 196/23

Convention for the protection of Human Rights and Dignity of the Human Being with regard to the Application of Biology and Medicine: Convention on Human Rights and Biomedicine (adopted 4 April 1997, entered into force 1 December 1999), ETS No. 164

Convention on the International Recovery of Child Support and Other Forms of Family Maintenance, OJ 2011 L 192/51

Council conclusions on common values and principles in European Union Health Systems, OJ 2006 C 146/1

Council conclusions on Health in the Digital Society—making progress in data-driven innovation in the field of health, OJ 2017 C 440/3

Council Decision (CFSP) 2016/1182 of 18 July 2016 concerning the Staff Regulations of the European Union Institute for Security Studies, OJ 2016 L 195/31

Council Decision (CFSP) 2016/51 of 18 January 2016 in support of the Biological and Toxin Weapons Convention (BTWC) in the framework of the EU Strategy against Proliferation of Weapons of Mass Destruction, OJ 2016 L 12/50

Council Decision (EU) 2017/955 of 29 May 2017 amending Decision 2008/376/EC on the adoption of the Research Programme of the Research Fund for Coal and Steel and on the multiannual technical guidelines for this programme, OJ 2017 L 144/17 [Council Decision Research Coal and Steel]

Council Decision 2008/210/EC of 18 February 2008 on the principles, priorities and conditions contained in the European Partnership with Albania [etc.], OJ 2008 L 80/1 [Council decision Albania]

Council Decision 2013/743/EU of 3 December 2013 establishing the specific programme implementing Horizon 2020—the Framework Programme for Research and Innovation (2014–2020) [...], OJ 2013 L 347/965, as corrected by OJ 2015 L 102/96

Council Recommendation 87/176/EEC of 9 February 1987 concerning tests relating to the placing on the market of proprietary medicinal products, OJ 1987 L 73/1 [Council Recommendation proprietary medicinal products]

Council Recommendation of 2 December 2003 on cancer screening, OJ 2003 L 327/34

Council Recommendation of 22 May 2018 on key competences for lifelong learning, OJ 2018 C 189/1

Council Resolution of 14 December 2000 on paediatric medicinal products, OJ 2001 C 17/1

Court of Auditors, Special Report No. 1/2000 on classical swine fever, together with the Commission's replies, OJ 2000 C 85/1

Decision (EU) 2015/433 (ECB/2014/59) of the European Central Bank of 17 December 2014 concerning the establishment of an Ethics Committee and its Rules of Procedure, OJ 2015 L 70/58

Decision (EU) 2016/456 (ECB/2016/3) of the European Central Bank of 4 March 2016 concerning the terms and conditions for European Anti-Fraud Office investigations of the European Central Bank, in relation to the prevention of fraud, corruption and any other illegal activities affecting the financial interests of the Union, OJ 2016 L 79/34

Decision (EU) 2017/1324 of 4 July 2017 on the participation of the Union in the Partnership for Research and Innovation in the Mediterranean Area (PRIMA) jointly undertaken by several Member States, OJ 2017 L 185/1

Decision 2012/235/EU (ECB/2012/6) of the European Central Bank of 29 March 2012 on the establishment of the TARGET2-Securities Board [...], OJ 2012 L 117/13, as amended by OJ 2017 L 199/24

Decision No. 2/92 of the ACP-EEC Committee of Ambassadors of 22 December 1992 laying down the Staff Regulations of the Technical Centre for Agricultural and Rural Cooperation under the Fourth ACP-EEC Convention, OJ 1993 L 53/33

Decision No. 3/90 of the ACP-EEC Council of Ministers of 29 March 1990 adopting the general regulations, general conditions and procedural rules on conciliation and arbitration for works, supply and service contracts financed by the European Development Fund (EDF) and concerning their application, OJ 1990 L 382/1

Decision of the Board of Governors of 12 May 2010 on the amendment of the Rules of Procedure of the European Investment Bank to reflect the entry into force of the Treaty of Lisbon and of the new Statute of the Bank, OJ 2011 L 266/1

Decision of the Board of Governors of 20 January 2016 on the Amendments to the Rules of Procedure of the EIB to reflect the Strengthening of the EIB Governance [2016/772], OJ 2016 L 127/55

EC 'A New EU Framework to Strengthen the Rule of Law', COM(2014) 158 final 11.3.2014

EC 'European governance—A white paper', COM(2001) 428 final, OJ 2001 C 287/1

EC 'On the precautionary principle', COM(2000) 1 final 2.2.2000

EC 'Promouvoir les conditions de la compétitivité des activités industrielles basées sur la biotechnologie dans la Communauté', SEC(91) 629 final 19.4.1991

EC amended proposal for a Directive on the legal protection of biotechnological inventions, COM (97)446 final 29.08.1997

EC *communication de M. le PRESIDENT, en accord avec M. BANGEMANN, M. FLYNN, Mme CRESSON, Mme BJERREGAARD, M. MONTI, M. FISCHLER et Mme BONINO: Création d'un groupe Européen d'éthique des sciences et des nouvelles technologies*, SEC(97) 2404 final 12.12.1997 [EGE mandate I 1997]

EC communication on the application, from 1 August 2013, of State aid rules to support measures in favour of banks in the context of the financial crisis ('Banking Communication'), OJ 2013 C 216/1

EC communication on the collection and use of expertise by the Commission: principles and guidelines—"Improving the knowledge base for better policies", COM(2002) 713 final 11.12.2002

EC decision (EU) 2016/835 of 25 May 2016 on the renewal of the mandate of the European Group on Ethics in Science and New Technologies, OJ 2016 L 140/21 [EGE mandate V 2016]

EC decision (EU) 2018/813 of 14 May 2018 on the sectoral reference document on best environmental management practices, sector environmental performance indicators and benchmarks of excellence for the agriculture sector under Regulation (EC) No. 1221/2009 on the voluntary participation by organisations in a Community eco-management and audit scheme (EMAS), OJ 2018 L 145/1

EC decision 2005/383/EC of 11 May 2005 on the renewal of the mandate of the European Group on Ethics in Science and New Technologies, OJ 2005 L 127/17 [EGE mandate III 2005]

EC decision 2009/757/EC of 14 October 2009 on the extension of the mandate of the European Group on Ethics in Science and New Technologies and of the period of appointment of its members, OJ 2009 L 270/18 [EGE extension of mandate III 2009]

EC decision 2010/1/EU of 23 December 2009 on the renewal of the mandate of the European Group on Ethics in Science and New Technologies, OJ 2010 L 1/8 [EGE mandate IV 2010]

EC decision 2014/792/EU of 13 November 2014 on the Early Warning System to be used by authorising officers of the EC and by the executive agencies, OJ 2014 L 329/68

EC decision establishing horizontal rules on the creation and operation of Commission expert groups, C(2016) 3301 final 30.5.2016 [EC decision experts]

EC decision of 31 January 2018 on a Code of Conduct for the Members of the EC, OJ 2018 C 65/7 [EC CoC]

EC decision on the setting up of the High Level Group of Scientific Advisors, C(2015) 6946 final 16.10.2015, as amended by Decision amending Decision C(2015)6946 on the setting up of the High Level Group of Scientific Advisers, C(2018) 1919 final 5.4.2018

EC *note pour les membres de la Commission 'Groupe européen d'éthique des sciences et des nouvelles technologies (GEE)—modification du mandat'*, C(2001) 691 final 26.3.2001 [EGE mandate II 2001]

EC proposal for a regulation on HTA and amending [Directive patient mobility], COM(2018) 51 final 31.1.2018

EC recommendation 2005/251/EC of 11 March 2005 on the European Charter for Researchers and on a Code of Conduct for the Recruitment of Researchers, OJ 2005 L 75/67 [EC Charter researchers]

EC recommendation 2008/345/EC of 7 February 2008 on a code of conduct for responsible nanosciences and nanotechnologies research, OJ 2008 L 116/46 [EC recommendation nanosciences]

EC recommendation 77/534/EEC of 25 July 1977 concerning a European code of conduct relating to transactions in transferable securities, OJ 1977 L 212/37 [EC recommendation securities]

EC recommendation of 26 March 2009 on data protection guidelines for the Internal Market Information System (IMI), OJ 2009 L 100/12

EC Rules of Procedure of the Commission (C(2000) 3614), OJ 2000 L 308/26, as amended by OJ 2011 L 296/58

EP annual report on human rights and democracy in the world 2014 and the EU policy on the matter, P8_TA(2015)0470 [EP report human rights]

EP Code of Conduct for Members of the European Parliament with respect to financial interests and conflicts of interest, http://www.europarl.europa.eu/sides/getDoc.do?pubRef=-//EP//TEXT+RULES-EP+20180731+ANN-01+DOC+XML+V0//EN&language=EN&navigationBar=YES [EP CoC]

EP draft report of 19 July 2018 on State of the debate on the Future of Europe (2018/2094(INI)), PE625.528v01-00

EP draft report of 2 August 2018 on differentiated integration (2018/2093(INI)), PE626.719v01-00

EP legislative resolution of 23 April 2009 on the proposal for a directive on the application of patients' rights in cross-border healthcare, OJ 2010 C 184E/368

EP resolution of 13 June 1997 on the mandate of the Group of Advisers on the Ethical Implications of Biotechnology to the EC (B4-0484/97), OJ 1997 C 200/258 [EP resolution GAEIB]

EP resolution of 16 February 2017 with recommendations to the Commission on Civil Law Rules on Robotics, P8_TA(2017)0051 [EP resolution robotics]

EP resolution of 2 February 2017 on an integrated approach to Sport Policy: good governance, accessibility and integrity, OJ 2018 C 252/2

EP resolution on compulsory gynaecological examinations at the Dutch-German border, OJ 1991 C 106/113

EP, Council and EC, 'Explanations relating to the Charter of Fundamental Rights', OJ 2007 C 303/17

ESA decision No. 290/12/COL of 11 July 2012 on restructuring aid granted to Landsbankinn (Iceland), OJ 2014 L 144/121

ESA decision No. 291/12/COL of 11 July 2012 on restructuring aid to Arion Bank (Iceland), OJ 2014 L 144/169

European Convention for the Protection of Animals during International Transport (revised), OJ 2004 L 241/22 [Convention animal transport]

European Convention for the protection of vertebrate animals used for experimental and other scientific purposes, OJ 1999 L 222/31, as amended by OJ 2003 L 198/11 [Convention animal experiments]

European Convention, [Draft] Preamble, CONV 722/03 of 28 May 2003

European Council, 'A New Settlement for the United Kingdom within the European Union', OJ 2016 CI 69/1

European Council, Stockholm presidency conclusions from 23 & 24 March 2001

European Data Protection Supervisor Decision of 3 December 2015 establishing an external advisory group on the ethical dimensions of data protection ('the Ethics Advisory Group'), OJ 2016 C 33/1

European Union Guidelines for State aid in the agricultural and forestry sectors and in rural areas 2014 to 2020, OJ 2014 C 204/1

Executive summary of Opinion No. 4/2015 of the European Data Protection Supervisor, 'Towards a new digital ethics: Data, dignity and technology', OJ 2015 C 392/9

Framework Agreement on comprehensive partnership and cooperation between the European Community and its MS, and Indonesia, OJ 2014 L 125/17

Free trade Agreement between the EU and its MS, and the Republic of Korea, OJ 2011 L 127/6 [Agreement Korea]

Interinstitutional Agreement [EP, Council, EC] on Better Law-Making, OJ 2016 L 123/1 [IIA Better Law-Making]

OLAF Rules of Procedure of the OLAF Supervisory Committee, OJ 2011 L 308/114

Protocol setting out the fishing opportunities and the financial contribution provided for by the Agreement between the European Community and the Gabonese Republic on fishing off the coast of Gabon for the period 3 December 2001 to 2 December 2005, OJ 2002 L 73/19

Resolution of the Council [etc.] of 11 November 1991 concerning fundamental health-policy choices, OJ 1991 C 304/5

Resolution of the Council [etc.] of 3 December 1990 on Community action to combat the use of drugs, including the abuse of medicinal products, particularly in sport, OJ 1990 C 329/4

Resolution on children's rights and child soldiers in particular, OJ 2004 C 26/17

Resolution on support for the peace process in Burundi, OJ 1999 C 271/49

Resolution on the "Enlargement of the European Economic Area (EEA)—institutional and legal issues", OJ 2003 C 308/16

Resolution on the future of ACP-EU relations, OJ 1999 C 271/35

Resolution on the impact of sanctions and, in particular, of embargoes on the people of the countries on which such measures are imposed, OJ 2002 C 78/32 [Resolution embargoes]

Resolution on the impact of tourism on the development of ACP countries, OJ 2006 C 330/15 [Resolution tourism]

Resolution on the situation in Southern Africa, OJ 2003 C 231/53

Resolution on the social and environmental consequences of climate change in the ACP countries, OJ 2009 C 221/31

Response of former EC president Barroso on a parliamentary request ('Criteria and methods for the selection of the members of the [EGE]', P6_RE(2006)0430, answer from 17.3.2006)

Strategic Partnership Agreement between the EU and its MS, and Japan, OJ 2018 L 216/4

Supplementary Code of Ethics Criteria for the members of the Executive Board of the European Central Bank, OJ 2010 C 104/8

Trade Agreement between the EU and its Member States, and Colombia and Peru, OJ 2012 L 354/3, as amended by OJ 2018 L 1/1

Venice Commission, Report on the Rule of Law, CDLAD(2011)003rev

Vienna Convention on the Law of Treaties (United Nations, Treaty Series, vol. 1155, p. 331)

World Medical Association, WMA Declaration of Helsinki, https://www.wma.net/policies-post/wma-declaration-of-helsinki-ethical-principles-for-medical-research-involving-human-subjects/

www.ingramcontent.com/pod-product-compliance
Lightning Source LLC
LaVergne TN
LVHW082339200926
848481LV00012B/3393
9781013275524